THE VILLAGE IN THE VALLEY

TRAVELS IN MEXICO AND ITALY

THE VILLAGE IN THE VALLEY

TRAVELS IN MEXICO AND ITALY

Corinna Sargood

PROSPECT BOOKS
2021

First published in 2021 in Great Britain and the United States
by Prospect Books, 26 Parke Road, London, SW13 9NG.

Some of the material in this book has previously appeared in the following articles:

'Crunch: *Chapulines* (Crickets, Grasshoppers, and Locusts), a Mexican Delicacy',
The Art of Eating, Issue 82, 2009.

'Mexican Vanilla: Sketches in Papantla', *The Art of Eating*, Issue 72, 2006.

'The Sweet Factory', *Petits Propos Culinaires,* No. 73, July 2003.

'The Uranium Spider', *Petits Propos Culinaires*, No. 77, December 2004.

BRITISH LIBRARY CATALOGUING IN PUBLICATION DATA:
A catalogue entry of this book is available from the British Library.

Typeset and designed by Catheryn Kilgarriff and Brendan King in Baskerville.

Cover design by Prospect Books.

ISBN 978-1-909248717

Printed and bound by the Gutenberg Press, Malta.

CONTENTS

THE VILLAGE IN THE VALLEY

Travels in Italy

For Richard,
my stalwart companion

THE VILLAGE IN THE VALLEY

INTRODUCTION

It was time to go away.

Angela Carter had asked me to make another series of linocuts to illustrate the second *Virago Book of Fairy Tales* that she was editing. As I had calculated that it would take about three months to complete, it seemed a good opportunity to decamp to another country and to work there.

Angela was a great friend of mine. We met in our mid-twenties when we both lived in Clifton, Bristol. The once grand Georgian terraces, often now divided into quite shabby tenements, still had the charm of past elegance. Even though the bathroom had been built under the stairs outside the apartment, the big rooms and huge windows compensated for this inconvenience.

My grandmother-in-law, Olive, had given me the best alternative to a nanny: a season ticket for the zoo. Every afternoon I'd pack up the pram, with my two small children, pens, pencils, crayons and paper, and set off to draw. Often, we'd meet Angela, who at that time worked there. Each day at 5 pm we'd walk home together. This was the 1960s: she was writing; I was working as an illustrator. We were both full of enthusiasm.

Our lives diverged, but we kept in touch. By the 1980s we were both living in London.

Two years before, I had spent three months in the Amazonian forest of Peru, making botanical illustrations of the jungle plants. I was excited as I prepared the pictures for a small exhibition in London. My partner Richard and I were beginning to think about going to the mountains in Peru.

Angela came to the private view with a friend, a literary agent from

New York. She looked with a shrewd eye at my paintings and prints. I told her that now I had a book to illustrate, and it was time to go elsewhere. She asked where we were planning. As soon as I told her we were thinking about returning to Peru she became quite emphatic, almost commanding.

The agent stepped in: 'Go to Mexico. Don't ask why. Just go.'

Angela was already too ill to take on such a journey herself. 'Do Mexico for me,' she said.

The next week we bought tickets for a flight to Mexico City.

We packed our bags: Richard's with woodworking hand tools as he is a furniture maker, and mine with the wherewithal to draw and paint and make linocut prints. Within a month we were in Mexico City astonished by everything we saw. We rented a cottage in a small town. It was the ideal place to work.

Richard moved his tools into an outbuilding, and with wood from the local forest, as well as our garden, began to make furniture. The men in the barrio quickly became curious. It was arranged that after their day working in the orchards and fields, our new neighbours would come to the workshop where, with a bit of help, they made their own beds, tables and cupboards. There, we worked for a year.

Since then we have spent most winters well occupied in Oaxaca.

That was the recommendation that has shaped our lives for thirty years.

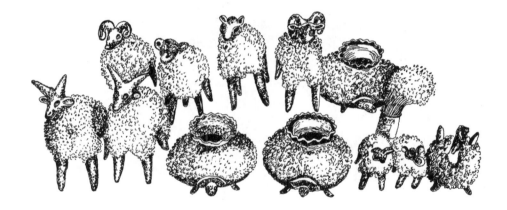

ONE

Mexico

El Distrito Federal

I f we had expected to leave the grey gloom of England behind, we were
right.
The descent into Mexico was through a stratum of thick orange fog.
Once inside, it felt as if we were in a great grubby marquee where only a
faint diffusion of sunlight could penetrate.

The city of Mexico was packed. It was packed to overflowing. It was
packed with unfamiliar, bewildering sights. It was so packed and so strange
that we were frightened.

Standing dumbfounded, we watched the spectacle that unrolled before
our eyes. We felt that we had dropped straight into the Big Top of a circus.

Insinuating themselves between the pedestrians and vehicles, clowns and
acrobats juggled and tumbled. Families climbed up and down each other
to form human pyramids. All held out their hats for small change.

Hurdy-gurdy players wound up their endlessly persistent instruments in
conjunction with their sidekicks, the quick sweeping 'bottlers', a matching
pair of money collectors always wearing the obligatory paramilitary
uniforms of the profession.

Full-grown men dressed as hobbyhorses cantered by. Youths leaping on their own legs masqueraded as credible ostriches, while others were stuck all over with shredded newspaper and resembled chickens. But it was not this battalion alone that menaced the pedestrians for money.

Those who could afford crepe paper sported brilliantly-coloured costumes, giving fleeting performances as exotic birds in the momentary gaps between the cars, crowds, pedlars, hawkers and other itinerants.

A small troupe of gorillas danced along the road to the jangling rendering of a waltz coming from their ghetto blaster. Top volume with the knob missing, the music was diluted to the odd screech that drowned in the roaring traffic.

Everyone was alert with a keen eye for even a hint of a traffic jam. The fire-eaters waited for a pause to threaten the idling drivers with a sheet of flame.

A moment's hesitation in the momentum of the traffic was enough for the fake fakirs to drag their beds of broken glass onto the highway and feign the repose of forty winks.

The red traffic light was a bonus for which every performer waited.

The red traffic light was the moment every driver made sure his windows were wound up.

Armed policemen, resplendent in outstanding steam-ironed uniforms looped about with braid like so many loosely strung parcels, sweated under

elaborate confectioneries of pith helmets as they directed the dense traffic. Done up like dogs' dinners, they energetically blew their whistles as they flailed their arms in the air, giving mysterious messages to banks of cars and taxis, buses and trucks that make only the briefest of stops before grinding and graunching away.

Exhaust fumes, expelled in black clouds, lay low on the ground. There was no fresh air into which it might have risen and dispersed.

Each day the newspaper produced a pie chart, showing the disproportionately large slices of foul chemicals that saturated the air. Trees, their spindly branches shedding leaves every month of the year, corroborated the story.

The airspace was filled with barrages of helium balloons. Every colour and shape known to the imagination of the Mexican balloon designer tugged at the tightly-held strings. Hearts and giraffes, bears and dinosaurs, saints and virgins, all hustled for limited airspace. A crucifix, duly bleeding, jostled plain spherical balloons in brilliant metallic colours. Each strained at the leash. On this same elevated height waved tall poles full of fluttering lottery tickets, held on high by vendors licensed by the municipality.

In and out of all this strode the stilt walkers. Adhering to an unspoken tradition, the majority wore baggy suits of loud checks. Already way above human level, they raised regulation top hats from their heads, as if to greet and patronise old friends.

Pickpockets moved stealthily, indistinguishable from the pedestrians they may or may not have just skilfully robbed.

Street markets were set up on the pavements like so much stair carpet unrolling before your eyes. Professionally demeaned but insistent beggars, their thin palms outstretched, pushed miserable suckling babies and filthy, scabby children towards you, as on craned necks they peered up from beneath the level of the passing hemlines. They roused our guilt and we paid.

As we eased our way through the crowd, the selling hubbub of thousands of traders reached us, as if tubes of sound were being piped from the seething side streets.

Ambulant vendors stepped into our pathways and pushed their trays under our noses. Heaps of homemade toys, jumping jack skeletons, beer can helicopters, space ships on sticks that whirred round your head, were piled together with suction propelled witches, hopping frogs, clockwork gnashing dentures – the latest imports in plastic from China. There were watches, clocks and shaving brushes, tubes of toothpaste, ribbons and wallets, glittery hairgrips and religious gewgaws.

I would have liked to wander and take a closer look, but even a moment's hesitation, the slightest turn of the head, and the street traders would close in as if for the kill. Despite itching with curiosity, we walked on in studied indifference. We walked by the shoeshine boys, crouching on their haunches in every available space. We walked straight by as they sneered at our scuffed shoes.

We came out into the vast draughty grey expanse of the *zócalo*: La Plaza de la Constitución. After Red Square, it is the biggest square in the world.

No trees, no seats, no bandstand. This military arena was not built for the benefit of nannies to proudly wheel their protégés for a breath of fresh air. Over the centuries, much more sinister dramas have unfolded on this windswept parade ground.

In the centre of the *zócalo* the federal flagpole rose so high it was lit as a warning to aircraft. And from the top billowed about half an acre of frayed cloth. Red, white and green, it is emblazoned with an eagle perched on the spiny racquet of a nopal cactus. The bird of prey is struggling with a writhing serpent clenched in its beak.

This is the flag of *La República*. A thin line of people had settled down on the paving to shelter in the shadow cast by its supporting mast. Almost imperceptibly they shifted anticlockwise, bunching up as the sun moved higher and arched through the sky, shrinking the shade.

The militiamen's shoes were laced in such a complicated way it outshone any fancy rope-work invented by becalmed sailors. Whiteness was chalky with blanco; brass buttons glinted from the effort of powerful rubbing. The parading soldiers made sure that the head of every civilian man was bared and every woman's covered. Talking subsided to a whisper and walking drifted to a halt. Children were brought to heel as drums rolled and the bugler blew the fanfare that pronounced night had become morning or day had turned into dusk. Grinning was frowned upon.

With pomp and dignity the flag was unfurled and raised every morning. It was lowered and refolded at dusk. The seriousness and importance of this military ceremony must not be underestimated. It took the strength of twelve cadets to shoulder the weight of Mexico's colours. And in time to the slow death knell of the lone drummer, these boys smartly high-stepped their straight legs as they carried their precious cargo in and out of the government building, an edifice that occupied an entire side of the great square.

Not one of the magnificent buildings that surrounded the *zócalo* remained vertical. At sixes and sevens since the earthquake of 1985, they are still sinking slowly into the mire of the lake on which they were built in the mid-sixteenth century.

The heavily baroque interior of the cathedral gleamed darkly in the candlelight. Since the earthquake, a dense forest of green-painted scaffolding poles supported the massive ceiling and roof. Only the very slender could pass through this thicket.

A side chapel dedicated to Saint Joseph still contained, in addition to its rightful incumbent, Our Christ of Sorrows. This miserable figure sits in the glimmering half-light. His elbows sink into his knees and his drooping head is cupped in his hands. Even glimpsed through the poles, his despair is as infectious as it is cathartic. Modelled from *pasta de caña de maiz* – a plaster-like paste derived from cornstalks – in the seventeenth century, he was daily carried out of the cathedral and processed round the Plaza before being sat on the *zócalo*, to collect donations for furnishing the chapel.

The slightly larger-than-life solid wooden saints that stand in every ecclesiastical niche are very heavy. When taken out on processions, they need constant relays of strong men to transport them. It was from Indian craftsmen, as early as the sixteenth century, that the New World Spanish manufacturers of saints learned how to make convenient, easy-to-lift versions. A deity the size of very large fat priest assumed the weight of a cherub when modelled from *pasta de caña*.

To construct a saint, dried stalks of maize were stripped of their outer husks and brought to the boil in water. The pith was separated and put to one side. Armatures, made from suitably curved branches of pine, were tied together with grass to form a support. Onto this were glued small sections of the maize stalk, and over this were pasted bits of rag or scraps of paper until the basic shape was ready to be modelled. During some recent repairs, it was discovered not only that strips of a sixteenth century codex had be used for this job, but also torn up pieces of the receipt for the purchase of Raphael's *El Pasmo de Sicilia* (*Christ Falling on the Way to Calvary*). This painting now hangs in the Prado, Madrid.

A gesso was made from powdered rehydrated lime, the cooked pith of the maize and the sap of the nopal cactus. With this, the details of the face, feet, arms and hands could be painstakingly built up, layer upon layer. When dried and painted, the surface was polished with a solution made from the juice of the nopal. This finish is the reason for the characteristic, almost translucent complexion of the fully portable *pasta de caña* saint.

The lightweight Christ of Sorrows lifted into the *zócalo* each day was very successful in gathering alms. Even as late as the eighteen-hundreds, long after it was legal tender, the *campesinos* – local farmers – would drop off their spare *cacao* beans, which had paid for the finely carved and painted wooden statue of Saint Joseph holding his son high on his left arm. In the cathedral in Mexico City, still sitting in a side chapel, is the sixteenth-century statue of *El Señor del Cacao*. He is the only Christ dedicated to chocolate.

Chocolate. *Theobroma cacao* ('food of the Gods'). *Theobroma* was the Greek description that Linneus tacked onto the front of the adapted name *cacao*. The original Nahuatl word *xocolatl* meant 'bitter water'.

The cocoa bean was not only a drink and a food. It was held in such high esteem that in preconquestial times it was used as a currency. Cortés quickly cottoned on to its value, and even with his lust for the evasive gold, he realised he could pay the wages of the Indians with this money that conveniently grew on trees.

The *cacao* trees grow in the crepuscular understory gloom of the forest. Throughout the year, the cauliflorous pods develop from the delicate flowers that sprout directly from its trunks and branches. As they become ripe they are harvested before each pod is cut open with a machete to reveal up to sixty beans embedded in fluffy white pulp. All this is scooped out and placed in wooden boxes, covered with large leaves and left in the shade to ferment. After about a week, the beans are spread out in the sun to dry before being sent to market. Here, they are sold before being roasted and ground. It could be with *piloncillo*, the unrefined brown sugar that is bought in small cones, while cinnamon, cloves, vanilla or almonds may also be added. The resulting smooth paste can be pressed into moulds or patted into cakes, ready for storing. To make the drink, pour hot water onto crumbled chocolate and whisk with a *molinillo* until it is dissolved. (The *molinillo* is the intricately handcarved wooden whisk which, when briskly revolved between the palms, transforms chocolate drink into a light frothy foam.)

In all markets another delicious drink is sold. Chocolate Atole is scooped from a huge green glazed bowl and served in small dishes made from the

dried shell of the calabash. They are called *jícaras* from the Nahuatl word *xicalli*, meaning 'gourd'. Each one is beautifully decorated, inside and out, with enamel paint. You can drink your way down to a swan or other aquatic birds on a lake in a mountainous landscape. Maize dough, *masa*, is beaten together with crumbled chocolate into water.

Champurrado is a chocolate drink thickened with maize corn and sweetened with *piloncillo*, the unrefined brown sugar cones found in every market. It is often flavoured with cinnamon, ground nuts and zest of orange. As in prehispanic times, it can be spiced with chillies. Hot chocolate drinks have become a delicious melange of prehispanic and colonial ingredients.

In every market, frequently on street corners, at bus stops in the mountains, or from one of the many chocolate shops, a huge variety of chocolate goods can be bought and imbibed. It is a popular beverage to offer the dead, and glasses of chocolate are a staple on many Day of the Dead altars.

One of the delicious and famous dishes of Mexico is the remarkable turkey and chocolate *mole*. Although *mole* is taken from the Nahuatl word *molli*, a generic word for sauce, and the turkey native to the New World, the recipe for chocolate *mole* was a concoction of colonial times.

There are several myths that tell of its creation in the seventeenth century. It is said that the nuns of the poor convent of Santa Rosa in Puebla were alarmed to hear that they were expected to produce a fine meal fit for the archbishop, when he came to pay them a visit. In their panic they put the entire contents of their larder – nuts, chillies, fruit and chocolate – together and made the sauce which, together with the old turkey they had roasted, turned out to be a great success.

Since then, the recipe has become more and more elaborate. A fine range of *moles* made by professional local women is found in most markets.

Chocolate does have a mild psychoactive effect. It helps the body produce serotonins that evoke a state of well-being. It also releases natural opium-like endorphins that give you the same elated feeling as falling in love.

It was the Spanish who introduced sugar cane, as well as the cow (and therefore milk). Thus the enforced collaboration of the Old and New Worlds provided the ingredients for the statutory bedtime drink of the English nursery. Cocoa, vanilla and honey were added to water for this prehispanic Royal beverage.

The staple diet of Indian Mexico has remained little changed since the period before 'The Conquest'. Maize, squash and beans are still grown together in the small fields worked by families.

Maize grows straight and tall, and supports climbing beans, which in turn provide nitrogen to fertilise the earth. The large leaves of the calabash shade the roots and keep in the moisture. They have been grown in this way for centuries. It was not until the Spanish introduced cattle, with the consequent ready production of manure, that the land could benefit from other methods of enrichment.

In the palace of Moctezuma over three hundred different plates were prepared each day for his personal consumption. While the Emperor was served at his own table by 'four very handsome and clean women', the rest of his court helped themselves from a choice of over a thousand dishes. Whereas only turkeys and the strange little bald and mute dog (now rare enough to be bred as a fashion accessory) had been domesticated, game was profuse. Rabbits, deer and peccaries abounded, as did pheasants, crows and doves. Those who lived near lakes or marshes ate wild fowl and frogs. And the much sought-after axolotl.

Lake Xochimilco is almost the only remaining part of the great lake that Mexico City covers, and is now one of the last few natural habitats of the axolotl or Mexican walking fish.

A-xolotl is a Nahuatl word meaning 'water monster.'

This curious creature resembles a huge crested newt, with its dorsal fin extending from the back of its head to the tip of its tail and continuing round the underside. Growing up to a foot long, it sports three pairs of magnificent feathery external gills and four tiny legs that are too weak to be of any real use. One of its stranger habits is to bite and tear off its own limbs. In this legless state, before the new set had regenerated, the Aztecs thought the feathery axolotl was associated with the god Quetzalcoatl, the Plumed Serpent.

The axolotl breeds in water neotenously, and it is as a giant larva that this delicacy remains all its life. A very few metamorphose into adults, but as gill-less air-breathers stumbling over the land, they make a far less appetising dish.

Young girls were forbidden to swim in lakes inhabited by this phallic-shaped *Salamandroidea* for fear they would become pregnant.

The axolotl itself fell victim to this myth of sexual potency, being rendered into a syrup by simmering with *piloncillo* and taken not only as a general tonic, but also as an aphrodisiac.

Axolotl, together with strips of chilli veins, was the main ingredient for the prehispanic ceremonial dish called *tamales*.

Both the Pacific and the Atlantic Oceans form the coasts of Mexico. Those who lived by the sea had further additions to their diet and ate sea fish, turtles, crabs and oysters.

The prehispanic Mexicans did not fry, for they had neither fat nor oil. Their food was grilled or boiled. It would have been highly seasoned with peppers and chillies. Dried and freshly picked chillies lie in huge piles in every market in the land. Fresh, dried pickled or toasted, there are dozens of different varieties.

Chilli is a *Capsicum*, a genus of *Solinaceae*. Used in cooking, it not only improves flavour, but aids digestion and – mercifully – prevents flatulence. Used as a medicine, it helps to ameliorate indigestion. As a tincture, it is useful as a local stimulant, especially when gargled. Sometimes it is used as a liniment. It is rich in vitamin C.

In this vast country it is not surprising that the names of each variety of chilli changes along with the landscape.

Chillies contain the same alkaloids as chocolate, and can also produce the same giddy feelings as falling in love.

Wild herbs were gathered and used by rich and poor alike. This tradition continues today. Amaranth, tomatillos – a native plant bearing small, round green fruit of the same name – and sage were very important ingredients.

Amaranth was made into a stiff paste and modelled into small idols, to be eaten as part of pagan rituals. Discovering this, the Spanish prohibited its use. They hastily replaced it with the distantly-related plant from Europe that is still in use today.

The ultimate Emperor of the land, Moctezuma, would lie back replete after the eating fruit, to receive his royal cup of cocoa laced with honey and vanilla: 'Then dwarves and hunchbacked buffoons produced their tricks and their jokes. Moctezuma took one of the painted, gilded pipes that had been placed within his reach, smoked for a short while, and went to sleep.' (Jacques Soustelle, *The Daily Life of the Aztecs*.)

The Spanish were very impressed by the curious sight of tobacco smoking.

For most of the population, the basic food remained maize. Today it is the same.

Homemade food and drinks could be bought on every corner: *tacos, tlacoyos, huaraches, tostadas, elote, quesadillas, chilaquiles, gorditas, jugos, aguas* and *licuados*. At the intersection of every road we caught sight of something edible that we had never seen before. At many stalls we bought these mysterious delicacies. Rarely were they not delicious.

We grew a bit more courageous and turned into the back streets of this gargantuan city. There was a constant and exhausting clamour for your attention. And by any means, be it fair or foul, for your money.

Soon we noticed that there were little areas where clusters of specialist shops filled the streets. Behind many of these windows were the workshops where the goods to be sold were made.

Wandering along, we were soon enclosed in the marriage attire quarter. Frothy gowns hung on racks that had been wheeled out and that overflowed the pavements and spread onto the dusty streets. Bridesmaids' dresses, in a full range of pastel shades and in all sizes, flounced and floated in the breeze of exhaust fumes. Frills were an integral part of all garments, and shirts stuffed down the fronts of morning suits were puffed out like a strutting cockerel with a lace interpretation of feathers. Tiaras and coronets, blossoms and blooms, sequins and jewels were all cunningly made from paste and paper and glass, plastic and glue – this glitter quite convincingly took me into this fairytale land, where to be a princess for one day in your life is better that never being one at all. Then a lifetime left with the photograph, the dress, the dainty shoes, and the veil. But what of the more lasting expectation?

Each of us left this dreamland thinking of our broken marriages. Neither of us had even a photograph with which to anchor our memories. And neither of us had the temerity to mention this to the other.

Out of the claustrophobia of nylon gossamer tucks, pleats and gathers, we came into a square filled with dozens of tiny clattering printing presses. Under the portales – the arcades – small wooden kiosks had flapped down their sides, and printer's devils were working hell for leather, printing cards and notices and invitations to every conceivable function. Emblazoned and embossed, gilded or bejewelled, you could choose a suitable illustration to be overprinted with any words that came into your head. Men sat outside the little sheds meticulously cutting and sticking ribbons and flowers onto the most elaborate of fancy envelopes.

Thinking hard, neither of us could come up with a single occasion suitable for having our own cards printed. It was as if we were standing on the watershed between the past and the future, as great swirls of confusion obscured everything but the immediate moment.

*

In the centre of Mexico City we stumbled across an abandoned sweet factory. The whole eighteenth-century building, including the works, the family home and all contents, were being sold piecemeal. A linen sheet hung out of an upper window announced it in large painted letters as a sale of antiques.

We turned into the building through the huge open doors that must have witnessed a whole history of transport.

Established over 150 years ago, it had abruptly stopped functioning when the proprietor died in the 1980s. The nephew who came into this curate's egg of an inheritance had little interest in the factory. It was his sons, who displayed even less involvement in the family business, who were selling up. Real estate in the city does not go for a song.

We walked into the central courtyard that had been roofed during the early part of the last century with a stained-glass canopy. The whole atmosphere was faintly sticky. The air was still and grey as if it were saturated with sweet glue.

Piles of documents in the process of spilling from huge desks onto the floor had been stopped in mid-flow, like cooling lava, as they had become a single mass with general stickiness. Just lifting our feet to walk across the tiled floor was a surprising fight.

There were cantilevered towers of account books filled with copperplate handwriting, surmounted by windup gramophones with cardboard favourites ready on the turntables.

Piles of old labels had been neatly tied into bundles with faded ribbon, maybe a hundred years ago. There were boxes still full of sweets. Lifting a few lids revealed that most contents had turned to a syrupy dust, while others had crystallised with age. There were several whose delicately serrated remains indicated that they had been partially consumed by mice.

Other boxes lay unassembled, as delivered by the printers. They were segregated into types, showing wonderful embossed and dainty pictures, each recommending an appropriate place for consumption. Amorous couples adored each other in a box at the opera, satisfied their appetites with an alfresco lunch in a glade, or rested, having been exerted by rowing on the river. Each vignette suggested that to buy a box of such delights would secure undying passion.

Further designs, stacked as flat as the others, showed coloured botanical illustrations, not only of cocoa beans, but ingredients such as vanilla orchids, almonds or cinnamon.

Sheaves of mourning paper and similarly black-edged envelopes overflowed from drawers, which hung out of desks jammed permanently open by damp stickiness.

Some sheets had been covered with euphemistic language written in pen and ink with a similarly florid hand. A few had been sealed in their addressed envelopes. Why were they left unposted? I wondered what had stopped the flow of this news of death.

There were letters received by clients over a hundred years ago, jumbled together with plaster saints, spent candles, a box of winged collars, bottles of medicines and other patent cures.

Large decorated sugar skulls, grey and decayed, weighed down legal documents that had been sent from foreign lands in the 1920s. There were several umbrellas among a hoard of signed photographs of 1930s film stars.

In the dark bowels of the back rooms was the sweet-making machinery: chocolate toasting machines, milling machines, and other more complicated devices with curly pipes and pressure gauges imported from Dresden in 1922, a giant cast-iron table formally used for rolling out caramel, were all similarly embedded in the thick viscous dust.

Back in the main courtyard, dozens of rolls of lithographed posters and theatre bills would have rolled across the floor if only they had been free enough from stickiness to do so. Three small sewing boxes containing a few rusty needles, several pins and a tiny roll of lace, were likewise adhering to a wicker table.

Receipts and lists of workmen's pitiful wages inappropriately shared a table top with family photos, batches of which had tumbled out of bulging albums.

The dead uncles had been captured and pictured as young men, pomaded and slicked fit enough for parts as early Hollywood gangsters, while the long decayed aunts appeared immaculately turned out in the latest fashions of the same era. They all smiled with confident arrogance.

But it was hard to tell if the ranks of employees, lined up against the wall in tiers, displayed a collective expression of submission or dumb insolence.

All were monochrome fading to sepia.

Nailed to the wall just beyond the retired clocking-in apparatus, surrounded by rosewood frames and blurred by sticky glass, were the final documents by way of a series of formal photographs of this manufacturing company.

Arranged in chronological order, the first showed the ultimate proprietor on his deathbed. He was surrounded by women dressed entirely in black, as was the costume of the professional mourner.

The next was the proprietor's bunting strewn hearse, which was an elaborately decorated tram. Even then the younger members of this extended family were to be seen jockeying for a good spot and hanging off the running boards to make room for the more decorous members to ride inside.

Then followed the final portrait of the last director-manager of the sweet factory. Displayed among the flounced lining of the open coffin, the uncle was seen to have lost nothing of his unequivocal authority in death.

The terminal photograph showed the magnificent coffin, its lid now in place being interred in the family mausoleum, a tomb that must surly owe its design to the art of confectionery.

We were once again standing in the vestibule. A monstrous chandelier, grey with sugared cobwebs hung down on massive chains from the ceiling high in the gloom.

Outside and framed by the ecclesiastically proportioned entrance, modern daily life, glowing in the late afternoon sunshine, continued unawares.

The nephew who had followed us through the rooms of his family secrets then spoke.

'They are all dead,' and a smile of relief passed across his face.

But when it came to buying anything, nothing was really for sale. The prices were outrageous.

*

Under the shadow of the cathedral, on a corner of this enormous expanse of paving slabs, stood a line of tradesmen, ready to ply their skills. Plumbers, electricians, carpenters, and stone masons, among others, patiently waited to be hired, the bags containing the tools of their trade lying at their feet. And for their entertainment or yours, one- or two-wheeled trick-cyclists slowly and circuitously pedalled by, dressed in costumes of skeletons, dragons, pantomime dames, panthers, bears, and crocodiles – which we now realised was everyday wear.

Wandering a little further, we peered into the dark caverns of shops crammed with the day-to-day accoutrements essential to meet the requirements and fervour of the Catholic Church. To me, this was another mythological land, foreboding and cruel maybe, but for a literal believer it was a terrifying lifetime of nightmares. The Mexican church has gone to town with their interpretation of the crucifix. No agony spared, no gash without its fountain of blood, no wound free from suppuration. A whole gammut of saints *in extremis*. Fully-fledged martyrs to outshine the disasters of your own life and to pin for reassurance on your kitchen wall. Or tiny versions to dangle in your car, to ward off the results of inattentive driving.

The nearer to the cathedral we drew, the more candles and votives with legs and arms and hearts and livers, or goats crudely stamped out of soft alloy there were. Keyrings and bedside lamps depicting Our Lord in various stages of his life were being sold, along with shrines to all and sundry, flashing lights or no. It was breathtaking.

Formerly, in the shadow of the leaning walls that still support the great edifice, sat the cripples, the deformed, the hunchbacks, the dwarves, and the dirty orphans. And in the chill of the gigantic portals, gathering their black rags to their sickly bodies, crouched the spinsters and widows, plaintively beseeching the better blessed to give them a coin before they entered this cavernous House of God.

In embarrassed misery, I picked through trays of trinkets: keyrings, tangled rosaries and saints embedded forever in resin.

Away from this lucky charm quarter, was a cluster of dentists advertising their skills with pictures painted by hand on the walls of their clinics. Fast denture repairs, extractions, fillings, diamond insets, gold framing and bejewelled encrustations to wear at parties, all graphically illustrated in full colour murals. And if that wasn't enough to encourage the nursing of excruciating toothache, some surgeries had display cabinets full of trophies that looked as if they had been robbed from an ancient tomb.

Once passed this batch of orthodontists, we came across the *papel picado* zone. Here, with frenetic energy, strings of hundreds of thousands of shaped and brilliantly coloured paper 'flags' were made, each of them cut by dies passed down the generations, stamped out in one of an infinite variety of filigree patterns.

Every fiesta, every religious or secular occasion could be catered for with appropriate silhouettes. From swathes of cherubs to rows of skeletons, from kissing lovebirds to wicked witches, from Miguel Hidalgo – the leader of the Mexican War of Independence – to Benito Juárez, the first indigenous president of Mexico. From the sublime to the ridiculous, all as ephemeral as anything cut from gossamer-thin paper would be. Eagles on cactuses, flowers and hearts and virgins and Madonnas, crucifixes and toothy smiling

pumpkins, all fluttered on thin strings right down to the darkest interiors of the shops. From these back rooms resounded the dull thuds of stamping dies as thousands more flimsy flags were punched out.

Slowly we were beginning to understand that our familiar boundaries, those that make up the bedrock of sensible prosaic Britain, were of little or no relevance in Mexico.

But this was not a circus: this show was real life. Whereas no expense or effort had been spared to teach us the difference between reality and fantasy, here, they were happily rolled up in bed together.

Soon we came upon the great cake area. Bakeries were displaying castles made from sweets, glacé fruits and biscuits. Shop windows were filled to capacity with tiered cakes dripping stalactites of shockingly bright icing, their tops serving as tiny stages for sugar dramas. Football matches, weddings, cemeteries, flowers, fast cars… There were scenes to commemorate or celebrate every aspect of life, every fiesta. Little cakes modelled like swans or babies, cup cakes full of fruits, pastries with patterns in sugar, tarts and flans, sponges, coronets and sticky slices. Inside, you took a tray and a pair of tongs and helped yourself until having travelled the full circle of temptations, you arrived back at the entrance and the till.

Exhausted by the sights and the noise and the polluted air, we walked towards the Alameda, the formal public gardens, and sat on a cast-iron bench. Already our chests had become painfully tight; our prickling eyes watered and our noses ran. We felt overwhelmed.

Huge fountains played between the tall trees and the municipal sculpture. A brass band struck up as ice-cream sellers on wavering bicycles, ready to halt, rode by. There was food and drink, more toys, more beggars, more clowns, more balloons.

A street theatre set down its suitcases of props and costumes and we joined the gathering crowd to watch their mime. We too wept with laughter, until as quickly as they had appeared, the troupe unmasked themselves, restuffed their suitcases and vanished. After a satirical attack on the government, they'd jumped out of sight at the first sign of a policeman sauntering into view.

We did not sit down and wonder what we were doing here, but we did begin to think the task of finding somewhere to stay for a few months was plainly quixotic.

The country, *La Patria*, is vast. Our plans had looked quite straightforward as we scrutinised the maps before we left England. Now, with our feet inside this country, we knew we had badly misunderstood the scale.

The next day, we went to a bus station and bought two tickets for seats on a battered looking charabanc. Its direction, its destination, was immaterial.

Still exhausted, bewildered and frightened, we left the city that had kept us on a knife-edge between laughing and crying, delight and horror.

As we started out on the journey, sitting side by side on the bus, peering through the cracked windows, looking out amongst the ruins and the rubbish for a speck of something beautiful in the landscape, it struck me that this was to be the beginning of our common history.

Our individual rucksacks were tied to the roof. Apart from a certain fondness for each other, we shared only a two-litre plastic bottle of electronically purified water.

The bus slowly and laboriously clambered over the hills, grinding its gears until we were almost deafened. Our muscles ached with the jolting. Then up and up the bus climbed until we could see a range of snowy mountains. Here, the fresh air and clear blue skies began. We could see forests full of trees displaying luxuriant leaves...

TWO

EL ORO
CARUSO SLEPT HERE

Two days and several second-class journeys later, we climbed stiffly down from the Silver Horseshoe Company bus (their motto, 'BETTER DEAD THAN LATE', is printed in large letters in the cabin, above the windscreen).

We waved goodbye to the ebullient driver, and thanked the company issue shrine to the Virgin of Guadalupe with her surrounding fairy lights pulsating in time to the beat of whatever music was blaring from the stereo speakers of the company issue tape machine.

Standing shakily on the *zócalo* of El Oro, a town some 100 miles west of Mexico City, we watched the back end of the bus roar away, staring absent-mindedly as the billowing clouds of dust settled.

Enveloped in the brilliant light, we listened to the rustling leaves of the magnificent trees and the singing of birds high in the canopy. It was a few minutes before it struck us as eerie. For a town, it was unnaturally quiet. There were no people to be seen. A polythene bag caught by the breeze idly flipped over and skated across the pavement; it had been made into a kite.

It was noon. Richard went to look for a place to stay, while I sat with the luggage on a wrought-iron bench in the *zócalo*. In the centre of the municipal square rose the bandstand. Its iron curlicues were exquisitely wrought. The shape resembled a fine blancmange mould. Great flowering trees covered with brilliant blooms, both orange and cerise, towered over the ominously dark lumpy topiary.

If I'd had the foresight to bring a beer with me, it could have been swiftly opened with the bottle-opener thoughtfully nailed to the tree trunk next to where I was sitting.

Richard returned, having made a provisional booking at the Grand Hotel. Before this could be confirmed, they wanted to make sure we were married. As our passports revealed this not to be the case, it was with trepidation that we entered the foyer of the only hotel in the town, ready to throw ourselves, presumed sinners, on the mercy of the management. The Silver Horseshoe we had watched leave town was the last bus of the day.

La Padrona greeted us and smiled warmly, while a conspiratorial cluster of men in the shadowy background nodded to each other, conveying to my companion something that could have been approval, but may have been sympathetic disappointment. As they grinned, their tombstone teeth caught the light of the midday sun as it filtered through the heavy crocheted curtains. No man in his right mind would take such an elderly woman to a hotel on a Sunday afternoon if she were not his wife. Therefore, we must be married.

So we felt very relieved to be escorted up the gentle curves of the staircase and onto a wide balcony, which ran round three sides of the quadrangle that made up the hotel. It hung over an enclosed garden and was supported on delicate iron pillars. Our room led from here, through a pair of french windows.

The bed was iron, and consisted of a combination of elaborate wire swirls surrounding the ogee cartouche on the headboard. Flaking and faded, it depicted a scene from the scriptures in a softly erotic style. There was a similarly designed washstand, with a jug of water ready in the bowl. The wardrobe seemed to be only moments away from turning to dust, but the bedside tables, each with its candlestick and box of matches, were solid enough to support our books.

The whole building had been constructed from wood in about 1900 – long enough ago for its timbers to have dried and shrunk considerably. With each movement, with each breath of air, the whole edifice creaked like a wooden ship on the high seas. Suddenly a draught of wind filled the white muslin curtains that hung in front of the glass doors. They billowed out like sails.

We lay on the bed, affecting the moribund condition required by the apparent longevity of our married state. We now realised that every eye in town, although invisible to us, must have followed every movement we had made since we stepped off the battered bus. And now every ear in the vicinity must be trained in our direction.

While the Grand Hotel might have been only a memory of its past grandeur, its courtyard was still a working kitchen. Chickens, turkeys, peacocks, and their various chicks, pecked among the vegetables and herbs growing in the garden. Coops of rabbits and hares were stacked up against a shady wall. A well and a washing place were piled high with draining pots and pans. Several braziers, their flames being fanned into life by small girls, stood surrounded by a patch of beaten earth. Nearby, *azulejo*-tiled charcoal grills supported various steaming pots.

Sun-bleached white linen hung stiffly from lines that were looped between flowering fruit trees whirring with hummingbirds.

From the centre of the garden, welded together from lengths of steel, rose the tower of the artesian well. It rose high above the garden, high above the building. It had been carefully coated with aluminium paint, and sparkled silver against the clear blue sky.

An elderly woman, La Padrona's mother, moved quietly around, overseeing the nimble work of La Padrona's daughters and the preparation for the Feast of Corpus Christi.

The meal was to be served in the late afternoon, so we wandered out into town.

The town of El Oro had been built in the last decades of the nineteenth century by a French goldmining company. We walked up the deserted main street in the warm sunshine. The quietness was unnerving; the emptiness was becoming disturbing.

The last of the powdery paint was being blown away from the wooden buildings. Everywhere the wrought-iron scrolls, now wasted away to delicate filigree, hung from the structures they had originally supported.

The bare wooden bones of the Mairie seemed hardly able to bear the weight of its once glorious, now listing turrets. Grand castellated villas flanked the town hall, set back in large impenetrable gardens, locked behind rusty iron gates. The window shutters were closed as in death. The weather vanes that topped the pinnacles of the imitation French towers were rusted immobile and pointed in various directions.

The short rank of shops must have been closed for years. The elaborate letters of their Parisian names almost faded away. Through the twilight of dust and cobwebs we peered through the plate glass, where we could just make out the sad chaos of the abandoned interiors.

Opposite the Grand Hotel stood the Grand Opera House, only a short soft-shoe shuffle from the former to the stage door of the latter. The extraordinary was becoming familiar. So we walked up the sweeping steps to the magnificent entrance, now only a bleached and peeling reminder of its original glory. The Corinthian columns were leaning out from the exterior panelling, gilded only here and there. Pushing open the heavy mahogany doors inset with a rococo arrangement of bevelled panes of glass, we stepped inside along with a few rays of sunshine. For a fleeting moment we caught sight of the curved dress circle and protruding boxes, the thin supporting pillars, the stucco cherubs and friezes of olive branches. A tangled chandelier hung lopsided over the little auditorium of red plush seats. Heavy velvet curtains were draped across the proscenium arch.

The entrance doors slowly swung shut. But for our breathing, it was as still and silent as the tomb. Gradually, as our eyes grew accustomed to the gloom, we began to see everything again, this time in monochrome. A pungent smell of decay rose up as our feet disturbed the dust that lay, slightly sticky, on the foliate designs of the carpets.

These stirred-up dust particles were visible only in the thin, parallel shafts of light that slanted through gaps in the shrunken wooden planking of the walls. A magnificent theatre had been built in a big shed.

It was said that Caruso had sung here, but only the once.

Returning to the hotel we were invited by the eldest son of La Padrona to pass the hour before the meal visiting the gold mine. We lurched off in a dilapidated American car, jogging over unmade tracks. The mining company had run into difficulties and closed in the 1930s, when the gold became uneconomic to extract. Apart from a thick layer of accumulated dust on every horizontal surface, it gave the appearance of a place just closed for the fiesta. Tomorrow the work force would be back.

A row of pay kiosks stood outside the living quarters. There were the bunkrooms, the mess rooms, the games rooms, all perfectly preserved.

In the director's office, chart drawers were full of maps. The last survey of this failing mine was still spread out on the huge table.

A curly iron gate remained locked across the entrance of the mine, from which a small stream bubbled before cascading down to the river far below.

A row of privies hung over the ravine.

In 1861 the Zapotec Indian Benito Juárez came to power and as a liberal leader made many fundamental reforms. The Government was bankrupt, so he stopped all payments of foreign debt. The conservative opposition sent for outside help. In the event it was only the French who showed sustained interest. Napoleon III advanced on Mexico, and despite setbacks, occupied the City in 1863.

The proposed Emperor was to be the Hapsburg Archduke Maximilian. He arrived a year later, with his wife, the Empress Carlotta. They knew nothing of the politics, intrigues and feuds of the country. All they had learned about Mexico on their long sea voyage had been culled from a book on court etiquette.

Missing familiar refinements of Europe, they immediately sent home to Maximilian's brother Franz Joseph in Trieste for two thousand nightingales to be sent from his garden, where they had enchanted the luckless pair before their departure for the New World.

As it turned out, the new Emperor was too liberal to repeal any of Juárez' ideological changes. The conservatives dropped the Emperor like a hot potato.

Everything went from bad to worse, and while Maximilian stayed with his out numbered troops, the Empress was sent to Europe to rally support. It turned out to be a hopeless quest.

In 1867, the Emperor was defeated, captured and executed. His wife never returned to Mexico. Carlotta refused to believe her husband was dead, and lived out the rest of her life in a Belgium lunatic asylum, where she died in 1927.

Although the Empress had such a fleeting reign, her passion for food and the introduction of French cuisine still has its influence on Mexican cooking. It continues to be an excellent partnership.

By the time we returned in the jalopy to the hotel, a large trestle table had been set up on the balcony and covered with one of the starched linen tablecloths we'd seen pegged on the line. Little conical towers made from napkins sat by each place setting. Tequila bottles stretched down the centre of the table; a line well punctuated by large jugs of water.

Beethoven's fifth symphony played, as if by an invisible musician, on the pianola in the darkened salon behind. Two macaws screeched like opera singers, warming up their voices in preparation for the evening's vocal entertainment. Each gripped its perch with great talons. Their stands had been placed symmetrically, one at either end of the table.

The same elderly men we had previously seen in the foyer had now changed into their Sunday best. Already ensconced, each wore a dark striped suit and a camel hair waistcoat that was looped around with heavy gold chains that led to watch-shaped bulges in various pockets. Their newly waxed and pomaded mustachios curled in a way that echoed the wrought-iron brackets of the balcony canopy. They greeted us effusively as we rushed by to change into our best clothes.

Glancing under the table I could see that the gentlemen kept their ankles warm with grey spats, buttoned up over cracked patent leather dancing shoes they had forcibly laced onto their artificially pointed feet.

La Padrona appeared almost as a vision and we took our places at the table. Just as we lowered ourselves onto our chairs, the three gentlemen rose in unison. Stiffly, and with a bearing that while it appeared to be military could have been rheumatic, each held a tiny glass filled with tequila high in the air. Licking a small cache of salt placed in the hollow at the base of their thumbs and sucking briefly on a segment of lime, they threw the apéritif down the back of the throat, before each in turn extolled the rare beauty and numerous virtues of their hostess.

La Padrona was indeed, a very fine woman. Her breasts, the only part of her trunk not confined by stays, quivered with appreciation beneath a lace blouse. Surmounting her proudly-held head was the magnificent spun gold hair-do of a Southern Belle. She drank a glass in gratitude to each compliment. While her numerous children waited at table, she presided with magnificent style.

Each one of us unfolded a table napkin and spread it on our knees.

A tableau had been set. The meal was served.

We ate festive hare served from a great cauldron, with bread that had been brought to the table in baskets. Water was drunk as well as the tequila. The toasting came thick and fast, and included La Padrona's mother, who was still scurrying around down below in the outside kitchen. This feat involved the gentlemen in seemingly reckless gestures as they leaned unnecessarily far out over the balustrade. The parrots joined in with screaming echoes of disjointed words, mimicking the guests. As the party grew more and more excited, it grew louder and louder. Louder than the cardboard rendering of Beethoven's fifth which, having come to the end of the roll, left the pianolo resting in unacknowledged silence.

As the plates and dishes were carried away, another of La Padrona's daughters was now charged with the duty of winding up and changing the three-minute tangos on the gramophone. This was much more in keeping

with the exuberant mood of the evening, and the parrots too screeched
their appreciation. The gentlemen's feet tapped out the tricky rhythms as
lightly as when their youthful bodies were able to join in.

The toasts grew more frequent and were pronounced with increasing
passion. As the tequila-fuelled fervour reached new heights, another
gentleman, the mayor, turned to us and asked why we were visiting El Oro.

We told him we were looking for somewhere to live for a few months.

As if in answer to this, the mayor stood up and with an operatic gesture
drew a sheaf of paper from an inside pocket. Barely glancing at the script
that was known by heart, he began to declaim. It was as if the words were
a love song, as indeed they were:

ODE TO EL ORO

Niguna Mitología	No Mythology
fue capaz de darte nombre	was able to give you a name
tu nombre El Oro lo escribió Dios	your name 'El Oro' was written by God
y lo esculpió en tus entrañas	and he engraved it on your heart,
lo convirtió en un tesoro	turned it into treasure
y cubrió con montanas.	and hid it beneath the mountains.
La riqueza de tus minas	The riches of your mines
te dio la fama mundial	gave you fame across the world
y sólo se comparó	and are equalled only by
con las minas de Trasvaal.	the mines of the Transvaal.

Then there was clapping and agreeing and more toasting, this time
holding the glasses high in the direction of the mayor. And just as they
were being refilled in preparation of even more appreciation, La Padrona's
mother made her first formal appearance. Dressed in deep mourning, she
swept in, holding up in front of her tucked and rouched black taffeta bodice
a great silver dish, on which, oscillating like her daughter's breasts, lay the
pudding. From this crème caramel rose the wonderful aroma of vanilla. It
was shaped like the bandstand.

I like to think that the Empress Carlotta brought a plain custard recipe from
France and made it quite delicious with the addition of an indigenous plant.

The crème caramel was served onto each of our plates by La Padrona.
And as the delicious pudding slipped down our throats, a huge full moon
began to rise, and the sinking sun gradually drained the colour from the
landscape. Bats in the air took the place of the swallows that had spent the
early evening swooping through the ironwork of the artesian well.

The night fell quickly and the air grew quite cold. By the time I had
fetched a shawl, the mayor was on his feet again. He nodded in our direction

and told us that we should look no further for a place to stay. He would assume this mantle of responsibility.

El oro de tus entrañs,	The gold from your most innermost being
se lo llevaron a Francia	was taken to France
y de alla nos devolvieron	and from there we acquired
la Cultura, el perfume	the culture, the perfume
y su fragrancia	and its fragrance.
Tus mujeres se vestían	Your women were dressed in
Con esas modas de Francia	these French fashions
Y siempre se distinguían	and were always distinguished
Por su porte…y su elegancia.	by their bearing…and their elegance.

Everyone was clamouring for us to stay. Each of the gentlemen was loudly recommending a different house. La Padrona sat back from all this without concern. We either stayed at her hotel, or we didn't.

The mayor took his position squarely on two feet, he silenced the excited guests. He cleared his throat and reassumed his authority:

'Oro' Joyas, piedras preciosas,	Gold jewellery precious stones,
mujeres hermosas, como las hay	beautiful women as there are
en esta tierra hermosa.	in this beautiful land.
Tu escribiste tu propia historia	You are the author of your own story
en la grandeza.	and of your greatness.
Tus moradores vivian en la riqueza,	Your inhabitants will live a life of riches
y no se fijaban en la pobreza,	and will not be trapped in poverty,
porque era una epoca de oro	for it was a golden age
y de grandeza.	and one of greatness.

In the background, a heated discussion had erupted about where we were going to live: in the town, by the lake, a new house, an old one… Yes, we could do some repairs, we said, and the argument shot off in another direction. Presumably about whose house were we going to rebuild. Everyone spoke at once, and as the language grew faster and faster, incorporating all the short cuts and codes of the local colloquial tongue, we were quickly out of our depth.

The mayor whetted his whistle and glared until there was calm and the only sound was the ticking of the clock coming from dark recesses of the music salon. It produced the same measured tension as a time bomb.

As if it were a refrain, everyone except us joined in the poet laureate's rendering of the last verse of the *Ode to El Oro*, as they must have done many times before.

Por eso tu nombre 'EL ORO',	Because of this, your name 'EL ORO'
lo escribió DIOS	was written by GOD
y lo esculpió en tus entraña	and He engraved it on your heart
lo convirtióen un tesoro	transformed it into treasure
y lo cubrió on montañas.	and covered it with mountains.

A town, built for 150,000 at the turn of the century had been reduced to a ghostly shadow, in which 3000 people were scratching a living in its decay.

It was the end of the evening. In unison, the gentlemen all stood up and as the sound of chairs scraping on the boards died down, bade us a very good night, the first of many they hoped. They formed a queue to the left of La Padrona, and only a little short of genuflection, each pressed his lips onto the back of her hand.

La Padrona caught my eye and we smiled warmly at each other. She hadn't been in the least concerned as to whether our union had been blessed by God, or indeed by anyone. Her concern, quite rightly, was the risk of being upstaged. If chalk and cheese had ever dined together, it had been on that night. As the company trooped out, and as the daughters finished clearing the table, the parrots tucked their heads under their wings to produce a bookend symmetry, and a welcome silence pervaded the hotel. We could retune our ears to the sounds of the night.

The full moon had risen high in the sky and the stars were brilliant. We returned to our room by candlelight. Among the flickering shadows the sagging matrimonial bed, its legs splayed out, looked as if it had been drawn in black pen and ink. We stepped up and lay between the linen sheets fresh from the line. Our bodies pressed their weight with pleasure against each other, as they rolled into the single trench.

Caruso must have slept in the Grand Hotel. It certainly felt as if he had slept in and moulded our bed.

The next morning we fled El Oro and its politics. The Silver Horseshoe removed us from the quarrelling inhabitants of this town at six o'clock in the morning. As we paid La Padrona's son, he smiled with duplicity. Had we stayed, we too, would have had to run with the hare, and hunt with the hounds.

The polythene kite, sucked into the whirlwind of dust caused by the bus's wheels, joined us momentarily, before sinking back onto the road.

Blithely we jogged on through the Mexican countryside. We did not yet know how much we had to learn.

THREE

LAS BRUJAS
THE WITCHES

The next few days were spent travelling in ramshackle buses up and over and down the mountains. Our faces pressed against the often shattered windows, we hoped that the 'perfect place' would appear. In our mind's eye it was always over the hill, over the mountain, in the next place, at the next stop.

Our initial hesitance to jump off at the stop turned into a reluctance to brave the unknown. Inertia overcame us, but we did not dare speak of it to each other. We drew great comfort from a proximity to the driver, and sat as if drugged by the go-faster music, music which seemed to inflict a sleepy contentment on us. All decisions, all problems, retreated to an imaginary perfect place, over the hills and far away.

Bright red curtains divided the driver's cabin from the passenger area. They must have been made with love and care by his wife. Or maybe she didn't want her husband to be seen travelling about the countryside in a badly draped front of bus. The ensemble continued with a deep crocheted pelmet, pinned the entire width of the windscreen. A row of infants' first shoes, each one of a pair, dangled from its fringes, showing him to be a prolific Catholic father.

A shrine to the Madonna in her elaborate niche was fixed in the centre. The lights were switched on only when trickier hairpin bends had to be negotiated. Sometimes we passed the roadside shrine of a fatal accident. Alone in not vigorously crossing ourselves, we watched hopefully to see if the lights in the Madonna shrine were illuminated.

The buttocks of the driver had an almost fluid quality; tightly contained in their trousers they spread and slopped over his visibly sprung seat. He crouched like an animal ready to pounce on its prey, but in reality he was only ducking his head low enough to be able to see the road as it rushed past beneath the flounces of the hand-made curtains. We watched as he fought with the gears and struggled to turn the steering wheel, pulling on the horn as we sped through more remote villages.

Sweat poured down his face and neck into his shirt before he could spare the time to mop himself with his towel.

This large taciturn man sat driving us in a cabin that reminded me of the reception area of a very pretty bordello – one that you might mistake for a hotel, stay in, and never be any the wiser.

It was late afternoon when we came to the end of the line. We were tipped out into a small market town. The driver did not acknowledge our thanks. He looked transfixed with exhaustion. We weren't quite sure whether to think of him as saving our lives with his skill on the road, or nearly killing us with his reckless driving. What we'd really wanted was his assurance, a response to our gratitude.

These are the first signs of apprehension coupled with tiredness. Neither of us could confide our worries. We were still trying to present ourselves to each other as really nice human beings. To my chagrin I saw that my act was growing implausible, and in a panic I didn't know how long my best behaviour could last. As we trudged through the lumpy mud of the bus station and up a hill into town, each of us must have wondered if a possible place to stay even existed. The dream of a perfect place remained out of reach.

Then Richard had a good idea. This was to shelve the search for our Holy Grail and go to a nearby spa for a hot municipal medicinal bath. Mud would be an option. That night we felt much more cheerful and sat in the crowded *zócalo*, listening to the town band playing under trees full of the ubiquitous screeching black birds.

Early next morning we left our rucksacks at the hotel, and walked with a spring in our step down to the bus station. The dilapidated assembly of vehicles that formed the town's transport system was parked in such an ad hoc way as to momentarily make us think we had arrived at a scrapyard. It had rained heavily in the night and many of the buses stood up to their axles in mud. There was a lot of shouting, directing and hauling as the rocks kept for such emergencies were distributed and placed behind the wheels of the sunken *colectivos*.

Our request for the bus to the Hot Baths fell on deaf ears. It appeared to be the most frivolous question of the morning. But we were persistent. We waded through the mud until it sucked the shoes from our feet, before we spotted a driver winding his destination panel to read 'The Spa'.

We managed to retrieve our footwear by plunging our arms down into the closing mud holes and pulling hard against the vacuum that had dislodged them from our feet in the first place. To double check, we asked a breathless man passing by, carrying a large piece of demolished wall, if this was the right bus.

'Yes, yes, yes,' he gasped with annoyance, as he threw his load under the front wheel we were standing near.

So we climbed in, barefoot, among the upholstery. As the first passengers sat in the best seats at the front, we hoped the mud would dry enough to put our shoes on before reaching the spa town. That adhering to our arms could be brushed discretely away during the course of the journey.

The lump of wall did the trick. By the time the vehicle was full, the wheels had enough purchase to stop them spinning, and it was manoeuvred out of the bus station backwards. After sliding around on a slippery three-point turn, we headed out in the direction of the mountains.

The conductor gave a few stylish turns to the handle of the destination panel before insinuating himself down the aisle through a lurching multitude of passengers to start collecting fares from the back. It seemed that he not only knew most of the people, he was related to many of them. So by the time he had exchanged enough news to have worked himself back to the front of the bus and the end of his travail, we had been enjoying the spectacular views through the cinemascope windscreen for nearly an hour.

'Two tickets to the spa,' we requested. He stopped to politely suppress the faint smile from his lips.

'The Village in the Valley,' he corrected.

At that moment the road flew over the high pass, and we could see down the steep wooded hillsides into the plush green valley winding generously between mountains that resembled an exquisitely painted Chinese landscape. Birds of prey had swooped up on the morning thermal currents, and now swept in wide circles over the treetops.

Two tickets to the Village in the Valley now seemed an excellent option.

*

It's surprising how far a little mud will spread. Even so, we did not feel too out of place sitting in the cool shade, under the spreading branches of the trees in the little square and putting on our shoes.

While aware of the scrutiny, the discreet curiosity, the general sizing up, we did not feel in the least bit threatened. Nobody seemed to think that our attempt to brush, beat or pick the mud scales from our clothing and skin was in the least bit peculiar. The road cleaner hovered at a distance, waited to sweep away the earth of the Town on the Hill. But he smiled politely without criticism or resentment. This place was as calm and peaceful as Mexico City had been frenetic. The square and the surrounding streets were spotlessly clean.

It was market day. Still clutching the bags of now redundant bathing things, we wandered in the direction from which a general murmuring hubbub rose. Dozens of people sat cheek by jowl on low chairs, while others crouched on straw mats that had been laid on the road. Children clambered and ran around, while babies who weren't clamped to the breast slumbered in baskets or boxes. The market had been spread out in the shade made by large white sheets stretched taught across the main thoroughfare.

Gesticulating with operatic passion, everybody talked. Everyone talked fast, passing on the weekly news. The magnificent piles of fruit, vegetables, pottery, shoes, clothing – and anything else that you might need – spilled out onto each other. Without a break in the conversation goods were weighed and packed, and money exchanged. Explanations of the use, descriptions of the quality, the price and the price to you, all took place without disrupting the flow of murmurings of friendship.

Yet we felt no cold shoulders. Nobody even glanced in our direction with a look to persuade or coerce as we picked our way slowly through the market.

At the bottom end, where the piles of edible and wearable goods turned into the hardware section, were saddles stacked up in diminishing towers. Suspended from a rail were the bits and halters, bundles and reins, martingales and stirrups. Beads jangled and little brass bells rang out as you brushed by. Some were basic and plain, while those aimed to satisfy the self-consciously flamboyant dreams of the most machismo of riders displayed outrageous decorations in intricately tooled leather.

Deeply indented, the dramas depicted landscapes and bullfights, rodeos and magnificent stallions. Every visible piece of leather was covered with pictures. Sets of spats for hooves illustrated with floral patterns dangled at eye level, along with enclosed stirrups, and dagger and machete scabbards.

Fresh from the barbers, their mustachios clipped, combed and plumped, their chins shaved and perfumed, a cluster of men dressed in their festive flounces and spaghetti western hats were discussing the goods they were delicately fingering. Casually, each man wore a polished leather holster slung on the diagonal, and buckled loosely round his waist. These cradled beautifully decorated pistols.

Nearby, were tied up the dozens of donkeys and mules and horses that had travelled overnight across the mountains, from all directions, to deliver their loads and riders at this weekly market.

Across the road, a woman was cooking *tlacoyos* on a charcoal fire. These maize *antojitos* – snacks sold by street vendors – turned blue from the black fungus that is encouraged to grow on ears of corn. Known as *huitlacoche*, it takes its name from the Nahuatl and means 'sleeping filth'. Each thick soft purse was slit and, as the steam rose, filled with beans. There was a choice of salsa: red or green. Held in a square of sugar paper, crispy and hot, they were delicious.

On the way up the hill, a smiling man leaned out of a shop. This was his home with a window built into the front. Lowering the *tlacoyos* from our mouths we returned his smile, and took advantage of the moment to look through the glass into the tiny front room. It was crammed with the detritus of magic.

Monstrous masks and wizards' wands carved with glyphs. Glass jars crammed with dried insects. Carvings of puma faces and piles of tree bark. Cats mummified to skin and bone hung by their crooked tails from the low ceiling. Lamps designed to cast mysterious shadows made from oil tins. Sculptured deities with three eyes.

All this was displayed alongside a good selection of shrines to be lit either by electricity or candle. Flags and herbs, baskets and ropes, all were jumbled together. We looked until it seemed rude to merely stare with the astonishment that we felt.

Then the shopkeeper spoke. He asked if we were Protestant.

'Certainly not,' we were quite truthfully able to say.

And he shook our hands with warm enthusiasm.

We omitted to explain that neither were we Catholic.

We bought a small mask with three eyes, two noses. Its one mouth was fixed in an 'O' of surprise. There were grinning serpents where plaited hair might have been.

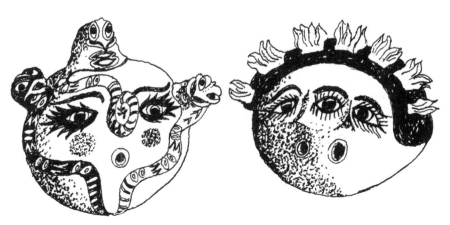

And as we walked back up to the *zócalo*, we felt that, now, everyone knew quite a lot about us.

This seemed to be a very promising place to try and find somewhere to rent.

Perhaps our unspoken wishes had reached the centre of the town before us. We had been told that any village pharmacist would know of an empty dwelling. As we walked through the square, past the bandstand and towards the chemist, a neatly dressed man detached his shoulder from the wall he had been leaning against. He looked at us and made a dramatic sweep with his right arm, indicating that we should precede him inside.

He introduced us to the pale, sad-faced man behind the counter. He seemed to be absorbed by more important things, and continued rubbing his hands together. Whether it was through despair or avarice, we could not tell. The pharmacist, *el farmacéutico*, then held out a thin damp hand in our direction. The man who had instigated all this was Don Cándido. We blurted out our names, and shook the proffered hand.

Feeling like a pair of eavesdroppers, we stood nervously on the periphery, understanding only the gist of their discussion. But this exclusion was short-lived, and soon we were following our new friend through the dappled sunlight of the mango, avocado and hog-plum orchards.

We sped along at the pace set by the excited Don Cándido, down little paths that followed the ancient irrigation channels. The water flowed down the mountainsides in curving canals, chased into the rock hundreds of years before the Aztecs fought their way into power. Once it had gushed down into the valley, an intricate system of tiny sluice gates and stone bridges had been constructed so that each farmer would receive a fair amount of water.

Joining a bigger track that must have once been meticulously cobbled, we rounded a corner to see an unoccupied adobe cottage. Dogs started barking. Don Cándido could only gesticulate and indicate that this was the place for us. The perfect place he insisted, as the barking gathered force and nobody could shout loud enough to be heard.

There was no way to communicate except by smiling and nodding in agreement.

Although smoke was curling up from under the tiles of the neighbouring roofs, we saw nobody. We heard shouting, which managed to cower the dogs into silence, and we thought we felt a score of eyes watching us. Soon we found that we had, by gestures alone, rented the cottage, a small workshop and a good-sized garden. All this was swiftly arranged without catching sight of a living soul. This was San Miguel, one of the seven barrios that constituted the Village in the Valley.

The next day we returned with our rucksacks, took up Don Cándido's kind offer and borrowed his spare mattress. He was very insistent that we visit him at any time and that his shower was at our disposal.

'Use any wood that you find in the garden, it is all yours.'

We shook hands, as if a job had been done well. He turned on his heels and departed at a trot.

We had moved into San Miguel. It was our first home together.

No sooner had our friend disappeared round the corner, than the neighbours began to appear. It was the boldest who introduced themselves. Several men had asked permission to come as far as the veranda, while two women politely stood by the gate.

We invited them into the empty room. Everybody looked around and after having spoken softly to each other, bade us good evening and gradually departed.

Not a single dog had barked; neither of us had felt any hostility. So we stood in the middle of the best parlour, trying not to kick up the dust of the earth floor and noticing, but not mentioning, the shafts of evening light slanting through gaps in the roof tiles.

There were no windows. Leading from this room was the other, the kitchen. Here, there were two windows, or rather rectangular openings to let out the smoke from a cooking fire that would be contained within a circle of whitewashed stones in the centre of the room. Various large tree trunks and planks made up the rest of the furniture.

In the garden was another smaller dwelling. This would be Richard's wood workshop.

Soon we beat a path around the herbs to the place where the lavatory, or rather earth closet, would be built.

Coffee bushes grew in the shade of tall mangoes, and 'plum' and avocado trees at the far end of the garden, while nearer the house was a small grove of lime and orange trees, as well as plantains.

We were lucky to have a fecund Chinese nispero tree, known in English as a loquat, casting its shade outside the workshop.

Nearby, grew a tree with cucumber-shaped fruit sprouting cauliflorously from its trunk and lower branches. Native to Mexico, the *Parmentiera edulis*, the candle tree, is locally known to us as *el guajilote*, 'the turkey'. Its fruit can be eaten cooked with *piloncillo* sugar, or made into chutney or pickles. At a pinch you can eat them raw, but they cannot be described as succulent.

A magnificent bush of rue (a useful 'morning after' drug) was tucked away by the wall. Night-scented Angel's Trumpets grew alongside delicate purple blooms of *Solanum*, or Nightshade, both relatives of the native potato. Over these scrambled Chalice Vine, whose giant golden leathery-looking cups give it its name. When spread out on your pillow, its petals are as good as any sleeping draught. Sprays of pink fragrant *centifolia* were tied to the posts supporting the veranda. And, above all this, towered sweet-smelling pines. From their canopy came the almost constant sound of buzzing honeybees.

We made some sort of bed with sleeping bags, unpacked our clothes, books and a few tools, and folded everything into neat piles on pieces of cardboard we had fortuitously bought on the way down.

Just as we were deciding where to pin the three-eyed deity, our next-door neighbour, Felice, returned, carrying two bowls of soup from which emerged the yellow scaly legs and feet of a chicken. Next to them she placed a pile of tortillas wrapped in an embroidered cloth. A minute later her husband, Sánchez, silently appeared, holding a tray with four cups of hot drinks. Together, we sat on the low wall of the veranda. Fireflies danced before our eyes. While we ate, Felice and Sánchez quietly and politely, between long, thoughtful pauses, began to ask us about ourselves.

The entire village must have been relieved that we were not evangelistic Protestants. The information we had unwittingly given to the owner of the magic shop must have travelled like wild fire.

With delicate but not unfriendly formality they asked us about our children and grandchildren, and must have sensed by the slight inconsistency in our answers that our lives were not as straightforward as we would have wished them to be.

Between us, we have six children and two grandchildren. Together, we are in the privileged position of having no issue. We kept these details to ourselves, and this reticence was clearly understood. Nobody was judgmental. After all, they weren't Protestants either.

The mugs were full of a maize drink, *atoli*. This warmed our insides just as the conversation warmed our spirits. They wanted to know what we were going to do here since we had no land.

Richard explained that he was a carpenter and planned to make furniture. I did my best to describe illustrating a book. And for a moment we all sat in silence.

It had grown dark; Felice and Sánchez got up to go. We found it difficult to find the words to thank them adequately for their kindness and their friendship. They left us their candle, and we sat for a bit longer on the wall, watching the insects almost fighting to be burnt to death in its flame.

Our neighbours had the discretion and charm of spies. Or maybe this is how the world turns smoothly, oiled by gossip.

That day, we had inadvertently effected our own marriage. That night, we slept well and long.

*

Las Brujas was the local name for the barrio of San Miguel. Built on an ancient necropolis, we were told that it had been a ghetto for the uncooperative Matlátzinca Indians, when, in 1476, the Aztecs conquered this highland valley. It was from this barrio that they took people to practise their ritual slaughter.

It was not long before we sensed their continuing anarchic resistance. The Village in the Valley had been a holy place long before the bloody tribal wars. It was famed for its sorcerers. Long before the rise of the Aztecs, it had been the place where these professionals had been taught their magic craft.

Most witches were male, their hero being the evil god Tezcatlipoca, or 'Smoking Mirror' as it's translated. The patron of sorcerers, Smoking Mirror represents the night sky. He is the God of sin and suffering with an interest not only in sorcerers, but young warriors. It was he who discovered fire.

It was said in ancient myths that the representatives of Quetzalcoatl, the Plumed Serpent, would appear as strange white men with unfamiliar clothing who would walk across the water. Their arrival was calculated to be in 1519, the year that Cortés coincidentally landed in Mexico. The fateful day was the 21st of April.

The Plumed Serpent was the god of Wind, Intellect and Education.

It was magicians from here that had prophesied the arrival of strangers. Some foresaw them as one-eyed men, while others insisted that they would have the bodies of snakes or fish from the waist down.

A man mounted on a horse was seen as a single beast. Some thought the creature was a dragon. Remembering the axolotl and its affiliation with Quetzalcoatl, it is easy to see where the confusion stemmed.

The women of Las Brujas would transform themselves into turkeys to outwit the enemy. This trick had been perfected and put to good use long before the Spanish fought their way through their land. Conquerors had been quite regular visitors to the Village in the Valley.

We were assured metamorphosis was still practised. Consequently, greeting a turkey in the lane became a more formal proceeding.

Hearing that rebellion was afoot, Cortés dispatched a fellow conquistador, Andrés de Tapia with eighty foot soldiers and ten horsemen to come over the mountains and incapacitate the military academy. The Aztec chiefs were routed and forced to take refuge in their beautiful temple, before the Spaniards continued on their journey to the city of Mexico.

The Aztecs started to build this unusual and magnificent sanctuary as late as 1500. Devoted to the cult of the Jaguar and Eagle Warriors, it was still unfinished when the Spanish swept through.

Today, this ruined site high on top of the mountain is the most wonderful place to visit. The temple had been carved straight out of the solid rock. A carved stone staircase flanked by jaguars leads steeply up to the entrance. A serpent guards the threshold, its forked tongue menacingly thrust out. Inside the circular sacred chamber is an extraordinary jaguar's pelt, carved with expressive detail into a round stone bench. This is flanked by two spread eagles. Another crouches in the centre of the floor. It was this that the first ray of sun would illuminate, as it rose above the mountains

on the day of the winter solstice. From here, there is a spectacular view overlooking the entire Village in the Valley. An entire earth-coloured village, well camouflaged in the landscape from which it was built.

By the time we had woken and dressed enough to appear decently in the full view that our veranda offered, our neighbours' day was in full swing. Useful things had been left on the wall, including a saucepan, two bowls, two cups, a spoon, a bunch of flowers in a jam jar, and a jug of hot coffee.

Well aware that the words 'host' and 'hostage' have the same root, and that we may have rushed in as fools, this did not feel anything other than a generous welcome. Maybe we would have had been more apprehensive had we known that, before us, no white person had stayed in Las Brujas. Barely realising that we were set apart as 'white', we had no inkling that until only five years ago no stranger had been permitted to put their foot over the invisible line at the end of the lane that was the boundary of the barrio.

A stranger of course is somebody who is not related by blood or marriage.

As we sat on the wall slowly drinking our coffee, we spun out the time wondering how to proceed. We listened to the giggles of children, fleetingly glimpsed as they hid in the bushes. And in the background, almost imperceptible, welled up the sound of the quiet *pat, pat, pat*, that would be the soothing backdrop sound of our stay in San Miguel.

Gentle was the *pat, pat, pat* of the *masa*, which is the maize dough used for tortillas. From every direction came this sound, as the tortillas were patted by hand. Thinner and thinner they were rhythmically patted between pairs

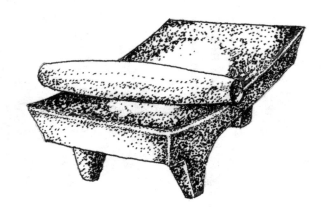

of palms, to form small, perfectly circular disks.

The smell of cooking corn floated out with the smoke from nearly every blackened aperture over every hearth. The village mass-produced hand-made tortillas for this whole mountainous area. The age-old methods and preconquestial utensils were still in use.

Every afternoon, the tortillas were wrapped carefully in embroidered cloths and stacked neatly in wicker baskets. The women fanned out by way of public transport to deliver them all over the countryside.

The rich only eat hand-made tortillas, so too do the very poor, because they cannot afford the machine-made variety.

Kitchens were usually contained in a small stone lean-to, outside the main house. Quite often it was hardly bigger than the raised fire platform. It would be an unusual kitchen not to be equipped with the following:

— The *metate* is a very ancient utensil. It is a tiny three-legged sloping table carved from stone. It comes with a stone rolling pin called a *metlapil*. These are not only used to grind maize, but also chillies, coffee and the multitude of ingredients used in *mole*. When grinding pumpkinseeds or cocoa beans, a small fire is lit underneath, so that the oil will become more fluid.

— The *molcajete*, a deep stone mortar with three legs, is often carved to the shape of an animal. The *tejolote* is the name of the pear-shaped pestle.

— The *comal* is the huge clay disk on which the tortillas are cooked. Unglazed and biscuit fired, they are sold in great quantities in the markets. To keep this from direct contact with the flames, the *comal* rests on small clay animal shapes, known as *tenamaxtles*. Not only tortillas, but chillies, fungus and even eggs can be cooked on this dish

without using fat.

— A *soplador* is used to fan and control the flames of the fire. Some are intricately woven in decorative patterns from palm or rushes, and may be dyed brilliant colours.

— *Tenates* or *chiquihuites*. These woven baskets help keep the tortillas hot. Cylindrical and with a close-fitting lid, these too can be very decorative.

— A tortilla press can be made from wood or cast metal. It squashes the small ball of *masa* flat, and so reduces the time taken in slapping the dough into shape.

The ubiquitous tortilla is made from maize cooked in water with unslaked lime. When it is tender, the skins are rubbed away before it is ground on a metate. While it is being kneaded, water is added to keep the dough malleable. Then it is left to rest.

Knead the dough again until it is slightly springy and does not form cracks when pressed. Keep damp. Roll little balls of the *masa* small enough to fit neatly into the palm of your hand and start patting, passing from one palm to the other until it is paper thin and translucent. If you do have a tortilla press, place the little round ball between two circles of polythene before closing the levers and applying pressure with the weight of your body.

(After our return to England a mill opened in the barrio, where *nixtamal* could be turned effortlessly into *masa harina* while customers caught up on their daily news. This invention must have been more welcome than the wheel that could spin straw into gold. For hundreds of years, every woman has suffered excruciating back and neck pains caused by slaving over a stone *matate*, rolling the *metlapil* with all their force. Not to mention damaged knees

from constantly pressing down onto the rough ground.)

Now gently lower this circle of *masa* onto the hot *comal*, being careful not to trap any air. Cook on the comal, turning twice.

When the edges become frilly and the tortilla is not sticking, carefully lift from the pan and place together with the others, as they are cooked, in a napkin. When the batch is complete remove from the cloth momentarily so they can let off steam. This should prevent them sticking together. Wrap again and put in a *chiquihuite*.

Felice asked us how many tortillas we would like every day. Six we thought, without knowing they were ordered in dozens. Their dog grew quite attached to us with our oversupplied kitchen. Every evening he would wait patiently outside, occasionally whimpering to remind us of his presence. When we had finished eating, we would spin the remainder of this staple food out through the apertures in the kitchen walls. It was impossible to stop the great flow of tortillas; Felice couldn't believe that we only wanted half. Only six?

While the women made and distributed their hand-made tortillas, the men worked in the orchards and fields, or generally repaired everything. Even if we only glanced, we could see that deals were being struck by small groups of serious men who met at the corner by our house.

By the time market day came round, Richard had brought out his hand tools and set up a workshop in the smaller cottage in the garden.

We had arranged to meet Felice at her stall in the market. Not so much as an introduction, but a public viewing. If, by an oversight, someone hadn't known by then that we were the two-white-people-not-Protestants living in Las Brujas, they did now. Felice and Sánchez were very respected people. Although we did not quite appreciate this at the time, their recommendation carried a lot of weight.

We set off through the bustling alleys, knowing that the prices we were going to be asked were fair, and that we had been spared the banter of haggling.

That morning we bought chairs and baskets, pots and pans, fruit and vegetables. Cloth and rush mats, rope and candles. Sticks of ocote wood and charcoal, two pillows and a pair of sheets. And a tortilla press, which I thought would be an excellent way of printing linocuts.

We piled up our goods under the surveillance of the magic man and began to carry everything back to the cottage. As we returned for the third and final load, we noticed Don Cándido standing alone in the road. Waving, he came up to us and picked up the last chair. By the time we turned round to thank the magic man he had vanished into his front room. The woman cooking *tlacoyos* suddenly became distracted by something on the other side of the wall, and the horse tackle experts, having made friendly jokes with us all morning, abruptly presented us with an impenetrable wall of broad backs.

We felt wary as we walked down Calle Emiliano Zapata, our lane. Not a soul was about. Maybe everyone had gone to the market. Don Cándido sat on the garden wall while we drank coffee, looking up and down the deserted road. He could only remark how much we must be enjoying the tranquillity.

A tight gaggle of turkeys waddled by, making their disapproving gobbling noises. We greeted them formally.

Don Cándido smiled and informed us that the residents of Las Brujas believe unequivocally that Protestants have cloven hooves and forked tails. I pointed out that we were not Protestants. Don Cándido, well aware of this, looked at us with astonishment.

Surely, in the outside world from where we had so recently come, it was part of accepted evolutionary fact, that women are women, turkeys are turkeys, pigs have cloven hooves and that the forked tail, in Linnean terms, is a myth. With a certain flamboyant courtesy we shook hands, before Don Cándido strode away down the ghostly stony track.

With his departure we felt more at ease.

That afternoon our neighbours enthusiastically crowded into our home as soon as they had returned from the market.

We had lit the fire and hung the baskets from the beams in the kitchen. Rat, cat and dog proof, they were filled with the food we had bought. Mugs and bowls hung from the nails we had hammered into the wall. The chairs set out on the veranda meant that we could now use the wall as a table. Rush mats were placed neatly either side of the mattress.

In one fell swoop, we had been able to buy ourselves a more or less complete home. We were embarrassed to be seen as rich enough to buy all this at the same time. But of course we were rich enough, and it did nobody any good either to pretend otherwise or to be squeamish about it. It was obvious to everybody that we hadn't chosen to come here out of poverty.

Our neighbours were more concerned that we hadn't been overcharged, they weren't the least bit put out by our ability to bulk-buy a home. They were amused.

Felice from next door and Dolores, the aunt from across the lane, took over the proving of the new earthenware. Vigorously, they rubbed the unglazed part of every cooking pot with juicy garlic, before laying each one out, bottom up, to dry in the sun.

While we waited, we talked. I was given not only a special twig broom, but also a very useful lesson in how to dampen and sweep an earth floor, how to brush with a gesture that left a pattern of great circular arcs.

When the garlic had been absorbed into the clay and felt quite dry, the pots were filled with water and set on the fire to boil. Tomorrow, they would be ready to use for cooking.

The tortilla press caused friendly laughter, as the women listened with the good sense of disbelief to my reason for its purchase. They knew it wouldn't work.

Living in the barrios, most people's dream home was shown weekly on the huge screens of their colour televisions. Their inspiration was the set of the TV soap *Dallas*. The strange thing to them was why I hadn't the same aspirations, where our apparent wealth would have really been put to good use. American soap dramas were their dream.

The interior of their homes, apart from the kitchen, was completely dedicated to saints. Every front parlour was a well-tended shrine. Everyone observed our wooden shelves that hung by rope from a crossbeam, and approved. Up and ready, waiting only for Our Saint.

We had been able to return all the things that had been so kindly lent to us.

That night we cooked our own supper using our own utensils. We sat on our own chairs, watching the moon rise.

The inhabitants of the barrio had settled us in with great kindness. Both of us felt confused about Don Cándido, but neither of us mentioned this, hoping that, unacknowledged, this unease would evaporate.

Independently, we thought of our pasts, our quite separate and different lives, wondering if it was possible for the saddest of ruptured marriages, long over, to ease and spill into new fondness. It was quite a time before we understood that, like a jail sentence, these feelings would long run concurrently.

The rush mats that we had laid out to protect our feet from early morning contact with the earth of the floor, served as beds for our neighbours.

In death they are their shrouds.

Up to now, there had been no history of furniture in Las Brujas.

Four

UTOPIA

THE GARDEN OF EDEN

The Village in the Valley was a small rural town of seven barrios. With seven saints to appease, fiestas came thick and fast throughout the Catholic calendar. In addition, there were weddings, baptisms, confirmations and wakes. There were celebrations for the children who managed to escape infant mortality by staying alive for the first treacherous three years of life. Then there were parties for fifteen-year olds to herald their entry into adulthood.

Seldom a week passed without a fiesta. Rates were levied on the length of the wall enclosing your house, and the money was spent on magnificent religious festivals. Bespoke fireworks and seventy-two hour non-stop *bandas* – bands of musicians – do not come cheaply. These are the outward expressions of the coalition of prehispanic and Catholic cultures; the exuberant expression of religious syncretism. The streaky bacon of two cultures forced to live together.

In the main centre of the town, leading through a grand portal in massive walls, stands a vast Augustinian convent. Built with fervent zeal in the first part of the sixteenth century by mendicant friars, its grassy atrium was now the perfect place to sit and quietly enjoy the shade of its magnificent trees.

It was no longer a monastery but there were always people coming and going from the church, which still provided succour, especially from the vibrant bustle of market days. I would leave my shopping outside, under a tree or by the wall, before wandering into the church. It was wonderfully tranquil to sit in the dim, candlelit nave, listening to the low whispered babble of prayers, the shuffle of knees, the quite sob, or the muffled sound of weeping.

Here, at the feet of an old and beautiful saint, was the barely audible telling of grief, of fear, of sickness and of tragedy. I would sit peacefully in the cool, my bottom sliding down on the polished pew as I looked up at the almost fairground baroque decorations. Then I would take a turn round the chapels, light a candle, and walk out into the dappled light as the sunshine made its way through the foliage of the green garden.

We felt very lucky that we had accidentally found ourselves in this little town the day we didn't manage to get to the hot baths. Whereas the Aztec temple was high on the mountainside for all to see, the town's other great religious treasure was a complete surprise.

One day I left the church, and with growing curiosity felt bold enough to walk through the archways of the 'Open Chapel'. Here was a two-storied cloister. Underneath the arches, painted on all sides of the quadrangle, was the Garden of Eden. Without a breath of warning, not expecting anything in particular, I was face to face with the most staggeringly beautiful sixteenth-century frescoes.

Exuberantly painted, the Trees of Life were filled to capacity with flowers and birds and animals. Flowing up and across the walls, the vines furled among the trees and proceeded across the vaulted ceiling until not a square inch was spared from this sub-tropical growth.

I sat down on a low wall of the cloisters.

During a recent restoration, these beautiful frescoes had been rediscovered. They had lain protected under twenty-two layers of lime wash. Painted by local artisans between about 1535 and 1585, when the mendicant power had been at its height, they constitute the most fascinating interpretation of Paradise.

The Augustinian friars had used the skill of Indian craftsmen, who had been trained locally in pre-Columbian times, to design and paint this didactic mural. Although obviously forbidding pagan symbols, this sumptuous fresco is a monument to the inevitable duplicity of syncretism.

The sapote – a tree native to Mexico – becomes the Tree of Knowledge, its fruit being conveniently spherical like the apple or apricot. Ostensibly a Christian symbol, it therefore continued to play an important part in indigenous ritual.

From the branches of this Tree of Life, grew the fruits and flowers that had the narcotic and hallucinogenic properties essential to indigenous ritual and medicine. But having so recently arrived in the country, the Catholics weren't to know. Such things would have been absolutely outlawed by the Spanish.

But even today, every market will have stalls where these plants can be bought.

*

Once finished, the Garden of Eden fresco had been almost immediately concealed under the first of its many coats of lime wash. Perhaps on more educated scrutiny it had revealed too many unacceptable pagan symbols. Maybe the new fashion for gilded *retablos* – devotional paintings above an altarpiece – and Flemish oil paintings made the murals look outmoded. Or had the competitive friars, who after all were meant to be unencumbered by riches and rely on begging, been among those asked to tone down their exuberant tastes? Questions were already being asked at the highest level about their extravagances.

The enormous task of converting the entire heathen population to Christianity had been done at the most astonishing speed. Arriving in the New World with the ideas of Erasmus and Thomas More fresh in their minds, the friars had only to catch sight of this strange, exotic land before deciding that it could be Utopia.

In about 1530 the most ambitious building programme the Europeans had ever planned was begun. Again, using the skills of the indigenous craftsmen, enormous cathedrals, monasteries, and thousands of slightly smaller churches, were built and decorated. Often, they were erected on the sites of temples that had been destroyed by the conquistadors. These temples quite often lead out onto a large flat area where people could assemble. This idea was incorporated into the Christians' plans, and this atrium was where the unconverted could stand while the clergy proselytised from the security of the open chapels.

Pagans were not allowed inside the churches, but the Indians were accustomed to worship under the open sky. With no choice in the matter, thousands of people were converted simultaneously. In a manner of speaking, everyone kept quiet.

Soon after their arrival in Mexico, the Spanish removed the Aztec priests, who were considered to have the power of gods. Without these direct lines to their gods, pre-Columbian rituals could not take place. Most of the customary festivals, those for specific gods as well as those to mark births, marriages and deaths, were abandoned.

The friars, under great pressure from the Pope, were quick to spot

the advantages of encouraging syncretism, and where there seemed to be common ground between the two religions, the similarities were welcomed. So prehispanic rituals continued under their new guise of Catholicism.

The clergy had their work cut out in mustering enough approved saints to replace the numerous native deities. Although these were accepted, the Aztec cosmology subsisted. Aztec songs and plays were adapted to illustrate Christianity. Native gods were cunningly transposed. The indigenous people accepted the Virgin Mary and a whole panoply of Christian saints, and their own gods were returned to them transformed into devils. By 1580, the powers that be considered the conversion to Catholicism complete.

Each religion had extremely differing views of the supernatural world. While the Catholics believed the relationship between God and man to be the bedrock of Christianity, the Aztecs saw their gods as having total power over their lives. Whereas both believed in eternity, with the soul continuing into an afterlife, the pre-Columbians, rather than being presented with a Heaven, a Purgatory and a Hell, had to contend with a nine step ladder. It was the manner of their death, not their behaviour while they were still alive, that designated them to a particular rung. Warriors killed in battle and women who died in childbirth were the most venerated.

Christians thought that clouds, mountains, water and fire were without life, the Indians believed them to be animate. The Spanish accepted coincidence, randomness and accidents as a way of life, while the Indians believed them to be part of a pre-ordered state.

Whereas the two religions appeared as different as chalk is from cheese, they have somehow rubbed along together for five hundred years. Did the impressive conversion ever really take place? No wonder Mexican Catholicism has a flavour all of its own.

*

A fallen avocado tree in our garden had been recovered and sawn up into planks by a carpenter in a neighbouring barrio. With this wood, Richard had made a bedstead which I painted with *trompe l'oeil* folds.

Now we could sleep as enfeebled Europeans off the damp floor. We made a swing that hung from the rafters. The shelves supporting our few books were now filling up with trinkets bought from the market. Our clothes were stored in boxes or baskets suspended by ropes from the roof beams.

Children would come after school in the afternoon, and take turns on the swing. There was always a 'captain' to make sure that the turns were rotated fairly, and to oversee the curiosity-spurred investigation of our strange belongings and our unfamiliar way of life.

Even as they watched its construction, everyone thought the blue bed was a sensation. Every young man wanted one just like it, and quickly hurried round to the workshop to ask Richard to make them a similar model. And that is how the 'Men's Club' began. Every day at about four o'clock, when their work was over, men from Las Brujas would meet at the workshop. They brought their own wood and, copying Richard's design, built their own beds.

Others would stand outside, teasing and joking with those sawing and planing inside. From the veranda where I was cutting linocuts, I could hear their hilarity, which I knew wasn't for their wives' ears.

Dolores, the aunt from across the way, was keen that I should be aware of her disapproval. I could tell from the slight puckering of her lips, the minute raising of her eyeballs towards the heavens, that she wanted me to see her disapproval. She could well do without carpentry, all its works and pomp. While the banter that welled up from the workshop was quite beyond my basic grasp of the language, Richard was learning the vernacular fast. The matrimonial bed for Dolores' nephew was one of the first off the production line.

Dolores became my friend. She had spotted my solitude only a week or two after our arrival, as I was on the brink of starting my work.

'Where is your mother?' she asked.

On learning that my mother had died more than twenty-five years ago, she took up the vacancy. What was for me peace and quiet looked to Dolores like abject loneliness. And having picked up her embroidery, its hoops and threads, she came to sit with me and keep me company. For her to be alone would have been a social disgrace.

I tried to point out that Richard was only working in the garden, but for her this was an irrelevance:

'I shall sit with you in your hours of solitude.'

I liked Dolores. For many days of the week, as soon as her own domestic work across the road was done, she'd sit by me, looking at my drawings and peering at the process of cutting lino blocks.

The tortilla press was, as had already been noted, not a printing machine. The pressure was one-sided, so we reverted to the well-tried and invariably successful method of rubbing the paper on the inked-up block with the back of a wooden spoon.

'Have you an aunt?'

'Far too busy, and far too far away,' I reassured my new apprentice, as she peeled away the print, looking at it with delight, before pegging it on the string to dry.

*

On Sundays, we took a much more languorous approach to the day, enjoying a breakfast that extended well past the church bell ringing, and greeting people with a wave as they passed by on their way to church or elsewhere. We ate bread rolls made by the bakery next door but one, honey taken from our local bees, and coffee that was grown in the village and bought unroasted in the market.

All the wood, the fuel used by every household for their cooking, was brought down the mountain into the barrios on the backs of mules. It was said that the Village in the Valley needed seven tons of fuel each day.

About twice a week, Salvador or his son Arsacio arrived at our gate, mounted on a magnificently dressed stallion, towing a long string of heavily laden mules. They had come down from Monte Grande, whose steep wooded sides rose immediately behind the lookout promontory, *el mirador*.

These were the two formidably machismo-looking men we had admired on that first market day, clustered round the horse tackle stall, near the magic shop.

Each visit we bought wood to burn. And as Richard helped unload the branches onto the woodpile their common interest in merchandise, as well as a natural curiosity, softened the alarm they had at first felt in each other's company. While I kept to the shadows, Richard began to be friendly with the men who were always referred to as 'the Bandits of Monte Grande'. Arsacio began to arrive early and, with the dozen or so beasts of burden strung out along the lane grazing in the nearest garden, stop for a cup of coffee.

Before long, the muleskinner would be returning to the mountain with templates that Richard had cut from old vinyl floor covering, with a special request for bent branches: particular pieces were ordered to make curved furniture.

Before long, the coffee was taken into the workshop and the visit extended to the soup at mid-day. My companion was always excited at the prospect of these visits and a new supply of curved branches. To thank the two men for their kindness, Richard offered them a bow saw, with the idea that it might make their woodcutting easier.

Emphatically, no. It was declined.

'No thank you,' they said, producing their machetes sharp as razors from between the layers of saddle. 'No, thank you very much.' Richard's rather theatrical demonstration of the effortless saw faltered and trailed off into silence.

We began to understand. Very slowly it dawned on us. While a machete is a laborious way to fell a tree, if saws were generally used, the machete would then look like a weapon. The 'Bandits from Monte Grande' were impeccably polite, and that afternoon we were left only with feelings of friendship.

The machete is more silent than the gun.

*

Rumours spread out across the town that furniture was being made in Calle Emiliano Zapata, San Miguel by white strangers. This brought a various selection of visitors to our door. Curiosity was the most straight forward of the motives.

Apart from the market, it was the ironmongers and hardware shop that became pivotal to our way of life. It was owned and run by an energetic young man called Jaguar. He must have been a bit startled when, not only the white stranger, but also a dozen or so members from Las Brujas Carpentry Club (with whom he had had only a nodding acquaintance with in the street) took to buying the woodworker's equivalent of haberdashery from his shop.

There were no paint charts full of seductively named colours in Jaguar's shop. The choice was Red (Red Oxide or Colonial), Blue, Yellow (Ochre), Turquoise or Black. The red made a good pink if used sparingly. I bought red, yellow and a lot of blue. Lime without pigment makes the most brilliant white.

Soon every adobe surface of our home, inside and out, was painted. Those that didn't sparkle white, glowed with colour. Our house became known as La Casita Azul, 'the Blue Cottage'.

The beds were quickly finished and the manufacture of chests of drawers began in earnest. The rumours must have reached as far afield as the Town on the Hill, because a cart piled high with mattresses was pushed and pulled up the lane. We bought a handsome satin model with already squeaky springs, and were able to return Don Cándido's loan. Our neighbours helped us lift it through the garden and onto the bed. Then we all stood back and admired. Admired everything. The mattress salesman shook Richard's hand very warmly as he continued through the village, making sales that would have been unthinkable before the 'Men's Club' became so productive.

One Sunday, Jaguar and his wife, Guadalupe, sauntered down to make their first visit to Las Brujas. Admiring the interior decorations of La Casita Azul, they politely remarked how old-fashioned it looked. It had been an initial disappointment that we hadn't invested in their new line in gold-embossed flock wallpaper. But seeing the cottage he understood: only lime paint would stick to the walls. This was to be the first of many Sunday visits.

It became quite a party, and Dolores put down her embroidery and helped me serve the cool refreshing drink that had been made for the occasion. Jamiaca is an infusion made from dried hibiscus flowers, sweetened with sugar.

After Seventh-day Adventists tried, once or twice, to convert us, we bought a weatherproof plaque from the shop with a picture of the Virgin of Guadalupe on it. Beside her image, these unminced words:

ESTE HOGAR ES CATOLICO

NO ACEPTAMOS PROPAGANDA

PROTESTANTE NI DE OTRAS SECTAS
VIVA CRISTO REY
VIVA LA VIRGEN DE GUADALUPE
MADRE DE DIOS

('This is a Catholic home
and does not accept propaganda
from Protestants or other sects.
Long live Jesus Christ.
Long live the Virgin of Guadalupe
Mother of God.')

Now, like every other home in the barrio, we had this firmly nailed to the garden gate. It certainly did ward off any other tiresome visits from opportunistic Evangelists.

When it rained, the children dug holes in the garden, and brought in the most beautiful little clay heads they had found. Unearthed from the necropolis, some of these prehispanic grave treasures were very ancient. Called *caritas*, these 'little faces' were miniature portraits of the dead. Most of those that were given to us predated the Aztecs by many hundreds of years.

The children put them carefully on the shelves, and sat on the bed while they waited for their turn on the swing. Our shrine was unconventional, but becoming more interesting.

The children of Las Brujas were unusually small for their age. Often they were slightly crippled. Outside Las Brujas they were called *los duendes* – 'The Elves', or 'The Goblins'. We were growing very fond of them and encouraged their visits.

It felt as if our life together had flowered. We were busy with our work, our neighbours were friendly, and our house was seldom empty. Enough curious things were happening that we were always amused. It was a beautiful place. We were delighted to be living in La Casita Azul. Las Brujas began to feel like home.

FIVE

DON CÁNDIDO

HIS FATHER & THE HUMMINGBIRDS

A bare earth floor was all very well and good, but for a real appreciation of this old-fashioned method of living, it would have been better not to have imported any newfangled modern items into our life. For instance, books or paper.

Soon every surface was covered with fine earth particles, and extremely unpleasant to the touch.

Although Richard had built a washing place, behind a curtain stretched on a string across the corner of the kitchen, our general grittiness acted as an increasingly poignant reminder of Don Cándido's offer. After ten days we gathered together our towels and spongebags, and walked out of Las Brujas for 'The Shower'.

Don Cándido lived outside our barrio, about a mile down the road heading out of town.

It would take us some time to realise that there is no such thing as a free shower. But that late afternoon as we stood outside the heavily padlocked gates of Don Cándido's mansion, pulling on the wire that ran all the way through the orchard and gardens to finally ring in the kitchen, we had no way of knowing to what the strings were attached

We brushed our instincts aside and our apprehension to the back of our minds. I didn't want Richard to think that I lived in some fantasy world of irrational fear, fuelled by a hysterical imagination.

Poking our noses through the thick mesh wire, we saw through the trees that the house was fairly new, and had been planned in a lavish way with two storeys, balconies and a veranda, which ran the length of the downstairs.

Squinting sideways, we could make out that the design for the garden beyond the orchard included not only lawns and flower borders, but grottoes, gazebos and statuary, along with terraces that led down to the swimming pool. Its grandeur only withstood a brief sweep of the eye, for at a second glance its decay became obvious.

The balconies had fallen away from the walls and the roof of the veranda was barely hanging on. Later, we were to learn that it was too dangerous to use the upstairs. Only a few inches of viscous green water stagnated in the bottom of the swimming pool. The nymphs and other allegorical ornaments were a pitiful sight of rust-stained armatures, as if bloodied from a recent massacre. All this built-in fast decay had spread to the grotto caves and the gazebo tearoom. It was accentuated by the pervading smell of rotting concrete.

The builders hired to construct this dwelling were not the first of that profession to take advantage of the lack of constant supervision, and had sold off much of the cement supplied for the job. With such a low ratio of cement to sand, the entire estate of our friend had quickly become a fissured ruin, a liquefying sandcastle.

In spite of hearing the bell ring far off in the kitchen, it was some time before Don Cándido sauntered towards his gates. He appeared attired in impeccably laundered and sharply ironed clothes, accompanied by perfectly polished shoes. A bunch of keys was hooked onto his belt, and with these we were eventually admitted to a palace that would only ever be a figment of the imagination. Once inside the gates, we followed our host nervously down the path through the fruit trees.

Escorted by Don Cándido, we came to the rim of a huge pit that had been dug in the garden. Here, we were invited to peer over the unstable looking perimeter into its depths. He said he'd discovered an Aztec tunnel that he was sure led to the temple on the mountainside. He was adamant this was the most interesting and significant archaeological excavation in the whole area.

Try as we might, we were only able to make out various strata. Topsoil barely covered a modern rubbish dump. This gave way to earth, a layer of stones, dank clay and gloom. There was no sign of a tunnel entrance. Although we tried to see what he saw, we found it impossible to empathise with Don Cándido's excitement and passion. Neither of us mentioned it at the time, but to both of us it looked suspiciously like an oubliette, dug just by the kitchen door.

'Only a bit more money and we'll show the sceptics,' said the amateur archaeologist.

Oh, yes, we were eager to agree. We already knew it was best to be on his side.

What was the Great Hole? We never found out, but there it remained, retaining more water than the swimming pool.

In the house of Don Cándido lived two diminutive young sisters, Carla and Paula. One was said to be his wife and the other his servant. He called both of them his 'Hummingbirds', so we never knew which was which. They shared the domestic work over which they chatted and laughed together equally. The Hummingbirds filled their days with relentless washing, cleaning, cooking and serving. All evening they would be waiting at table, skipping from the dining room to the kitchen in the best of humour. They were the most enchanting pair of miniature women.

'They come from the south, where it is quite different,' their patron said, in rather too dismissive tones I thought. While they were indigenous, this did not altogether account for their size. They were midgets.

Don Placido also shared the house. He was Don Cándido's father. This small and agile man, kind to everyone, was a dancing master. He was always ready to give a lesson in his soft pumps. At the end of the evening, after the table had been cleared, he pushed it back against the wall, where it became a stage. Each hummingbird pinned round their waists a taffeta

skirt, as deeply frilled with ruffles as the backside of a turkey. Don Placido then gently lifted them one by one onto this stage, before they slipped their feet into minute high-heeled shoes.

He then plugged in the gramophone, selected a record, and they danced, under his meticulously watchful eye, the intricate steps of his convoluted choreography. They bent deep back bends, swirled their skirts, and shook their breasts, stamped their feet and smiled as far as the cupid's bows of their scarlet mouths would stretch across their faces. Their teacher glowed with paternal pride as these tiny women performed with sensual grace. We all laughed and applauded with pleasure.

Most weekends Don Cándido's house was filled with visitors; people who arrived with supplies of food from Mexico City. They breathed the air that is in such short supply there, and with great enjoyment savoured the freedom that the countryside offered them. It must have been reassuring to see a tree with a full head of leaves.

Much later, we learnt that this was only possible under the skilled and watchful eye of our host, for the visitors were the grown-up children of the famous and wealthy. They were too vulnerable to kidnap and subsequent assassination to be allowed to roam the country unprotected. Our cottage was owned by a nervous young man far too frightened to stay in it. And as if to expunge the constraints of the fearful and envied, they were wonderfully friendly towards us. They never tired of our stories of walks over the mountains, of taking shortcuts through the woods, wandering in the market, or eating whatever we fancied from the wayside braziers. They drew admiring intakes of breath, immediately followed by mild warnings.

Our host was on the payroll of some of the most influential families in the country.

The visitors listened to the descriptions of our everyday life with the excitement that a 'What the Butler Saw' machine would have incited at the end of the nineteenth century.

On these evenings, which became a regular event, we stepped into another world.

We must have been a conspicuous sight on a Saturday, for at about six o'clock in the evening we left Las Brujas with our washing things, turned right at the end of Calle Emiliano Zapata before walking down the unmade road to Don Cándido's crumbling fortress. With a ritualistic clanking of keys we were admitted. We would then ask if it were convenient to take a shower. Afterwards, we would accept, as if with surprise, the formal invitation to *la cena*, supper.

We really enjoyed these evenings, even when there was some failure in the water supply and our pores remained clogged with grime.

Over the weeks, in between Don Placido's patient tuition as he tried to show us the intricacies of dancing to the sensual rhythm of the salsa, and prayed that we might fall in with the devilish syncopated hiccup of the tango, we listened to our hosts stories. Gradually, we pieced together some of their history. While we were much more reticent, we were in no position to answer anything but the truth when Don Cándido asked directly how long we'd known each other. Known in the biblical sense of the word, that is. About six months, we admitted. Although we didn't say it in so many words, the entire company understood this.

It caused the most touching response. Everybody smiled and laughed and hugged us. The general consensus was that we were still on our honeymoon, and they clapped their hands with enthusiasm. We smiled a lot, too, and hugged each other in a slightly stiff way. Don Cándido pointed this out: 'They must really be English.' As if we were some sort of rare species that only he had been able to classify.

This caused the company to hold their sides with mirth, while our host elaborated on the repressive nature of our countrymen. I longed to prove him wrong, and for the uninhibited woman inside me to leap straight onto the table and dance, without faltering and in rhythms so complicated that the company would gasp with amazement. But he was right. In reality, my body sat there, politely static, while I felt the warm familiarity of inhibition heavy on my shoulders.

So it was well observed and a fair comment. But while I am on the subject of national characteristics, it would be a good moment to point out that Don Cándido and his father were originally from the north, and were machismo Latinos of Spanish origin. Just to keep you in the picture.

Then Don Placido took charge, put a tango on the turntable, and lifted the hummingbirds onto the stage. We were all to be enthralled by their dance. That evening they wound they bodies round each other and performed like a pair of sensuous snakes.

*

When Mexican men want to get drunk, they drink spirits. The bottles of Tequila, Mezcal or Bacardi will stand shoulder to shoulder all the way down the centre of every respectable trestle table at every fiesta. Women tend to remain sober.

At Don Cándido's it was pleasure in the company, spiced up with a little hilarity, that fired the evenings. There was usually Mexican brewed beer to drink, but this did not flow down throats in the generous quantities habitually witnessed in an English pub. Although the beer was good, thirst could be quenched with much more delicious non-alcoholic, home-made concoctions.

Every fruit would be squeezed before your eyes, before it was poured into the glass. Mashed prickly pears with finely chopped parsley and lime juice is as delicious as it is popular. Pumpkinseeds and maize boiled in water, sweetened and ground is a very popular drink that is as thick and good as a food.

Postprandial stories of spectacular bullfights were backed up when Don Placido produced a folder of photographs. Dog-eared and black and white, the pictures were a record of Don Cándido's career as a classical toreador. Standing firmly in the balletic pose that we had all seen on lithograph posters, his crimson cloak held out to tease the infuriated animal already goaded with wooden picks, its hooves pounding the ground, and with seated curves of spectators, expectant and aghast. Our beautiful young hero, cool as a cucumber, stood side-on, slim as a scimitar with the stony expression of a theatrical sneer.

We looked closely from the photographs to Don Cándido, and back to the photos again. He had aged, and his youthful confidence, while remaining quite recognisable, was now veiled, more worn, more wry. The last fading picture showed us the young bullfighter flying through the air above the horns of the roaring beast. In the background, an audience, wide-eyed with horror, were screaming from behind the hands covering their open mouths.

The father looked at his son and gestured that the retired toreador remove his shirt. The reason he had to retire while still in the first flush of early manhood was revealed to us. A massive scar swept diagonally from shoulder to waist and curved around his entire torso. Back and front was displayed as the son slowly turned, pivoting on his heel to show us the lumpy tissue, cobbled together as if in panic and left to heal with no other help but the Grace of God. A terrible reminder of a horrific goring.

It seemed that Don Placido hadn't had much difficulty putting down his foot and ending the glittering career of the indomitable Don Cándido. The resourceful father had something else up his sleeve.

*

That evening, after we bade farewell, we walked with our host and entertainer as he jangled the keys up to the gates. Now we realised why Don Cándido had such a mincing gait. Following behind him, we could see the effort with which he tried to compensate the lopsided stiffness. His whole body was skew-whiff.

Don Cándido was still a young man when he and his father toured the south of the United States of America with their 'act'. They travelled with a thick blanket each, and hats to keep off the sun. Between them, they carried a folding throne, partially gilded and encrusted with crude copies of Aztec carvings, a string bag of fruit, and a cardboard suitcase pasted all over with woodgrained paper. Inside this, folded with the greatest of care, were two very similar, if slightly shabby, silver and white satin toreador costumes. The jackets had wide lapels and were nipped in to form a high waist. They were further adorned with gold buttons and gold braid, being further flounced with gold-ribboned epaulettes. The accompanying pants stretched to their limit over the neat muscles of their bottoms. Blood red cummerbunds covered up the short rift between these and the white embroidered frilled shirts. Without this attire, no one's attention would be arrested. People tend to drift off unless they are rooted to the spot by curiosity. There was also a thin pad, with a dressing gown cord tacked onto its edges.

At all times, Don Pacido carried a soft leather pouch, strapped for safety close by his genitals.

Seeing a possibly good pitch, they would set down and assemble the throne, plump up its threadbare cushion, and, with luck, find a handy bush or clump of cacti behind which to disappear, before emerging, transformed, sleek and puff-chested, into 'The Toreadors'.

Seeing that his son had clipped the rusted spurs onto his down at heel, high-heeled shoes, Don Placido would hand the leather pouch over to his son, before gently lowering his constrained bottom onto the throne. Sitting as straight and tall as his physique would allow, he found a pose he could keep. The son then selected an apple from the string bag, and placed it on top of the father's head. Looking into the sun, the older man froze.

From inside the pouch, Don Cándido unwrapped from its tissue a golden ring. A golden ring with just one huge sparkling diamond. A diamond cunningly cut, so as to leave the centre with a great reflective area. Over a pair of white gloves, our friend worked the ring onto the wedding finger of his left hand. With the flamboyant sweeping gesture that we had seen outside the chemist's at our first meeting, he showed his hand to the gathering, expectant crowds. Then he pulled a jewelled pistol out of the bag. After he had pressed the image of the Virgin engraved on its mother of pearl stock to his lips, he turned his back to Don Placido, who was now as still as if he had been carved in marble, or more realistically, modelled from papier-mâché.

Signalling to the audience for complete, yes, COMPLETE silence, he placed his right arm across his chest, round his torso, until the gun protruded from under his left armpit. Holding his gloved left hand at eye-level and lining up the gun's sights mirrored in the central facet of the diamond ring, Don Cándido carefully took aim.

Naturally, the punters held their breaths. Well aware, the former Olympic Gold Medallist waited. He searched the crowd with rotating eyeballs, as if to spot a dissenter in the almost overwhelming silence. He waited until he could sense their lungs about to burst. He held back until he could almost feel their pain, before making a last-minute adjustment in the sights and pulling the trigger.

The piercing shot cracked out, inflating every eardrum to painful capacity before the air was filled with exhalation of an audience-worth of held breath.

At the shot, the apple rose into the air, shattering into an ever-increasing sphere of pulp as it cleared the father's head.

The audience would turn their next breath into a roar of amazed relief. Whereupon the marksman would adroitly take a swift turn round the escaping crowd, and collect as much of their small change as he could in the leather pouch.

Don Placido, his life spared for another performance, was left to ease himself into an upright posture, before bowing deeply with mock servitude.

*

No wife, no mother was ever mentioned. And we were never forward enough to exhume such a person from the depths of their memories. It

was enough to sense the deep bond between the two of them.

After we had eaten on the evening the story of the 'act' had been told, and while we expected the dancing to start, Don Placido plugged not the gramophone, but a video recorder into the electricity supply. And in case we should have had the temerity to doubt the authenticity of the story, and to the delight of all of us, he showed the flickering film that *Texan Talent Spotters Weekly Television Show* had made of 'The Most Amazing Death Defying, Re-enactment of William Tell.' So here we were confronted with the truth, although we felt the Texans, while they had been quick to spot the talent, had missed out on the performers' deep sense of irony.

We began to understand that scepticism is a defensive mechanism, more applicable in Europe and North America than in Mexico. Here, believing is so enjoyable.

Usually, we arrived back in Las Brujas just after eleven o'clock at night. A couple of dogs would bark, but we liked to think that this was more of a welcome than a hostile reception. The rest of the barrio was so silent we were reduced to whispering. Turning quietly into our garden, we breathed in the wonderful night-scent of the big white Angel's Trumpets. We lit a candle before cleaning our teeth and pulling back the sheets to inspect the bed for white scorpions. We had been told they were the most dangerous, and would drop from the roof to hide in the warmth. The only sounds now, after a single bark, were the exterior tinnitus of cicadas and the screech or hoot of an occasional owl – if you were able to stay awake long enough to listen. It must have taken less than fifteen minutes between turning into Calle Emiliano Zapata, and extinguishing the light.

As our lives had shaken pleasantly down into comfortable repetition and mindless routine, our cottage became a home where you did not have to spend half an hour looking for the fork or the coffee, and the chairs were in the same place every day. Delicately, we worked out the balance of chores. It was usual for Richard to make the breakfast, which we'd eat together sitting on the chairs placed on the veranda. Then he left for his workshop. I cleared everything away, tidied up and swept the dampened floor. Then my linocutting could begin. Market on Wednesdays, shower on Saturdays. Every fortnight or so we would take a day trip and walk over the mountain to our postbox. The weeks began to roll by in a very pleasant way.

*

We had been settled in the cottage for several weeks, when one night, our pleasant drift into sleep was wrenched brutally into reverse by the terrifying noise of gunfire.

We lay rigid on the mattress. Rigid with fear but poised for fleeing, it felt as if only certain parts of our bodies were in contact with the bed. We lay there as if petrified. With every hair on our bodies painfully alert, we heard the bullets whistling over the roof. Time and time again we heard the batches of shots and the overhead whistling. We strained our hearing for distant screams, some muffled shouting that might offer an explanation, human noise that would give some clue to this sudden, shocking violation of calm. But there was none of the bellowing in fury or screaming in terror that welled up so vividly in our mind's eye.

Then it stopped.

We lay shivering, our cold sweat soaking into the bedclothes and mattress

as grim black silence closed in on us. Had it lasted half an hour, we asked ourselves? Ten minutes? Five? But we could not tell. We only knew that it had been long enough to keep us from sleeping that night, and very wary as we stepped outside to drink our habitual coffee the next morning.

Stick to the routine, we thought. We didn't ask any questions and no explanation was forthcoming. We'd learnt to just wait and see how things went. Life continued as usual.

That day, the next and many more days afterwards, proved to be as peaceful and friendly as the first few weeks of our stay in Las Brujas had been.

Only quite often, shortly after we had returned from our hot shower and been given enough time to get into bed, the gunfire would begin again. But we knew that they knew we were at home in bed.

Saturday night shooting practise, we learnt to call it casually. I could not say that we were able to sleep all the way through the firing, but it did not keep us awake for long. Most importantly, we realised it was certainly None of Our Business.

*

By 1968, Don Cándido, now on the brink of full-grown manhood, had enrolled with the police and lived with his father in Mexico's federal district. The uniform may not be as theatrical as that of a bullfighter, and the women may not faint at your feet with desire as often, but the outfit is very smart, the boots of excellent quality, and the helmet fit for a pantomime. It is a job that must be frequently coveted.

1968 was also the year Don Cándido won an Olympic Gold Medal for best shot. The Games were hosted in Mexico. Don Placido could see that his son's talents would help him go far. His chest filled with pride as he fumbled in the table drawer for the little box in which the gold medal on its red ribbon was kept. We took our turn to finger it as the elderly man passed it among the guests. 'The gold medal for best shot...' he muttered, until tears sprung to his eyes and he felt he had to turn away.

When Don Cándido came to visit us, he spoke in English. This we originally thought was to impress our neighbours with his culture, his worldliness, but when we thought about it again, maybe this was to ensure our conversations were secret.

Our initial suspicions of Don Cándido had all but vanished, and when he appeared in the lane, we always made him welcome. That our neighbours hid, seemed no more peculiar than other goings on. So we sat on the stone wall drinking coffee, enjoying the warmth of the sunshine.

'Mexico is Mexico,' said our friend. He started many of his stories with this phrase, until the words meant to us that we should make ourselves comfortable and believe the gem of a tale we were about to hear.

They were to become as irritating as they were enigmatic.

'Mexico is Mexico,' he began that day, when the sky was full of big silver-lined clouds bounding across the blue sky with determined speed. We breathed in the heavy scent of the pine trees and listened to the buzzing of the bees. His eyes glazed over and stared into the distance, as if it took careful focusing to conjure up a clear image of the past.

'Nothing is what it seems, for I have seen things, I have done things, that only later turned out to be quite different.' As the tone of Don Cándido's voice lowered, this confidence, however abstract or noncommittal, drew us closer not only by its dramatic effect, but by the necessity to actually catch the Gold Shot's words. Words he hoped would be conspiratorially inclusive.

Continuing in this newly-acquired sotto voce, he spoke of the Aztecs, whom he insisted we should never forget were the Nazis of Central America.

According to Don Cándido, they were carrying only small suitcases when they arrived on the banks of the lake. He said they saw the sign of the eagle sitting on a nopal cactus wrestling with a serpent, built their city, and taxed the population into poverty. 'Never forget...' And we wondered where all this was leading.

Nobody has ever seen an eagle perching on the painful prickles of the nopal cactus.

'Mexico is Mexico,' and we made ourselves comfortable.

In 1968, Mexico was preparing for the Games. These were the first to take place in what was then called a third world country. It was being taken very seriously. But the student pro-democracy movement refused to be bought off, it rose up and demonstrated in Tlatelolco Square in the city. In fear of losing face as the eyes of the world turned in the country's direction, the demonstrators were well and truly silenced. The government had them executed in their hundreds.

'Hundreds and hundreds. First came the Police, intermingling with armed marksmen. As their work finished, every ambulance in the city rolled into the square. Finally, the army of municipal road cleaners came in and with the help of the fire brigade, washed away the bloodstains left by the brilliantly orchestrated massacre. Within a very short time only the fabric of the square appeared to have witnessed the apocalyptic nightmare.'

It seemed to be such a private story it seemed better for us to appear not to have heard. It was so terrible a tale that part of our brains hadn't taken it in. We also understood our friend had been there.

It was planned, planned to the last moment, when all that was left visible were the wet roads, shining as they caught the rays of the evening light. We waited while Don Cándido searched for the right words to explain that he had been as young and unprepared as the students. He had been one of the dozens of cadets, commanded, ordered to go to the demonstration wearing civilian clothes to direct, lead or coerce the demonstrators into Tlatelolco Square.

'Each one of us was asked to wear one of a pair of white gloves in the epaulets of our shirts.' And that, he explained, was how none of them was shot.

'I went home,' he continued, 'and removed the white glove from The Act.'

Don Cándido said that he had not dared come out for weeks, and had been unable to speak for a year.

'I was young like the students,' he said quietly, by way of an apology.

But whatever the logistics, he did manage to emerge triumphant at the Games.

After the Olympics and the big win, it would have been almost impossible for the Gold Medallist, mute though he claimed to be, not to have made a meteoric ascent up the police promotional ladder. Before long, Don Cándido was working in close proximity to the President.

We shelled sunflower seeds and tried to assimilate the story. It was all the more shocking to us, who had arrived so recently from a country where the police force were rarely armed. A land where most people have never even seen a gun, let alone a person shot dead.

A seed shell got caught between his front teeth as Don Cándido manoeuvred himself round to ask the question. It was as if his tale had meant to soften us up, to put us in the right mood.

'Have you heard shooting?'

Only now did we understood why he had been perched on the wall half the afternoon. It had not been merely for the sake of our company. All the time we had known, but only as a doubtful shadow. In the half-light of realising that this was the crux of the matter, we remembered our initial nervousness and confusion in the company of this man.

And as our reply was not immediate, Don Cándido continued:

'Of course, everyone in Las Brujas will have a gun tucked away under the bed. Uzi Israeli made submachine guns.'

I thought in panic that he might hold us responsible for this space 'under the bed', that he might accuse us of introducing this secret hidey-hole along with the new cult for wooden furniture.

But Don Cándido swept on: 'They are waiting for the uprising. They are revolutionaries. They are Matlazinca Indians.'

And then in a desperate effort to convince us, he bellowed in frustration: 'They are all anarchists!'

Then, noticing that we had become a little shaken by his outburst, he added:

'They have to practise sometime. Have you heard them firing at night?'

We both thought of Felice and Sánchez, their family and their fruit trees, of Dolores and her little nephews and nieces. And we saw our neighbours working so hard and barely making a living. We thought of their generosity towards us.

'Surely you must have heard them? They're supplied with ammunition.'

Without being able to consult, we each gave a firm answer.

'No,' we said, not finding it very difficult to look bewildered. 'We've not heard a thing.'

Politeness went into automatic and the afternoon was, on the face of it, saved.

Don Cándido took his leave.

We felt shaken, not only by our off-the-cuff lie, but also by our surprising ability for instantaneous collusion.

Without knowing why, we both agreed it had been the correct answer.

Anyway, we thought he must be able to hear the gunshots from his own house. That meant he now knew our allegiance was to our neighbours in Las Brujas.

Six

THE END OF THE WORLD
A FLURRY OF RUFFLES

The rainy season started late, at the beginning of June, and continued in full spate. While everyone had been gasping with the heat at the end of May, complaints about the weather were not brought to an end when the rains, with all their steaming and chilling, arrived.

It was exceptionally wet, we were told, especially on days when it rained all day. Very unusual, but then so had been the heat the month before.

The men in the village, certainly not welcome at home, stood around in miserable groups under the trees, the rims of their hats pulled down and their shoulders hunched up as they passed the jug of *pulque* amongst themselves.

For at least two thousand years this drink has been fermented from the sap of the maguey, a succulent that resembles a cactus but is a member of the *Agave* family.

Before the Spanish imposed its alcoholic culture, *aguamiel* or *pulque* was drunk as part of a ritual. Ordinarily, only the elderly and nursing mothers were allowed to imbibe. While a plebeian drunk was publicly stoned to death, an inebriate from the nobility was strangled (in private).

But after the conquest, when these restrictions were removed, the colonial regime was not slow in blaming the consumption of *pulque* on the rapid decay and demoralisation of their subjugated workforce. While the control of the industry brought in magnificent profits and tax revenue, the alcoholic state of the population had to be addressed.

In 1672, licensed *pulquerias* were opened. These bars were located in open areas and had no doors. The government imposed a host of controls: these drinking establishments were to close at dusk, play no music, nor allow dancing. Men and women had to drink on different premises.

Today women have nowhere to drink. The *pulquerias* are exclusively male. Gradually these dens of iniquity, under the auspices of the powers that be, became socially acceptable. It could be argued that the fine tradition of modern Mexican mural painting has its roots in the customary exuberant paintings on the inside and outside walls of these establishments.

The cultivated maguey thrives well in the cooler dryer conditions found in the mountains. Each plant is grown from a *mecuates*, one of the numerous side-shoots that grow from the base of the parent maguey. When they are about three and a half feet tall, they are wrenched from the earth, and their tattier leaves and spines removed. Here, they are left uprooted for several weeks, so that they dehydrate and lose enough weight to be carried and transplanted in grid patterns in their own field.

*

Maguey – *Chicuetecpacihuatzin* – Eight Flint Women

> Welcome now, noble women of eight in a row,
> for here is a very fitting and very good place.
> I have tilled and cultivated in order for you
> to be very much at your pleasure.

This was the incantation intoned as the small magueys were transplanted into the chequer-board pattern of eight by eight.

These 'names that the Wizards used' greatly alarmed the Catholics, as they swept through the land evangelising and converting. The church sent out its emissaries to learn the language of Nahuatl, to get to the bottom of these devilish incantations.

When the maguey is between ten and twelve years old, the heart of the plant, the centre shoot, begins to become elongated as it prepares to become the twenty-foot tall bloom.

This is the sign that the *aguamiel* – the sap of the maguey plant – is nearly ready to be siphoned out. The central section is cut away, 'castrated', to prevent flowering. For protection, the outer 'leaves' are folded over the aperture and fastened with a spine. The plant is then left for six months to recover before the wound is reopened with numerous punctures.

After a week, the fibrous pulp that develops to plug the holes is removed. And the *aguamiel* sucked out with a long hollow gourd, called an *acocote.*

Twice a day, the sap is removed: early in the morning and late in the afternoon.

About two litres daily is the yield from each plant, although eight litres is not unknown. After about six months of production the plants will die.

In the past, the sap was then transported in animal hides to the *tinacal,* the processing plant, where it was hung up to ferment.

Nowadays, this takes place in oak vats and takes between seven and fourteen days. With the speeding up of modern life, a 'starter' yeast can be added. While *aguamiel* is quite capable of fermenting on its own, the process is delicate and fermentation secrets are fiercely guarded.

Because it can easily go sour during the making, the process abounds with superstitions. Strangers are not welcome, and women are not allowed near the brewing. As it has to be drunk within a few days of making and travels badly, the best is tasted near the *tinacal.*

*

In the Village in the Valley the gloom persisted.

Streams of soil were running off the deforested mountains and accumulating in the lanes, which had become knee-deep in the sticky mud. Walking to the bakers became a major expedition.

Muddy children appeared more regularly with the most beautiful *caritas* that had been washed out of the ground by the running water. Ceremonial flint arrowheads were also brought to our door. The asking price for these had been fixed by one of the elder *duendes* at the equivalent of ten pence.

Our collection was becoming quite impressive and took up nearly a foot of the hanging shelves.

All agriculture and construction work had become impossible.

Soon there was to be a total eclipse of the sun. Don Cándido told us with great enthusiasm and invited us to his house for a good view.

The chemist's shop had a notice in the window warning people not to look at the sky with a naked eye.

'View the phenomenon with one of *el farmaceutico*'s smoked glass squares,' it recommended. These were displayed in the window, wrapped in paper and built up into a house of cards. 'Buy while stocks last.'

In preparation for Don Cándido's astrological spectacular, and being sensibly nurtured under the auspices of Aneurin Bevan's National Health Service, we naturally took this professional advice.

But we must have been one of the few to make the recommended purchase. The worst aspect of this was braving the damp handshake of the pharmacist and enduring the palpable loathing of his old mother. Dressed from head to foot in black crepe, sparkling with jet jewellery, she greeted us, as had become customary, with a mute, stare of hatred. The son's manual greeting slithered away from my hand as if it were a dead fish.

There was an infectious miasma of despondency in Las Brujas. The trees were constantly dripping. Few people had roofs more waterproof than ours. Even so, we began to feel sorry for ourselves as the water poured in through the same chinks that had previously let in rays of sunshine. We tried to catch the cascades in bowls, so that the floor didn't turn into mud and flow out of the door to become the garden. I moved my work under the table.

But as the leaks became more numerous, and rearranging the tiles only redistributed the gaps, we covered everything with sheets of patterned plastic.

With the start of the wet season the market had come up with a huge and varied selection of brightly printed, often photographic, designs on plastic sheeting.

It was with enthusiasm that I bought my first length of the stuff. I chose an endlessly repeating image of red-hot monument valley.

The next week we chose the silver sands of a sun-drenched beach, following this with a reproduction of Edwin Landseer's painting *The Monarch of the Glen*, standing majestic in plump purple heather and repeated at three-foot intervals.

But as the wet weather persisted, their absurdly cheerful and acutely optimistic designs helped plunge me into a deep despair. As it was too wet to sit on the veranda, Dolores disappeared into the dark depths of her shrine, and I began to miss her company.

My continuing resolve to be light-hearted, even-tempered, and unflinchingly agreeable came to an abrupt halt one morning, when I woke up to see the floor covered with the tiny pyramidal forms of freshly laid worm casts.

It took only a moment to recognise the sight not as an ariel view of the Valley of the Kings in the Sahara desert, but as a manifestation of our disintegrating home.

It wasn't as if I had any dislike for worms. Before this, I'd been fascinated by their methods of earthmoving, the way they churned up and blended the soil.

But one foot over the side of the bed and the clammy, slightly slippery surface of the earth floor was, ridiculous as it then seemed, the last straw.

'It's the last straw!' I screamed, as Richard returned with the coffee.

And I began to cry. Like a vast wave, the flip side of my nature began to roll and rise. Although I could still appreciate that this was only the result of the wet weather, the black mood overwhelmed me. I feared I might drown. I felt that it was the end of my world.

'What were we doing here?'

Richard sat on the edge of the bed and patiently listened to my tirade.

The paper was too wet, the lino too brittle, the cutting tools too cold, my hands swollen and stiff. The new plastic coverings were somehow smirking with satisfaction as they hid everything from view.

Please don't mention the washing. It hung over ropes in the kitchen, heavy with water. Its everlasting dripping pitted the floor. The fire produced smoke that was too damp to rise to the height of the openings. It fell to earth and choked us.

The wood was swelling and the saw wouldn't cut. The drill wouldn't make a hole, while the wood shavings were too damp to light the fire.

Waiting for the next drip to splash into those already in the bowl turned the screw of anxiety still further, until you could have played the *Flight of the Bumblebee* on our nerves. And the luminous green patina beginning to grow on the floor was making it first clammy and then slimy.

'This is where we live,' said Richard sensibly. 'It's only a matter of the wet. It won't rain forever.'

For a moment there was just the tinny sound of the drips landing in the recently emptied tins.

And then, added as if it was a throwaway line, 'And I love this life.'

My spirits rose and put an abrupt end to the self-indulgent gloom.

Once we had accepted that it was too wet to work and the best option was to go back to bed, we pulled the blanket and the plastic silver-sanded beach over our heads to exclude the outside world.

The only heating available to us was each other's bodies. Slowly the chill was warmed away.

We had survived a black day.

*

The next day we became slaves to the local fashion and bought two more (particularly garish) plastic squares. By this time in the season there was no choice of design. We cut holes in their centres, pulled them over our heads and went for a long walk. In our new lurid rainwear, our appearance nothing less than technicoloured Gardens of Eden, we headed up into the swirling mist to Don Cándido's mirador.

As arranged, we arrived at his home in good time to see the total eclipse of the sun. We must have looked like the ultimate contradiction in terms, as

the rain gushed in rivulets down our tropical beach patterned, wet weather attire. Our host, clad in blue plastic sheeting, dashed up the path to let us in.

From the flat roof of the house there was an unusually wonderful view of the mountains. If the sun came out it would be spectacular. With the present weather conditions, we all had very low expectations of the event.

The Hummingbirds handed each of us a mug of hot *atole*. It warmed our hands as well as our insides.

The sky was totally overcast by dark grey clouds, slung very low over the landscape. Nevertheless, we gathered in the gloaming, our smoked glass squares looking more and more like an unnecessary purchase.

Don Cándido took charge and stared at his wristwatch as it ticked us nearer and nearer the exact moment when, above the clouds, the moon would come between us and the sun.

Standing in a huddle we watched in monochrome gloom, as Don Cándido described how the moon would be approaching the sun.

And as the sun and the moon grow nearer and nearer, the dark blanket of clouds drew slowly back and dropped behind the mountains.

The wettest weather in living memory had come to an end as we stood in amazement and watched a perfect eclipse of the sun against a backdrop of the freshest looking mountains and the clearest of skies.

There was a brief dusk when the swallows swooped after the insects, before they gave way to the bats that darted before our eyes. An owl hooted and the cows lay down in the meadow for seven minutes of eerie night.

Eclipsed, the sun had been a sparkling diamond ring in the sky. This was reflected a dozen times or more in the puddles of rainwater that had collected in the undulations of the roof's perishing cement. Steam rose from the wet. Everyone agreed that a spectacular miracle had occurred.

The air pressure felt as if it had risen to unfamiliar heights. If so, everyone's spirits had been lifted with it.

We all went into the house for lunch. How quickly one becomes used to routine, I thought, as we all sat round waiting expectantly for the Hummingbirds to serve the meal – *la comida* – they had prepared earlier.

After this, we returned home with a new sense of well-being. People were out and about in the lanes of Las Brujas, but there was still a rather subdued atmosphere. Although the sky was beautifully blue and the air much drier, it seemed as if the wisps of mist had been replaced with tattered worry. That evening we learnt from Sánchez that most people in the barrio had thought the total eclipse of the sun was an extremely bad omen. Some believed it would herald the end of the world.

Gradually, everyone began to accept that the occultation had passed without causing immediate disaster.

It was with fear and awe that Moctezuma II saw a comet arc across the sky. He remained deeply unnerved by what he thought to be a terrible portent. When the conquistadors landed, he was further convinced that his premonition had been correct.

The dice were cast in Cortés' favour.

*

While the wet season was not due to end for two or three months, the rain became sporadic and the sun shone quite often from a blue sky full of speeding, billowing clouds.

In the chemist's window, the smoked glass house of cards remained intact.

Richard and I were able to fold up many of the waterproof sheets to reveal what lay underneath. We could now return to work.

I was delighted when Dolores reappeared on the veranda with her embroidery.

This was the life that I, too, loved.

*

I think it was the fine day that prompted us to make an unscheduled visit and take an early morning shower.

It was afterwards, while we were sitting in Don Cándido's kitchen savouring our cleanliness, that an insistent ringing of the gate bell surprised us.

Our host must have been expecting this visitor, but it wasn't until the imperious ringing above our heads that we noticed he was dressed to the nines. All flounce, with the regulation machismo bearing.

Don Cándido fairly flew up the path in his excitement.

We were left sitting in the kitchen, with an excellent and uninterrupted view through the garden to the entrance. After a moment's nervous fumbling, both gates were unlocked and drawn aside. Slowly, majestically, a four-square, all-gleaming American limousine rolled through the entrance. An unusually deferential Don Cándido had ushered in an important guest.

While the host rushed round the back to secure the defences, the electric windows slid shut and the low-slung, powder-blue door swung open.

Out stepped a small, stocky man whose tailor must surely have been responsible for the design of all those wedding cakes we had salivated over in Mexico City.

Taking an embroidered handkerchief out of his jacket pocket, he exhaled gently onto the the fin-shaped chrome flashing and, polishing away the condensation, took an admiring glance at his own reflection. By this time the estate had been made impenetrable, and the host joined the guest.

The pair arrived in the kitchen without even a swift glance in the direction of the oubliette.

We both stood up as they swaggered through the door.

In the scullery, we could hear the Hummingbirds clattering away as they prepared the *antojito*, the snack.

The moment he saw us, Don Cándido's friend stopped in his tracks and stared with irritation in our direction. In fact, he glared at us with such aggression that we began to think about a decorous escape from the situation.

But with swiftly applied etiquette, our host introduced us as his great friends from England. 'Perfectly harmless,' he added.

The visitor's demeanour became less impetuous. He puffed himself up like a fine Chantecleer. A skilfully tailored jacket was worn over a flounced shirt, the gilt buttons of which were only slightly strained over the abdomen. The high-waisted trousers had immaculately sharp creases. On his dainty, pointed feet were a beautiful pair of high-heeled boots, fully illustrated with fighting scenes, and cluttered with silver buckles.

His dramatic movements gave the impression that our Chantecleer was auditioning for a part as a flamenco dancer in a silent film.

Throwing his high-crowned white hat onto the table, he looked again in Don Cándido's direction, as if to make doubly sure that we were as silly as we must have looked. After the reassuring nod, Chantecleer began to make himself at home.

He removed his jacket to reveal, in addition to a leather holster, covered with pictures of bloody fights, that housed a pair of jewelled pistols, an arrangement of criss-crossing nylon webbing, which supported a much more sinister looking state-of-the-art firearm.

All this harnessing and weaponry was hung inside the food cupboard by a dutiful Don Cándido, who then, bunch of keys in hand, padlocked the doors.

As Chantecleer replaced his jacket, shaking out his form to extend into the shoulders, he filled his lungs and contracted his tummy muscles, and I caught a glimpse of what at first I thought was a shiny broach. Tucked well under the collar, it was his badge of office. He was no less than the Chief of Police of the whole district.

All firearms now secure from prying eyes, the Hummingbirds arrived with the eggs and tortillas, while our host opened the fridge and brought out the beer.

This interim meal consumed, it was decided that we should join Don Cándido and the Chief of Police, and drive to the butcher's to buy the meat for lunch.

We were offered the back seat of the Oldsmobile, and following the statutory unlocking and relocking of the gates, we set off at speed. Scattering chickens, turkeys, donkeys, mules, children and anyone else merely going about their own business on our way, we roared into the centre of town.

Here, the Chief of Police, incognito to the point of being obvious, bought beefsteak, a case of beer, a bottle of Bacardi, a crate of Coca-Cola and a bag of ice. Theatrically, he filled a large box with fruit.

We felt very awkward in the company of the two flamboyantly dressed 'plain-clothed' policemen. Our offers to buy things were sharply refused. All we could do was carry these rare riches back to the car, an ostentatious seven-day wonder that was parked in such a careless way it blocked the entire road. It was encircled by boys and young men who melted away as we reappeared.

We returned in the same dust cloud as the outward journey.

Even though we mentioned that it really was time for us to return to Las Brujas, our host was insistent that we had lunch with them. He became so intransigent that we felt like courteously imprisoned hostages.

The Hummingbirds had prepared everything, and were waiting to cook. The table had been laid with freshly starched cloth and the best china.

By the time the meal was cooked, Don Placido had returned from giving his dancing class at the local primary school, and sat beaming in anticipation of the feast. He and the Chief of Police knew each other well.

A short-wave radio had been set up on the windowsill; the beer and Coca-Cola put on ice. Through a collective application of method acting, the party began to take on an atmosphere of conviviality.

By the time we were sinking our teeth in the tender slices of beef, we were all genuinely enjoying ourselves. Don Placido was instrumental in this. He really liked every individual member of the company.

Gradually, even I began to think of other things besides, 'How can we get out of the locked gates?'

As the coffee was served, the postprandial conversation was being severely interrupted by the urgency of the distorted voices emerging concurrently from the crackling ham radio. Meaningless to us, it was all very clear to the initiated. We could only conjecture that the feast was over.

A helicopter passed by so near and so low that all communication had to take place by lip-reading. The trees whipped around in the artificial whirlwind, while the spiralling tufts of grass lay flattened against the earth.

The Chief of Police threw his last 'Cuba' – Mexican rum and coke – down his throat, finished his bottle of beer, wiped his lips on a napkin, buckled on his holsters and harnesses, and readjusted his body amongst the guns, before wishing us a formal, unrecognising goodbye.

Don Cándido, carrying the radio, followed his friend, trotting up the garden. We all listened for the jangling of keys, and for the car to roar into life, turn round in a shower of grit, and race away.

*

It was quiet when Don Cándido came back into the house. He seemed subdued; he seemed preoccupied.

The table had been cleared, but the girls were asked to make more coffee. We were signalled to sit down. Our host sighed.

He told us how long he had known his friend, how they had worked together as secret police. As he fumbled in his mind for a story to accompany the coffee and keep us sitting in the kitchen for just a bit longer, Don Placido remembered:

'Carlos the Jackal.'

So Don Cándido told us the story, while his father looked on with unconditional love and pride.

When the Chief of Police and Don Cándido were younger, when they were doing very well in the secret police, they had been sent to track down and arrest Carlos the Jackal.

It was now the middle of the afternoon, and our plan had been for a very early shower before returning home and getting down to 'a good day's work'. Would Dolores be wondering where I'd got to? Hardly. Not after our well-advertised excursion to the centre of town. Everyone would know exactly where we were and what we were up to.

I imagined that we would be able to light a fire with the taciturn disapproval we'd receive if we did get home. Very soon, it would be the time Richard expected his friends to arrive at the workshop to continue making their furniture.

Carlos the Jackal was the most wanted criminal on the face of the earth and somehow the story was not permeating the dense resistance of my brain. Only anxiety welled up inside me. As if in the distance, I could hear the narration drone on:

'We were dressed up as cleaners,' (the idea that the Chief of Police could dress up as a cleaner was rather unlikely) 'and sent to the main airport in Rome, where intelligence had informed them the terrorist would be arriving shortly.'

Back at the table, Don Cándido looked at his watch and then at the studiedly expressionless face of his father.

Continuing to an audience with untethered, wandering attention, our poor friend was left to mime the sweeping and sweeping that the impostors had to do, while they kept an eye out for Carlos the Jackal. 'Sweeping and sweeping,' said Don Cándido as he pushed an imaginary broom across the floor.

And then we heard the shots. 'Sweeping and sweeping,' reiterated our host.

In the distance, we could all hear the helicopter lift off the ground and this time, much higher in the air, fly overhead. Neither of us flinched.

'And then?' we asked, to demonstrate our rapt attention.

Don Cándido's reply would have been drowned, as with a deafening roar the Oldsmobile, its exhaust backfiring with the same vigour as gunfire in a spaghetti western, was driven frantically up the hill and out of town.

'And then,' Don Cándido pulled himself back from the brink of distraction. 'He gave us the slip.'

Gathering speed as his thoughts returned to his guests, he completed the motley story. 'We were not the first, and I do not imagine we were the last, but Carlos the Jackal had given us the slip.'

Gratefully, we accepted what seemed like our freedom as we walked with our host up to the gate, and thanked him for the shower and the delicious meal.

*

The next day, everyone was talking about the owner of the trout farm and restaurant, who had been arrested for dealing in drugs. Some say he was shot and killed, some say he had been shot in the head and was now an imbecile. Others thought he would spend a life in prison, others that he was a friend of the president, and would receive a medal.

Suddenly, there was a glut of trout in the town.

Richard bought a reel of black plastic hosepipe from the Jaguar's ironmongery and hardware shop. The pipe was connected to the intermittent water supply, and wound up the trunk of a lemon tree with its end tied pointing down. Round this was strung three of our wet weather sheets for modesty. After a full day in the sun the water in the hose would be quite hot enough for a shower. These, we took on alternate days.

Our new independence gave us a good feeling of confidence.

SEVEN

HIDALGO & EL GRITO
'MEXICANOS VIVA MEXICO!'

The village shop had a new stock of patriotic ribbon, in red, white and green stripes. I bought a few yards to wear in my hair to show solidarity.

By the morning of the 15th September, there was a sense of excitement in the air. The men of Las Brujas were hanging around in the lane, getting into the holiday mood. *Copitas* – glasses of mezcal – whetting their whistles as they stood, idly shooting their pistols into the canopies of the massive mango trees.

Red, white and green flags, as well as bunting, were for sale on every corner. Plastic *papeles picados* depicting Miguel Hidalgo in a choice of national colours hung in bundles outside the shop. Red, white and green prints of the Mexican hero, and bunches of similarly coloured children's windmills, were all selling like hot cakes.

By lunchtime every dwelling, every yard, every lane, and many of the lower branches of the trees, were draped in these patriotic decorations. I'd stuck a pair of crossed flags in each of the pots of geraniums on the veranda wall. This met with Dolores approval. I was relieved, because I often found myself trying to please her, and this was the main reason they were there.

Nobody seemed to be working that afternoon, so we sat together only occasionally putting a stitch into our embroidery hoops. So the return of Richard with the sticky cakes put an end to our pretence, and we started warming up for the party.

By the end of the eighteenth century, the world order had fundamentally changed. North American independence had been acknowledged in 1782. In 1789, the French Revolution took place. By 1796, the British Navy had forced free trade agreements on all the colonies.

Napoleon successfully invaded Spain in 1808, whereupon he sacked the king and gave the throne to his older brother, Joseph Bonaparte.

The rulers of Mexico, putting their heads in a bucket of sand, were in denial that the country which had conquered the New World was fast losing its power. They continued to support Ferdinand VII, hoping the status quo would remain unaltered, and that life would continue in their favour.

The Creoles and the Mestizos became more and more enraged.

Now that the ports were open, new political ideas were travelling fast. Even though the works of political philosophers were forbidden, they were eagerly read and discussed in the newly-formed literary societies.

From one of these emerged Miguel Hidalgo y Costilla, a creole Catholic priest, and Ignacio Allende a young and resentful army officer, who became the first leaders of the independence movement.

When their plans for a coup d'état were discovered, they had to rush into action. Standing on the steps of his parish church in Dolores, Hidalgo first shouted out the words that would become the cry of independence: 'Mexicanos, viva Mexico!'

On the night of 15th to 16th September 1810, the support of hundreds of Indians and Mestizos was rallied, and the first step on the long road towards independence for Mexico was taken. It would not be declared until 1821.

It was nearly dusk when we joined the groups and families making their way to the centre of town.

The zócalo was solid with the heaving crowd. Many of the people milling around were dressed in red, white and green costumes. Red, white and green streamers were being swirled above our heads. Most of the adults were clutching, with just one hidden hand, something secret within their clothes. Meanwhile, their right hands were behaving normally in a useful way. Eating and drinking.

I adjusted the bow on my head, and we pushed through the crowds to the stalls that were cooking food and serving drinks. Steam and smoke rose into the air, along with the candyfloss that had been caught by the breeze and which drifted around until it became trapped in the branches of the trees. Along with everyone else, we jumped up and down, plucking the spun sugar out of the air. We, too, stuffed the tricolour wadding into our mouths as we waited for a space in the wall of bodies to appear, so we could lean over and reach for plates of rice. When they arrived, each was neatly laid out in the three-coloured stripes dictated by fervent patriotism.

The red was flavoured with tomatoes and chorizo sausage, the white was cooked with milk and cheese, and the green leeched its hue from macerated parsley, peas and avocado pear.

*

Our stomachs full, we returned to the melee.

Several local bands had joined forces and were fighting their way towards an empty spot that had been cleared for them. A cluster of five or six sousaphones could be seen, their great horns lurching above the heads of the crowd as it moved towards the presidential palace.

We were carried along with the flow of this slowly moving mass. The huge iron gates swung open and the populace, under its own momentum, moved forward and without a pause flowed into the grounds of the palace.

At precisely the same moment, to the rousing sound of a fanfare, the town president, resplendent in the bandana of his office, stepped out onto the municipal balcony.

In red, white and green stripes, the moiré sash hung diagonally across his chest. It sagged under the weight of his medals.

He was flanked by a dozen freshly laundered militiamen. Looped around with regulation white rope, they stood six on each side, their backs arched with rigid tension, the butts of their rifles firmly on the ground next to their right feet.

The people continued to press forward, taking us with them. Those that had reached the firmly bolted doors slowly turned and began to fan out into the gardens.

At one point we brushed passed Don Cándido leading his entourage. 'Stay with us and you will be safe,' he yelled in English, but we were swiftly separated by different currents in the crowd.

The band now modulated its style, from strident military to a more domestic oompah. This was the music that compelled the most reluctant feet to dance. And as the people moved into the gardens, more elbow-room was made.

The dancing of the seething masses got under way. Dozens of bottles were being passed from hand to hand, as mezcal was poured straight down the open throats of the men. It looked like part of the choreography.

And still each one of this apparently one-armed battalion of revellers clutched something hidden underneath their cloaks.

Red, white and green fireworks shot into the air. The sky was filled with domes of tricolour sparks. Portraits of Hidalgo and Allende appeared and faded in pyrotechnical arrays.

Finally, an avenue of roman candles above our heads poured out great cascades of sparks in red, white and green.

People fought to dance amongst these arcs of fire in time with the escalating and frenetic tempo of the band.

Then the music died away as the illuminations faded.

In the momentary quiet and the sudden darkness, our faces turned to the only illumination left. On the balcony, in the limelight, we saw the president elevate his stature by stepping onto a box.

Opening his arms and showing us the palms of his hands, he must have hoped to present a beguiling sight to the people of his town.

He began his oration. But his pompous words were soon drowned out. Even as his voice forced itself up the scale, it became a lost cause.

The bells of all the seven churches of the Village in the Valley began to toll. It was midnight.

Nobody could wait any longer to shout the great patriotic call to arms – 'el Grito'.

A gigantic roar went up: 'MEXICANOS VIVA MEXICO!'

'Mexicanos viva Mexico!'

'Viva Hidalgo!'

'Viva Allende!'

The president raised both arms, as if in benediction. In response, most of his town were only able to raise a single limb in his direction.

'Mexicanos viva Mexico! Mexicanos viva Mexico!', the chanting went on.

This in turn was brought to a fluffy end by the bands striking up the National Anthem.

At this moment, the soldiers lined up symmetrically on the balcony and smartly shouldered arms. Then slowly, simultaneously, they lifted their rifles high in the air and in well-trained unison emptied what sounded like a single volley over our heads.

In immediate answer, every man, and many women, produced their firearm. From cloaks, shawls, bags or bundles, out came an extraordinary collection of antiquated guns.

Hundreds of loaded weapons were pointed into the night sky and fired in the direction of the moon.

It was now the 16th September, Independence Day, the day of firearms amnesty.

We looked around for Don Cándido, but he was nowhere to be seen. If he had hoped to catch the inhabitants of Las Brujas in possession of the newest range in Uzi weapons, he was going to be disappointed. Our neighbours were sporting an historic assortment of muskets after which the most prestigious museum would have lusted.

From round the corner came a dozen men carrying bunches of huge flaming torches.

These were handed out to other enthusiastic men. The majority of people condensed into a procession. With accompanying flashes of gunfire and under the following cloud of thick smoke, the president, at a pace set by the band, led this small, raggle-taggle army along the lanes of each of the seven barrios of the Village in the Valley.

In the company of some of our neighbours, we followed the phalanx down the road. Keeping our distance, we saw the line of torches snake off into the orchards; we listened to the gratuitous gunfire, and saw the rockets shoot up into the sky.

An hour or so later we stood on our veranda and watched, as a rather slower group of men, their empty bottles discarded, their torches reduced to embers, staggered past, still marching in time to the flagging band. Coughing in the acrid smoke of spent gunpowder, the remains of the procession shuffled up the lane and out of Las Brujas.

The sound of gunfire echoed around the mountains all night. These were blasts from weapons more powerful than pistols and six-shooters.

It is said that this is the time to settle old scores. An accident could easily happen on this night when it is not illegal to use firearms.

*

The shooting was still continuing when we awoke, and it was raining steadily. A smokey fire smoulded in the hearth.

At midday, we covered everything in the living room with the plastic squares and put on those that we had adapted as raincapes. Looking like holiday brochures enticing tourists to visit the palm-fringed beaches of the Caribbean, we joined the drift of people gathering in the town. In our macs we became part of the technicoloured population. This camouflage helped us vanish into the crowd.

Early in their sweep through the New World, the conquistadors introduced a play dramatising the recent Spanish sacking of the Moors: *The Conquest Dance*. Over the years this had been subtly adapted by indigenous players. The colonialists began to be shown in a less triumphant light than was originally intended.

Following the main crowd, we reached the junction of roads that led in various directions out of town. Here, milling around the tall castellated tower that had been hastily erected in wood for the occasion, an extraordinarily varied cast was limbering up for the show.

The rain had stopped, but it was very sticky underfoot. Those playing the Spanish had bright red faces or masks with sky-blue eyes. Some had the goat horns of the devil. Those playing Moors, painted black, were sharing a bottle with some Aztecs dressed as eagles. They flapped around in huge wings made from palm fronds sewn onto their sleeves.

The heads of decapitated Spaniards, fashioned from papier-mâché, utilised a single pot of scarlet gloss paint to press home the point of complexion and gore. Stuck onto broomsticks, they quickly became useful weapons as they battered and bludgeoned everything in their path with enthusiastic force.

Men dressed in their sisters' frocks hitched-up their pointed bosoms, their lipstick smudging as they tipped the contents of peripatetic bottles down their throats. Their well-turned, hirsute legs strode through the mud, as the unexplained plastic dolls bounced floppily on their backs. These bit-part players, grouped in bunches, were casually laughing and eating tacos, while the main players rushed about as if they were searching for the best place from which to start.

Hidalgo, in black robes already dragging heavily in the mud, waved a print of Guadalupe.

Allende was recognisable from his tattered military uniform. A Roman gladiator rode a donkey up towards the theatrical set, for no other reason than to get a better view, and thereby offer thespian advice to the Spanish soldiers, who were already up in the tower, holding the fort. Black stovepipe hats now topped the immobile scarlet masks. The whole ensemble made from papier-mâché had been rendered water-resistant by layers of gloss paint. 'Jump to your deaths,' the gladiator had suggested. The replies were too muffled to catch. The battle had commenced.

Ripe fruit, soft avocado pears, plucked chicken carcasses, and lumps of mud were all among the projectiles being used for ammunition. At the height of this free-for-all, a band of Zapatistas galloped through the action, waving their rifles above their heads as they screamed,

'*MEXICANOS VIVA MEXICO!*'
'*MEXICANOS VIVA MEXICO!*'

And clods of earth flying off the horses' hooves splattered straight into the faces of the spectators. A roar of approval greeted these proud revolutionaries manqué.

Sporadic fireworks enhanced the unpredictable action. Rockets whooshed passed our ears on their way to the clouds, while Jumping Jacks lived up to their name as they exploded around our feet. An impromptu demonstration of lasooing filled up most of the pockets of space between the action. One Aztec succeeded in looping his spinning rope round the neck of a Spanish nobleman who had been leaning over the battlements,

trying to catch the attention of a transvestite with a bottle. This piece of fortuitous improvisation brought an even more enthusiastic roar of appreciation from everyone.

Moctezuma, appearing under a bobbing crown of ostrich feathers, and swirling a flared cape of cerise satin, displayed a spangled Spanish diva hanging bewitched on each arm. Wishful thinking had momentarily rewritten history. It was as if the Spanish had been the vanquished, as the mighty Aztec emperor took his bow, and savoured the adulation of the crowds. Each of the maidens was, however, only seductive up to their necks. Over each of their heads had been mysteriously stretched a nylon stocking. From the neck up, they had the squashed faces of bank robbers. Again, the action moved on too quickly to ask why.

Every door that opened onto the street was selling food or drinks. The colour choice of the latter – a crimson hibiscus and cinnamon tea, a rice *atole* rendered off-white with cinnamon, and a greenish beverage made from melon seeds, almonds and limes – came to us as no surprise, although the three distinctive cauldrons of *pozole* soup, flanked by great plates of tricoloured salads did smack a trifle of xenophobia.

We settled for patriotic ice-cream cornets, before we wandered off towards the pageant.

The king of Spain stood at the top of the tower, which swayed when the actors moved and lurched as projectiles hit the wooden walls. The whole set began to tilt alarmingly. Quickly a passing posse of infantrymen came

and tightened the guy ropes that held the whole hastily-constructed fortress upright and fixed it to the ground.

The king of Spain, with his shiny scarlet face, bright blue expressionless eyes, and especially long, black horns, gripped the battlements as if for dear life. Rotting fruit flew thick and fast. Their target was the silver bejewelled cardboard crown, firmly fixed to the royal head. Despite the whole stage set being near to collapse, and the conquerors clinging to the ramparts, the Spanish crown, the symbol of all repression, resolutely refused to fall this year.

The air began to clear of missiles. The action continued.

Squashed fruit and abandoned, crushed chickens were now well-embedded in the mud of the road.

A silver crescent, the moon, rose behind the tower on a long stick. It was now night, and the sound of a man hooting like an owl added to the feeling of expectation. The audience did well to stand clear, and we leaned with the others against the wall of a house.

Crawling up the road, sliding along the squelching surface, slithered our Indian hero.

On all fours, through the detritus of theatrical warfare, he headed for the fort. On his back was strapped the stage version of the stone block that in real life had protected him from the bullets of the viceroy's militiamen. A small Mexican flag stuck out of this cardboard box, as he held aloft a flaming torch to set light to the fuse of the dynamite hidden under the wooden Castillo.

Even though this story and its outcome are general knowledge, we, along with rest of the spectators and actors, held our breath.

We watched as the torch lit the fuse. It is silent as we wait. With a huge whoosh, a sheet of flames flashed up the sides of the fortification before an almighty explosion blasted through the air. The ground shook and the houses shook and we all shook, as we witnessed the Indians storm the castle. The king was captured, the Spanish were beheaded and Miguel Hidalgo appeared as an apparition, and for a moment becomes King of the Castle. He swept the flag of Guadalupe, the 'Queen of Mexico', above his head.

'*Mexicanos viva Mexico!*'

Behind him, a ten-foot wide circular ring of smoke slowly rose, and hovered in the air by the moon.

The spectators and the actors, masked and in fancy dress, merged as they swarmed into the eye of the storm. Members of the band divested themselves of their acting regalia, sat down and struck up. A night of dancing began.

During the trip home we realised how muddy we'd become. This thought reminded us of Don Cándido and his shower. But we hadn't seen him to speak to all day. Maybe it had been him disappearing round the corner. But we both agreed that he couldn't be avoiding us. But like all the rest of our neighbours, we washed at home.

EIGHT

A JOURNEY IN MEXICO
THE FRAGRANT VANILLA ORCHID

In Oaxaca there was a particular chocolate shop. No one had thought to modernize its beautifully faded deco, which must have dated from the nineteenth century.

The powerful smell of cocoa beans being ground drew us in as if we had been caught on a line. Here, we stopped for a cup of the warm whisked drink. As we sipped the comforting cup, an additional aroma rose on the dispersing heat and filled our nostrils with its heady fragrance. It was vanilla.

Later, we would buy a large block of vanilla-flavoured chocolate. This was chosen not just for the delicate botanical illustration of a vanilla blossom on the wrapper. At home, we shared the chocolate with our neighbour, the matriarch Maria. On hearing how much we paid for it she gave a scornful snort, and showed us the little pats of vanilla-flavoured chocolate she used to make her frothy drink.

'The vanilla orchid is grown in Papantla,' she said, enunciating the word for orchid before pausing to see how intrigued we were.

Immediately we wanted to know how far away Papantla was.

'Beyond Veracruz,' the powerful grandmother answered, throwing an arm out in the direction of the north east.

As a young mother, Maria had travelled with her family on many pilgrimages. For her, a holiday was a real Holy Day. We loved to listen as she described walking with her family across Mexico, carrying all the practicalities of domestic life. This included a full kitchen balanced on the back of a donkey. It would take a week or so, joining together with friends and relatives on the way until there would be thousands of pilgrims (many of the women having covered the distance on their knees) to amass at the shrine on the sacred day.

With the ease and speed of public transport nowadays, Maria could see no reason why we should not immediately visit Papantla, especially as she knew the routes and times of the buses as well as any company timetable. Soon we were planning to see vanilla growing for ourselves.

With our spiritual well-being in mind, Maria recommended the votives that should be left in the cathedral of Papantla. Meanwhile, we visited the library of the Oaxaca botanical gardens to find out more about this unusual plant. Carefully, we turned the pages of the magnificent tomes.

Vanilla planifolio, the variety generally cultivated in Mexico, is the most aromatic. The genus name *Orchideae*, from the Greek word *orchis*, means testicles, and describes the shape of its twin tubers. The Spanish word *vainilla* is the diminutive form of *vaina*, meaning sheath or vagina. This describes the dark brown cured bean, each of which encases thousands of minuscule seeds. The long, thin, pendulous seedpods are used for aromatic flavouring.

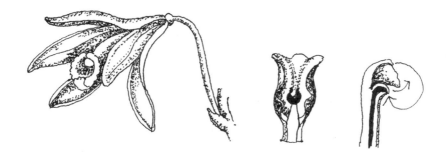

Every leaf emerges from the base of the previous one, and slowly unfurls into a succulent flat *planifolia*. Not only does the scent conjure desire, so does its etymology.

The Aztecs called chocolate 'the drink of the Gods'. While the cocoa bean was valuable enough to be used as currency, it was not rare. Vanilla has always been very precious.

It is said that a pod placed between the breasts will charm the handsome man of a young girl's dreams. There is certainly something strangely alluring about the scent, even without its reputation as an aphrodisiac.

Before the conquest, when the tropical rainforests covered a great deal of the New World, the vanilla orchid grew as far south as Honduras. It is along the coast of Veracruz that Mexico pumps out its oil. Since 1940, great swathes of the forest have been cleared to grow bananas, citrus fruit and coffee. The ubiquitous 'slash and burn' method quickly turned the slopes into pasture.

Nowadays, vanilla cultivation is reduced to odd spots in the few remaining wooded hills. The small town of Papantla is the centre of the Mexican vanilla trade.

Nahuatl is the Aztec language that still can be heard today. Papantla means 'many flags', as the glyph illustrates.

We caught the early bus and travelled north through the lands ravished in the sixteenth century by the Spanish, who cleared the primeval forests in their rush to supply enough timber to replace all the pagan temples with cathedrals and churches. It is still a deeply fissured desert. Next we sped through scorching cactus forests, before reaching the fertile valley of farms south of Mexico City. Turning east, we skirted the snow-topped volcanoes of Popocatépetl and Ixtaccihuatl, and headed towards the gulf coast of Veracruz. Reaching the bleak seashore, we passed the romantically named Laguna Verde, the country's only nuclear power station. In the dusk, we could just make out the plethora of emergency instructions with arrows pointing inland.

It was dark when our bus reached Papantla, after a spectacular journey. Like a sigh of relief, the air was expelled from its brakes.

Still swaying, we stepped out into the hot, damp, night. We took our first breath of the unfamiliar warm air and its accompanying smell of rot that is the hallmark of a tropical climate.

Walking towards the centre, we felt apprehensive. I feared that fervour had blurred my reason and the vanilla trade could be a thing of the past. But as we approached the *zócalo*, the air we began to inhale was laden with the familiar musky aroma.

The strong scent of vanilla pervaded the atmosphere. Musicians were playing from the bandstand and couples were still dancing under the trees. A small kiosk was doing a brisk trade in local produce. Vanilla pods, graded by length and girth, had been placed in small bundles either between bottles of essence for cooking or phials to atomize it as a perfume. All were laid out symmetrically around a tower built from boxes of vanilla-flavoured cigars.

The next morning, we crossed through the zócalo, insisted on a zigzag passage through the dense traffic, ducked under the awnings at the entrance of the market and into the twilight of its interior. Deeper and deeper we ambled, slow enough to take note, but at a pace so continuous that we were not brought to a halt and sold something that neither of us wanted. We passed stalls of tropical fruit, diaphanous dresses, braids, ribbons and buttons. There were a number of places selling a wide selection of vanilla artefacts.

Steering our bodies beyond the alarm clocks and shears, machetes and shoelaces, we reached the more rundown back end of the hall, where the cement path itself had broken into lumps. The ultimate stall just before the before the turn to retreat was in the darkest corner, and but for a postcard stand I would have already made a dive for the way out.

The display was entirely made from old photographs and we admired them. They had been meticulously printed by the elderly man who peered out from behind a glass cabinet. He responded immediately to our unguarded enthusiasm. Many of the pictures were of vanilla cultivation and processing. Most were of Papantla during the first half of the last century, when the wide cobbled streets that were now jammed with traffic were filled with hundreds of yards of neat lines of vanilla pods drying in the sunshine.

The man talked of the old days as I picked out a selection of cards.

'The harvest is short and in a few days from the tenth of December, when the pods are fat but still green, they are picked and brought down from all the surrounding villages to be sold in the town.'

On the twelfth of the month is the festival of Guadalupe, the most revered Virgin, the Indian Madonna. Papantla will have been overflowing with excited people flush with the proceeds of their vanilla crop.

The stallholder described being a young boy who, together with his friends, sorted through the huge piles of pods before placing small bundles on squares of cloths.

We understood from his mime that they were then plunged into scalding water for the few seconds that would stop further photosynthesis, before each bundle was quickly thrown into a great wooden chest and covered with sackcloth to keep them warm enough to 'sweat'. To prevent the beans from rotting rather than fermenting they were carefully laid out to dry in the sun.

The man pointed to the photograph I held. Fading to sepia were the neat lines of pods that filled the wide streets of Papantla when he was a boy. 'The streets were stained black with juice,' he added.

Each day the beans were rewrapped in clothes and returned to the closed boxes. This continued until they were dry enough to be stored in a cool dark place, where the familiar aroma would fully develop. It takes between six to eight weeks for vanilla to cure. The pods greatly reduce in size. All this is done with meticulous care, lest they should decompose.

Returning from his memories of youth, the old man drew breath and smiled. With the theatrical flourish of a magician he pulled out from under the counter a dark stick of beautiful glistening vanilla pod, about eight inches long. It was sparkling with givre, the frost of vanilla crystals. Our nostrils flared as we inhaled the accompanying aroma.

We paid him for the cards and the pods, and as we turned away towards the light he beckoned us back. He now held out three cellophane packets. In each was a small model of the crucifixion, complete with Christ made

from snipped twisted and tied vanilla pods.

I wondered if it would be possible to visit a vanilla farm. But the man had vanished. Vanilla is such a valuable crop that it is with good reason that strangers arouse suspicions.

Once out into the sunshine we drifted towards the *zócalo*, where the municipal benches are tiled with pictures of local scenes. We chose to sit slightly along from a picture of a beautiful young girl standing in a vanilla vine, gracefully fingering a flower. Now we could look at our postcards for the first time in a good light.

Among the collection was a touching portrait of a young couple, hardly out of childhood, standing in the photographer's studio, waiting for the shutter to click open and closed to capture them on their wedding day.

They looked very uncomfortable, and we tried to guess if this was deep embarrassment or the pain of unaccustomed footwear. Dressed in the traditional costume of the Totanac Indian, we wondered if this was the marriage of the elderly man we'd met in the market.

A boy selling vanilla ice cream bedded down in barrels of ice pushed his handcart in our direction, and soon we were licking the cones in the dappled sunlight under the trees.

Above a massive retaining wall on which the history of the Totanacs is set in the cement of a huge bas relief mural, rises the cathedral. In the atrium is planted the 135 ft mast from where the *voladores* fly. Craning our necks, we could see that the band of five men were nimbly climbing the pole. On reaching the top, the eldest stood up on the tiny platform capping and to the sound of his own pipe and drum, danced a jig.

The others perched and, preparing for their descent, carefully coiled the long ropes round the hub of the trunk and secured the ends to their waists.

When this ritual had been completed, and to the accompaniment of the thin notes of the whistle and the undercurrent throb of the drums, the flyers threw themselves backwards into the air. Like birds of paradise they slowly spun out with the centrifugal force to spiral gently down. Their blood red costumes, embossed with embroidered flowers, glittered in the sunshine. Behind them fluttered brilliant plumes of ribbons. Just before they touched the ground, each man tipped upright and lightly ran to a stop.

The conquistadors, mistaking this extraordinary ritual for a sport, had inadvertently let this religious ceremony pass their censor.

In the museum there are costumes of these *valodores* stitched with exquisite illustrations of vanilla vines.

Perhaps the tourist office would know of a vanilla farm we could visit. When we did find what must have been by normal standards a secret tourist office, they responded to our breathless zeal (we had just run up two flights of stairs) with friendly assistance.

After a short discussion, it was arranged for us to visit a small farm just outside the town early the next morning. 'Take the local bus and get off at the first shrine to Guadalupe, walk down the lane and the hacienda is on your right.'

It is said that Moctezuma greeted Cortés with a golden goblet of chocolate whisked to froth, sweetened with honey, laced with vanilla, and stirred with a tortoiseshell spoon.

In Nahuatl, the vanilla pod was known as *Tlilxóchitl. Tlilli* is the word for black, while *xochil* means flower. This misnomer occurred because nobody in the Aztec court knew of the orchid's beautiful creamy green blossoms.

Before embarking on the journey to Papantla, we had visited another library in Oaxcaca. Opposite the cathedral of Santo Domingo and with a reading room in a courtyard shaded by flowering vines is another treasure trove of books.

Tall ladders are needed to reach the top of the shelves, and from there were brought down the leather-bound facsimile editions of the sixteenth-century codices.

The first known description and drawing of vanilla is in the Codex Badiainus, the magnificent work of Martinus de la Cruz, a converted Indian and a Spanish botanist, Juan Badiainus.

This herbal was written in 1552, at a time when plants were medicines and the vanilla pod known as *tlilxóchtl* was not only used as flavouring, but carried to ward off infection.

Vanilla may have reached Europe via Cuba as early as 1500. In 1570, King Philip II appointed Doctor Francisco Hernández as 'First Physician of the Indies' and sent him to Mexico. The inadequacy of renaissance medicine made the Spanish very interested in learning about Indian herbal remedies. Once established in the New World, Hernández enlisted native guides, artists and physicians to teach him.

The Aztecs showed him their impressive botanical gardens and zoos so that by 1577, when he returned to Spain, he had written a comprehensive study of the indigenous flora. He presented a copy to the king but it was not until 1628 that *Rerum medicarum novae hispaniae* was posthumously published, allowing the royal physician's extraordinary work to be studied.

Hernández had never actually seen the vanilla plant and translated its Nahuatl name, describing the spice as *floe nigra aromatica*, the black perfumed flower. It was when the cured pods arrived in Spain that they acquired the now familiar name *vainilla*.

Gradually the pod became known across Europe. At the start of the seventeenth century Hugh Morgan, apothecary to Queen Elizabeth I, suggested it could be used to titillate the taste buds rather than restricting its use to medicinal purposes. From now puddings became much more delicious.

Whereas Spain was keen to import vanilla as a flavouring and perfume, the English plantsmen were vying with each other to cultivate the vine.

With the innovation of the hothouse, the gardeners of the competitive aristocracy struggled to rear the orchid plant.

It was not until the beginning of the nineteenth century that *Vanilla planifolia* flowered for the first time outside the New World. It was in the London hothouse of the passionate gardener Charles Greville. This caused a notable frisson through the horticultural world and many people wanted cuttings from this plant. Even though a contemporary painting includes not only the bloom, but the bean, without its particular pollinator this may have been the illustrator's informed flight of fancy.

When in 1809 Greville died intestate, his private collection of plants was dispersed. The *Vanilla planifolia* went to the botanical gardens in Liège, Belgium. From here cuttings were taken to the French Colony of La Reunion, but without the Mexican bee they remained barren. In 1837 the Belgian botanist Charles Morren successfully pollinated the orchid by hand.

But it was not until 1841 when a twelve-year-old slave called Edmond Albius, on the island of La Reunion, discovered the technique of manual pollination and thereby the mass cultivation of the precious bean.

Soon its production had spread to other neighbouring islands including Madagascar. Vanilla was to be cultivated not only in the French colonies, but in those of Belgium and England. Now this lucrative trade boomed. Vanilla ice cream was to become a popular treat.

It was still early when our bus pulled up opposite the shrine to Guadalupe. 'Parque Ecológico Xánath' was written on a scrap of paper given to us by the tourist office and the driver pointed us in the direction of a shady track that lead down to the farm.

A fable tells us that Xánat, the young daughter of a Mexican fertility goddess fell in love with a Totonac youth. Unable to cross the divide between mortal and the divine and mad with unrequited love, she changed into a vanilla vine. Now she could give eternal pleasure to humans. The Totanac name for vanilla is xánthi. The wild orchids are known as xa'nat.

To the right of us woodland covered the slope. To the left was the open country of small hills scantily covered with parched grass cut through with great fissures of erosion that is the familiar legacy of deforestation. These are the pastures for beef cattle originally brought from Europe.

Further on we came to an entrance. Here we were greeted by the smile and reassuringly firm handshake of José Luis Hernández. The gate squeaked open.

We sat on the veranda of a wooden hut and drank gourds of cool water that tasted not of wood, but of being in a wood. My companion being a furniture maker with a passion for timber, it was not long before the conversation turned to the trees growing around us.

This land had been in the family of Señor Hernández since 1872. It had been the municipal rubbish dump until twenty-five years ago when José Luis began to clear the sight and plant citrus fruit and vanilla orchids.

We walked all round the trees before being escorted by the proprietor up the hill.

Vanilla is a unique orchid. Not only is it edible (albeit after complicated curing), it is the only variety that climbs like a vine. Clinging to the trunks and branches of trees with aerial roots, it can reach the dizzy height of seventy feet. The plant's chief sustenance is obtained from the damp atmosphere.

Although we did catch sight of a simple ladder made from a thick bamboo pole, it is more practical to restrict their height by growing the vines over especially planted support trees of about eight feet.

It was April and the orchids were in bloom. Their pale creamy green flowers are extraordinarily beautiful.

Some vines were decorated with red ribbons tied to their branches. These are to ward off not only the destructive influence of the full moon but also the evil spirits that might ruin the harvest. The Totanac will take no chances and even an agronomist appeases the gods.

With the decimation of the rainforest, not only did the vanilla orchid loose most of its habitat, but likewise its natural pollinator; a particular bee. The Melipona bee is now only found in the area around Papantla.

Also disappearing is a species of bat, one of vanilla's essential distributors. The unusually hard seed of vanilla must pass through the digestive system of this flying mammal before it can germinate.

Equally devastating is the demise of mycorrhizal fungus without which the seeds of sapraophytic plants (those feeding on decaying matter) cannot germinate.

Nowadays vanilla orchids are grown from cuttings. This eliminates cross pollination thereby diminishing the genes pool, making them more susceptible to pests and diseases.

With toothpick poised Señor Hernández chose a perfect bloom from amongst the buds. It lay fragile and pale in his farmer's hand as he demonstrated the invaluable technique of artificial pollination. Inside the trumpet shaped petal and with the little stick he lifted the rostellum (the minute central flap) so that the anther carrying the pollen can be bent over to reach and adhere to the stigma below.

Having repeated this gentle action with all the flowers in bloom, we sat down in the wood and listened to our host's soft voice.

Although the plant may be in flower for a few weeks, only one in a cluster opens at a time. The vines must be visited every morning for the efflorescence lasts no longer than a few hours and will have certainly faded by the afternoon.

José Luis pointed out that by harvest, eight months later, more than a hundred beans may hang ripe from every plant, each blossom having produced but a single pod.

He told us the story of how during the first half of the nineteenth century, a local *campesino* was intrigued to see bees easing themselves into the flowers of the vanilla vines. He noticed that after the bees had paid their visit the blooms closed and the petals began to droop. Only then did the beans begin to develop.

With a small twig the man deftly imitated the actions of the bee. As this trick of the trade became general knowledge, the Papantla vanilla industry began to burgeon. It is possible that this method of hand pollination was the rediscovery of an ancient lost technique.

The Aztecs having subjugated the local Totanac population, demanded huge contributions of this rare spice. Discontented with the treatment they received from the Aztecs, the Totonacs were easily coerced by Cortés to help him muster indigenous troops to conquer Moctezuma.

The descendants of these tribes still inhabit this area of Mexico.

'Listen!! Listen!' cried José Luis, and we tried to make some sense of the forest cacophony. A large bird took to its wings and flew out of the branches high above us.

'Look! Look! A *papanes*, the bird that has given its name to Papantla.'

A little confused, we watched the crow-like bird fly out of the forest and swoop out of sight. This particular bird and the flag share the same Nahuatl word. Both flutter in the sky.

With twigs cracking underfoot, we strolled over the leaf litter and down the other side of the hill, taking a closer look at many of the trees, and listening to the singing and calling of the birds in the canopy.

'There is a hive of melipona bees in the roof of an outbuilding, their honey is good, but they are not reliable pollinators. Perhaps humming birds also played a part in this,' José Luis shook his head sadly, for these avian jewels are no longer to be seen in great numbers.

Passing by the barn, we saw for ourselves the beehive under the eaves, surrounded by these industrious insects.

Luis fetched and unwrapped from greaseproof paper his own vanilla. Here was the most luscious, dark selection of pods we had ever seen. Plump and gleaming, they were laden with glittering white vanilla crystals.

We each lifted a pod to our nose and inhaled its fragrance. No wonder young husbands were recommended to drink a beverage laced with vanilla before bed.

José Luis smiled. 'It is the cold snaps of a Veracruz winter (unknown in the Indian Ocean) that enhance the flavour of Mexican vanilla, making it the best in the world.'

My companion's attention was once again gripped as our host spoke of the devastation caused by cutting down the forests and the subsequent flaying of the landscapes. Both men nearly fell over each other in their effort to agree about the vital importance of replanting trees.

José Luis Hernández walked with us to the gate, and once again firmly shook our hands.

Together we stood and looked across the lane to the bony hills, where a few thin ruminants grazed. Shaking his head in a despairing manner, he added under his breath, 'What a way to treat the world.'

Turning into the now sunlit lane we walked to the bus stop, taking it in turns to open my bag and draw in deep breaths of the musky bouquet to delight our sense of smell.

NINE

SAN MIGUEL ARCHANGEL
HIS PORTRAIT IN FRUIT & VEG

Il Templo, the church of Las Brujas, was dedicated to San Miguel, Saint Michael. The barrio takes its official name from this warrior archangel.

Like the *ex-convento* in the centre of the village, this was erected very early in the massive ecclesiastical, iconoclastic destruction, conversion and rebuilding programme planned by the triumphant Spanish.

The grassy atrium was enclosed by high walls in the Moorish shapes of up and down ogee curves. Huge trees provided essential shade.

The 'open chapel', from which sixteenth-century priests preached to the heathen masses, was still intact on the side of the church.

One tree was several hundred years old, and possibly predated the conquest: *Frangipani Plumeria Obtusa L,* also known as the *Yoloxóchitl* Tree, or Heart Flower Tree. Its great trunk and branches were grey and wrinkled, like the limbs of an elephant. They bent over, leaning towards the church, as if the tree were trying to head that way.

Underneath the gnarled tree sat an ancient and equally gnarled man who, inheriting the position from his father, guarded this sacred tree. He barely moved from the squatting position. He appeared to be in a permanent trance as he muttered the neverending lyrical poetry of his incantations.

He alone was the herbalist allowed to pick the flowers. These he sold, fresh, dried, or made into tinctures. The tree blooms before the leaves appear, and the flowers play an important part at Easter.

Each bud resembled a small heart. Pounded and taken as an infusion, it has been traditionally used to cure heart complaints. Like foxglove in western cultures, it is still used today. When administered, the concoction produces alkaloids similar to adrenaline. This is a very effective treatment for diseases of the heart.

Flowers, ground and mixed with chocolate, are given to alleviate congested chests and fever. It is said that they expel bad humours and combat sterility.

Both the inside and outside of the church were decorated in great profusion by strangely unfamiliar symbols. The Spanish friars had sent emissaries to Antwerp who asked the Flemish engravers to supply the New World missionaries with prints that would educate the pagan craftsmen in Catholic iconography.

The sun and moon had prominent positions carved in bas relief on the tower. Wonderfully vivacious interpretations of indigenous plants swirled over the façade, outshining the very essence of European baroque.

I had the feeling that the didactic engravings were still on the high seas when *Il Templo* of Las Brujas was being built. It dates from about 1540.

Being Augustinian friars, followers of the Algerian Saint, the carvings of Christ as well as those of his mother were very dark-skinned. Whether the cause was centuries of candle smoke or not, these images had black complexions.

*

Before maize was sown, a few especially-chosen ears of corn were placed in a basket. With a stick of carved hardwood, holes were made in the earth, and with the following incantation the seeds were planted:

Come on possessed one,
whose happiness is in the rains (stick),
do your duty for the possessed ones,
for The Gods (the clouds), have already arrived.
Now I am going in order to leave the Possessed Prince (maize)
among others, for he is Seven Snakes.

Seven Rampant Serpents had been carved slithering up the cupola that crowned the bell tower.

Two days before the feast of San Miguel, a train of about fifty heavily laden mules wound up the road over the mountains, from a valley three days away. Half a dozen men led the train through the gates, into the atrium. They stopped at the open doors of the church.

The panniers were unloaded and the cargo of broad beans and pears were gently piled inside, against the walls of the nave. The animals were let to graze and, incidentally, to give the grass it annual manuring.

Their journey had brought them to an entirely different climate.

When the *arrieros,* the mule drivers, had prepared everything for the exchange, the bell in the tower began to ring.

Soon people from the village began to arrive with baskets of their own produce, which was exchanged for the exotic fruit and vegetable from over the mountains. We brought a large basket of limes that we had picked, overseen by Dolores and Felice, from our garden that morning. Not too much and not too little seemed to be the motto. This was so vague that we were relieved to have had more practical help from our guardian neighbours.

We carried our basket of limes along with the flocks of inhabitants from the barrios.

The Village in the Valley grew a wide range of produce and we watched as the centre of the nave filled with mangoes, hog plums, avocado pears, maize, black beans, bananas, citrus fruit, squashes, melons, tomatillos and tomatoes.

The *arrieros* wasted no time as they moved nimbly about, creating before our eyes a magnificent portrait of the patron saint.

Without ever coming across Arcimboldo, the portrait of San Miguel, entirely made from the fruit and vegetables, had been laid down the full length of the nave.

The bellringers continued pulling the frayed rope until everyone who was interested in broad beans and pears, had collected their quota. The priest arrived. Quickly pulling a black cassock over his head, he returned to the altar end of the nave and produced from the vestry a gramophone. Having wound up the spring, he carefully placed a 78 rpm Bakelite record on the turntable. Slowly he released the brake.

Indistinct through wear and tear floated the singing voice of Enrico Caruso. The nostalgic sound filled the space, and for three minutes we celebrated the exchange of comestibles with *O Sole Mio*. The song rose up into the dome and rolled round the vaulting, as if enjoying the sixteenth-century acoustics.

The clockwork was rewound and the flip side was lowered into place. It was no less moving, just a little less appropriate. The tenor's voice welled up with *La Donna e Mobile*, 'Woman is fickle'.

The walls of the nave were clear of food. The warrior archangel was complete.

It was evening, and as dusk became darkness we added our lighted candles to the banks of guttering flames that began to surround the fruit and vegetable form of San Miguel.

*

Early the next morning, we heard the bells ringing for mass. Before dawn, the muleteers had dismantled and stowed the portrait of the saint in the paired baskets slung over the animals' backs.

It was the eve of San Miguel. After the blessing in the church, the animals were raring to go. We found ourselves part of a small crowd letting off a sky full of rockets, and accompanying the small convoy to the edge of the Village in the Valley. The sun was just rising over the mountains as they started on their three-day journey home.

That afternoon, Dolores arrived with a basket. I collected mine and we joined the rest of the women from the barrio who were leaving to walk up the mountain to gather bunches of *cempasûchil*. This yellowy orange flower has the pungent smell of the marigold. It has many uses.

On that day we sat in a meadow above the mirador, and tied the plants together with grass in the form of small crosses. I carefully followed Dolores instructions and produced more than enough floral cruxiforms to pin above each window and door of La Casita Azul.

It was quiet. It was so quiet that even moderate voices travel right across the valley. Conversations can be conducted between people over great distances. I listened to the melodic sounds of the mysterious language, often a jumble of Spanish and Nahuatl, that was still spoken. To me, it was as revealing as the songs of the birds.

Our baskets full, we returned to Las Brujas down a narrow track. In single file we trooped passed the shrine to Guadalupe, under the fluttering decorations of the fountain, down to the wash place and into Calle Emiliano Zapata.

Most days, I considered Dolores to be my alter ego. Occasionally, I felt her to be an interfering busybody.

That afternoon, when she sent me off to the shop to buy two big prints of San Miguel in triumphant combat with the devil, I felt the latter. It did not annoy me that, without mentioning it, one would be for me and the other for her. But I knew that I was being sent to the shop so that she could snatch down the old and pin up the fresh cempasûchil above each aperture of my home.

So it was with her authority that our home was to be protected from evil. Under her auspices, the crosses were fixed over each opening. The standard print pictured San Miguel, his sexuality as ambivalent as ever despite his sword raised over the cowering devil. The indistinct lithograph nestled in its regulation frame of garlic heads.

With a deft hop, Dolores hooked the picture onto the nail above the door. I felt she was treating us like Protestants. But then, we weren't Catholics either, and it was important for our neighbours that everything be done correctly. In the event, we were all set and ready to ward off demons.

As soon as Dolores disappeared to dress her own home, my annoyance melted away. Later, when she darted back across the road, smiling and carrying a jug of Jamaica, I felt sickeningly ashamed of myself.

The church bell with its dead, cracked sound, peeled on.

In the atrium, the ancient herbalist had joined the two bellringers, who were lying under a spreading Indian fig tree.

Several lengths of rope had extended the bellpull so that it reached the supine men. Tying it to one or other of their ankles, and with a scissor motion of their legs, they were able to continue swinging the clapper and keep the bell ringing without interrupting their evening meal.

The mystic herbalist was in his usual crouching position. But that evening, he had moved ten yards across the grass and was stirring a pot of *pozole* that was cooking over a small fire. We watched as the trio of men enjoyed several helpings of the maize pottage, without interrupting the steady circulation of mezcal bottles. Nor, at any time in the long evening, did the steady rhythm of the bellringing falter.

*

Six men were needed to support the two shafts of the solid wooden saint. Several teams of strong men must have been expended before the slightly larger-than-life San Miguel reached the lane that ran by our cottage. Here, I joined the entourage.

It was well after dark; progress had been slow. The eighteenth-century saint was carved with magnificent gilded wings. These were spread open, as if the archangel was about to take flight. The wings, the elaborate breastplate, and the gilded flowers decorating his Roman skirt, glinted in the guttering candlelight. His eighteenth-century form, with its sinuous body and the muscular legs, had been freshly touched up with enamel paint. Human hair flowed down his back. The warrior archangel, with perfect feet and pink knees, brandished his golden sword above his head. The centre of gravity must have been quite high, and the wind resistance an exhausting problem.

Underneath, the procession stumbled along the stony paths deep between the stone walls that for hundreds of years had contained the orchards. Like everyone else, I tried to step from rock to rock, but like everyone else ended up wading through the morass of the irrigation channels.

The candles were being constantly relit. The eerie singing and chanting was interrupted by fits of coughing as we breathed in the dense smoke of the burning incense. The orchards and woods were very dark. There was no light with which your eyes might become accustomed. It was a disorientating pitch black.

At last we turned in the direction of the ringing bell and out of the dark we eventually saw the lights of the church. Like moths, we followed our patron saint into the warmly illuminated interior.

A single fiddler played the thin lament.

The inside of the church had been filled with vases and buckets of white gladioli. In hopeless imitation of the others, I prayed and chanted, droned and sang as the service was spun out until midnight. At last it was the Feast Day of San Miguel, the archangel who had fought the devil and won.

Outside the bellringers lay asleep, curled up together under the Indian

fig tree. The herbalist crouched motionless by the trunk of his *Yoloxóchitl*.

Next morning, the atrium was full of people busy with preparations for the Feast Day.

El Castillo, the castle, a tall bamboo tower that would support the grande finale of the pyrotechnical show, was being erected between the trees.

The finishing touches were being applied to *los Toritos*. The fireworks had been already tied in series onto the wicker frames that represented these little bulls. They were ready to be stored under the arches of the open chapel. Meanwhile, they were being tried for size. Held by the two front legs they lurched above the heads of various young men in excited anticipation of the evening.

The doorway of the church had been transformed by a great archway made from flowers, Spanish moss and small slices of cactus.

A wooden platform had been nailed together for the band.

The bellringers, nursing sore ankles and probably similar heads, were preparing to strike camp. Winding up the yards of rope, they returned with

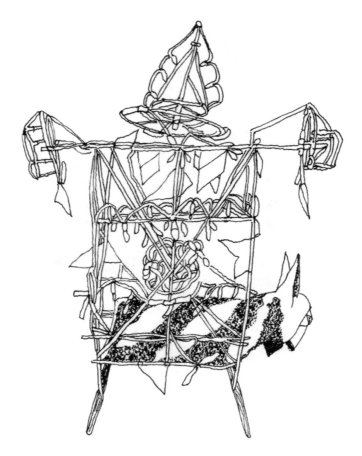

it to the tower for the day's work.

By lunchtime, the band was sitting on the elevated rostrum and ready to play.

But it was not until the late afternoon that we changed our clothes, locked up our home and joined the crowded festivities.

The ancient herbalist was squatting under his Yoloxóchitl tree apparently oblivious to his change of surrounds. With his eyes shut, he continued muttering his endlessly rotating cycle of incantations.

The tables from the store were out again and had been placed round the garden walls. Charcoal fires were lit and fanned under cauldrons of food.

We sauntered past the wall-eyed, severed head of a lamb. Decorated with herbs, it advertised the youth and health of the animal that was being served.

The mass had been going on for some time. Long enough for one complete change of worshippers. People moved freely in and out of the

building, along with the billowing smoke from the burning incense that was also escaping the thick atmosphere of the interior.

The ringers sat up in the tower, taking it in turns to push the clapper against the bell with their feet. Leaning down, they waved their recharged bottles with a gleeful bravado. Few looked up.

It is hard to better the Mexicans when it comes to recycling rubbish. Plastic cups became whirling toys on sticks; aeroplanes had been made from beercans, pull-along monkeys peddled furiously on tiny wire tricycles, and furry bears jumped up and down on elastic string, beating bottle tops. Coloured kites made from coloured plastic bags were already snared in the trees. Everyone was dressed in their Sunday best. It was a day of endless treats.

The band in full swing ran concurrently with the tireless tolling of the bell.

Mingling in the crowds were the men in fancy dress. There were a variety of clowns; one group were parading themselves in eagle costumes, while others were disguised in animal outfits. There were the glamorous, young transvestites and the old pantomime dames.

The giant '*locos*' – crazies dressed in long floral print dresses that billowed round their stilts – added themselves to the dancing melee.

A beautiful youth in a sequinned ballgown had added a huge papier-mâché tortoise to his ensemble. It was worn like a hobbyhorse with braces that hung over his décolleté shoulders.

Hundreds of eggshells scattering confetti flew through the air that was dense with conflicting sounds.

By dusk the pyrotechnics were ready. The combination of excitement and anticipation was almost electric.

As darkness enveloped the fiesta, the first rockets shot into the air and cupolas of coloured lights repeatedly appeared and faded in the sky.

Los Toritos were lifted onto the backs of eager young men, the fuses lit before they galloped away zig-zagging into the crowd. A not unexpected chaos ensued for the wild boys exploded in sheets of sparks and deafening bangs. They bucked and wrestled the wicker frames, before they were wrenched away by others.

There were huge waves of cheering and yells of support for the knots of fighting. This mayhem, along with the crumbling church and the huge dark trees, was exaggerated by the intermittent visibility, the monochrome light of the magnesium flashes.

The church had emptied. A long tongue of candlelight protruded from the wide open doors. The bellringers had joined the fiesta at last, leaving the band alone to saturate the air with sound waves.

We saw Don Cándido hovering in the shadows, but a moment later he had vanished.

It was time for the climax of the day. The fuse of 'El Castillo' was lit, and everyone stood back. A series of mighty Catherine wheels was set in motion. From the base, the fuses worked their way upward. Once ignited, each whirled in a sequence of revolving illuminations. An angel kneeling in prayer was followed by a toothy Bugs Bunny sucking a carrot. Next was a bleeding heart, a bottle of 6X, then the Virgin. One after another they flared up, spun and died down. Finally, the pinnacle caught fire and began to turn.

The band, still following the spectacle, rose in pitch and crescendo as the final wheel gained speed and traced out the incandescent shape of San Miguel the archangel brandishing his sword. As the brilliance faded, dozens of rockets were projected into the darkness.

The firework show had finished, leaving us looking at the stars shining against a background of soft dark sky.

We heard the band play all through the night as we turned in a fitful sleep.

The next morning, Las Brujas was quiet and still. No human sound could be heard. No dog barked. As we sat listening to the birds singing in the trees, we wondered why Don Cándido was making us feel so uneasy.

TEN

SAN LUCAS

THE GREEN ARCHITECT

The wet season was really over and only a distant memory in the past. The sun shone continually in clear blue skies. Each day was one in a procession of similarly beautiful days. It was warm, but not too hot. It was a dry heat, not humid. When the wind rustled the needles in the pines, we welcomed the breeze.

The fruit on the trees was ripe.

The orchards that have traditionally helped sustain the Village in the Valley are still watered by the same irrigation system that has for hundreds of years wound its way round the steep mountainsides. In narrow channels carved into the rock, the water slowly spirals down to the valley floor. Here, the elaborate system of mud and stones that serve as tiny sluice gates make for absolute equality as far as the water supply was concerned.

This efficient system of water distribution had been in place long before Cortés conquered these parts, and long before the Aztecs appeared and took control of this valley, too.

In the past, the many varieties of avocado pear had been an important crop, but recently the trees had become diseased. A virus had infected many of the orchards, and the results had become a familiar sight. Dead trees now lay rotting, their ghostly white, tangled limbs broken on the ground.

But the huge mangoes were laden, and the back path up to the *zócalo* was slippery with fallen fruit. There was a rather heady aroma in the air, along with the loud and threatening drone of wasps.

The orchards were full of lightweight boys clambering around high in the branches, filling baskets with fruit.

Felice's husband Sánchez had made dozens of small bamboo baskets on long poles that helped pluck the fruit from the most inaccessible places. This made the pickers perform enormously unstable stretches from tree to tree. A crowd of admiring peers, together with several anxious mothers, gave conflicting instructions from below.

Wicker baskets flew up and down on ropes. As quickly as one was full, another was sent flashing through the leaves up into the canopy.

A white canvas awning had been stretched over the lane just beyond our garden gate. In this shade the packers worked.

All day, men would arrive with big wicker baskets overflowing with fruit. These containers hung over their backs, the weight taken by a leather strap supported by the forehead. This put an enormous strain on the muscles of the neck. Pulsating veins were clearly visible, as was the sweat that ran in rivulets down their bodies.

Sitting on the garden wall, Richard correctly assumed that the workshop would be empty until the fruit was harvested.

Dolores was keeping to her own yard. We had become divided by the Sánchez family annual fruit enterprise. I waved, but my friend was pegging out her washing, as if to make a screen. *Los duendes* were swinging in the trees, not in our living room.

All day and every day, the steady flow of baskets would be carried up the lane. From each of the seven barrios the cargoes arrived, and were weighed by Sánchez's son, Servando. Together, they calculated the payment and recorded it in a small exercise book. The full basket was exchanged for an empty one, and the *campesino* was paid the few pesos owed to him.

Tons and tons of fruit were delivered. Hour after hour, Felice and her daughter-in-law, Gabriela, packed the fruit into rectangular wooden boxes. With the nimblest fingers working as quick as lightening they arranged each hog plum or each mango into neat herringbone patterns. Each layer was separated by a layer of banana leaves. Meticulously the boxes were filled. Not one fruit must be bruised, not one squashed by over-packing or being too loose.

At dusk, a lorry would back down the lane to the stack of boxes, and let down his tailgate. At this moment a dozen related people were there to load the fruit. Sánchez, with a resigned gesture, pocketed the meagre payment, while we all stood watching the cash crop head for the wholesale market in the city.

Although *ciruela* is the Spanish word for plum, this fruit is not from the Rosaceae family, but *Spondias lutea* from the *Anacardiaceae* family. It is known in English-speaking America as hog plum.

The ovoid yellow fruit that grows so plentifully in the Village in the Valley is native to Mexico. Its local name, *jocote*, comes from the Nahuatl word *xocotl*, meaning acidulous or sharp. (As distinct from *zapotl*, a sweet fruit.)

The stone inside the thin layer of flesh is much bigger in proportion to that of the plums we know. Cooked with sugar or eaten raw, they are delicious.

The *Spondias lutea* comes highly recommended by the Spanish historian Oviedo, who in his journal written in the early days of the conquest described the tree by its Caribbean name:

> The young shoots of this tree are good for shaving the face, as they are of exquisite odour. The bark of the Hobo Tree when boiled and used to bathe the limbs is astringent and relieves exhaustion due to travelling, for it is a healthful bath.
>
> And when the countryman seeks a sleeping place they try to have it beneath this tree, for its shade keeps off the dew and never causes headache as many others do. A source of water can be found by digging out its roots.

The orchards of Las Brujas were well-stocked with these trees.

The mango is another crop that grows prolifically enough to send to market. This paisley-shaped fruit reached Mexico in the nineteenth century from India, via Africa and Brazil. There are many varieties, several of which are familiar to the Village in the Valley.

It is the slippery, sensual texture of the mango, coupled with exquisite flavour, that made its consumption a legendary sensation.

On long dusty bus journeys, we kept a sharp look-out for the mango vendors.

The fruit will have been peeled and then sliced before it is handed to you in a bag.

The large yellow variety is often available on a wooden stick with an optional sprinkling of powdered chilli. It is cut in a way to make it resemble a rose, and will quench your thirst as well as divert your thoughts from hunger.

Then there are the declining orchards of avocado pears. Cultivated long before European intervention, these magnificent trees have been struck down locally with a mysterious disease and are dying.

The name *aguacate* is taken from the Nahuatl word *auacatl*. It belongs to the *Lauraceae* family and is indigenous to Mexico. Before the virus, the Village in the Valley produced abundant harvests. There are many varieties of this prized and nutritious delicacy. The flesh is a very good source of the vitamin Bs.

The skin can be pounded with honey to make a tincture that will expel intestinal parasites. The leaves are used in cooking in a similar way to bay.

The avocado has a reputation as an excellent aphrodisiac, although this may be due to its suggestive shape as it hangs from the tree. *Auacatl* is one of the Aztec names for testicle.

Just as suddenly as the fruit harvest started, it finished

One morning we looked over the garden wall and the lane was empty.

Dolores returned with her sewing, I got down to the linocuts, and furniture-making continued to be a popular hobby.

It did not surprise us that Don Cándido continued to keep a low profile. We had hardly expected to see him picking his way through the congestion that surrounded our cottage.

As we thought less and less about the comforts of modern life, we assumed that our lives were naturally diverging.

The preparations for the Day of the Dead start on 18th of October, with the feast of Saint Lucas. Sánchez and Felice came the evening before and invited us to their family celebrations.

About midday, we walked out into the fields below the cemetery. If we had lost our way, we would have been drawn there by the conflicting smells of burning copal – a tree with a very aromatic resin – and cooking meat.

Many members of the extended family had been here since early morning.

The footpath ran alongside the adobe shrine that stood in the open fields. That day, the curly iron gate that secured the saint had been unlocked and fastened open. The whole structure had been swept, scrubbed and mopped before a fresh coat of lime wash was brushed on the walls. By now, the tiny chapel glowed so brilliantly white in the midday sun, it was almost too painful for the eyes to bear.

The solid wooden incumbent stood with a little docile bull at his feet, entirely filling the niche. He had been edged forward not only to clean round his back, but also to facilitate wiping his entire surface with a soapy cloth. So today he stood in the sunshine and we could get a clear view of this beautiful polychrome carving. With human hair and realistic glass eyes, he struck me as a gentle and kind man. And I wondered if he had been standing in this rather isolated place since he was made in the eighteenth century.

There must be some market for buying and selling secondhand religious furniture and fixtures. I imagined the temptations of the catalogue.

Incense billowed out from the folds of his skirts, and he stood in a pool of melted wax. A colony of flickering candles was melting in the sun.

In the eyes of the Catholic Church, San Lucas, being of the profession, is the patron saint of doctors and surgeons. He was also an artist, so they are added to his list of patronees.

The outside of the shrine had been decorated with paper flags and strings of *cempasûchil*. The smell of the flowers was as pungent as that of the smouldering copal.

This was the *ejido*, or communal land, worked by Sánchez and his family.

A dozen or so young bulls grazing in the adjacent field had been crowned and garlanded with the sacred yellow plants.

The awning that until so recently had kept the sun off the fruit packers was now stretched between the shrine and a tree, and shaded the trestle table. Its white cloth was well anchored by jars of *cempasûchils* that alternated with the jugs of *pulque* and the bottles of mezcal.

Felice and Gabriela, together with one or two cousins, were cooking over an open fire. The children had laid the table. Sánchez was talking to a fat man whose glass needed frequent refreshing.

Benito Juárez is still the people's hero. He was a Zapotec Indian in the mountains east of Oaxaca. Both his parents died leaving him, still a small boy, in the care of his elder sister. Destitute, they left their village and walked to the city where Benito was adopted and educated by a priest. He became a lawyer.

In 1855, Benito Juárez came to power as leader of the Liberals.

At this time the church was vastly rich and very reactionary. The general population saw it not as a supportive Christian institution, but as the enemy of the people. The Catholic Church had totally neglected their responsibility to educate the peasants, so Jaurez set up secular schools. He instituted the Democratic Constitution, a copy of which he carried at all times.

The response of the Church was to threaten all supporters of the government with excommunication, thus ensuring that the ensuing civil war grew very bitter.

The government sacked the churches and shot the priests, while the Church responded by assassinating all the liberals they could lay their hands on.

In 1861, Juárez was deemed the winner – for the moment.

All churches became the property of the state, and the monasteries were closed. Weddings and funerals, which few could afford under the old regime, became civil matters with fixed charges.

Even though this wasn't the end of the matter, many of the reforms instigated by Benito Juárez are still in place today. Priests are forbidden to wear their canonical robes outside the sanctuary of church buildings.

We were introduced to the fat man. There being no outward signs, we had not been able to recognise him as a priest. He was no one I had seen before, but a peripatetic cleric doing his rounds on the Feast Day of San Lucas. A hired clergyman.

More relatives arrived, their numbers swelling the crowd. The cars, pickups and wagons belonged to those who had moved further afield, to where life is apparently more lucrative. Nearby, were tied the donkeys and occasional mule on which the more familiar family members had ridden.

Aunts, uncles, brothers and sisters were greeting each other, along with cousins, grandparents and children. Everyone was excited to meet again. They were kissing and hugging and talking with great speed. Most had at least a few genes in common. I thought it was visible even in the in-laws.

The priest swallowed his full glass in a gulp, and we noticed him turn his wrist and indicate that time was passing.

This was the cue for the relatives to disentangle themselves. The conversation petered out and all of us turned our faces to face the shrine.

Our man of the cloth stepped a few paces in the direction of the saint. Assuming a similar expression of piety to that which characterised the demeanour of San Lucas, he spread out his arms as if to welcome little children. With great rapidity, he rattled through a single rosary, a swift benediction, and blessed the occasion.

It was a mumbling sea anchor of a chorus that joined him in the Hail Mary, as he was helped to his chair at the head of the table.

With *el Sacredote* ensconced, the rest of the party sat down in readiness for the chillied soup, grilled kid, and the sweetest prickly pear water, to offset the dehydrating effect of the mezcal.

We found ourselves sitting next to the only people in the company, apart from the priest and ourselves, who were not related. Our surprise at meeting was mutual. So too, we discovered later, was our pleasure.

They introduced themselves: Joaquin and Ofelia. They were Mexican. And, like us, they were white. Because of this common defining quality, we felt a little wary.

He was an architect, and had designed and overseen the building of several of the fortified palaces that were springing up around the Village in the Valley. More estates for the rich, rushing their families out of Mexico City and into the dreamland of the Valley, were in the pipeline.

Joaquin must have taken in our formal smiles and noticed our eyes glaze over, for he immediately launched into a defence.

Guessing our reservations, he produced his mitigating circumstances. He was an 'ecological' architect, and primarily interested in vernacular buildings. Quick as a flash our interest was rekindled. He employed local craftsmen using traditional methods.

Ofelia was an anthropologist. They lived in Mexico City's federal district, and had a house in the Village in the Valley, just behind the *zócalo*.

Many of the men in Sánchez' family worked on his schemes. The 'Green Architect' as we began to think of him, was obviously well-liked by this family.

I noticed Sánchez and Felice smile.

The priest had consumed his food with the same urgency with which he had preached. Pouring a final glass of mezcal down his throat, he stood and raised his arms once again in the air. Everyone stood as the cleric turned and toddled towards his car. Bidding 'God go with you', he squeezed his body into a dilapidated Volkswagon. '*Adios, adios,*' we all cried to encourage his departure. We watched him jolt over the fields towards his next appointment, before we sat down and resumed our conversations.

All that remained of the priest's visit was the smell of his exhaust fumes. As the meal was finishing, two men began to play their guitars.

Esta guitarrita mia	This little guitar of mine
tiene lengua y quiere hablar;	has a tongue and wants to speak;
solamente le faltan los ojos	all it needs is eyes
para ponerse a llorar…	to break down and weep…

People took turns to sing. Comic songs and romantic songs and stories of woe or tragedy, were interspersed with clapping and laughter.

Dices que me quieres mucho,	You say how much you love me;
es mentira tu me engañas;	you lie, you cannot mean it
en un corazón tan chico	in a heart as small as yours
no pueden caber dos almas.	there is no room for two souls.

To mark the end of the feast and the beginning of the entertainment, batches of rockets were sent to explode in the sky. Outshone by the sun, they were marked only by corkscrew trails of smoke.

Boys had been sent to catch the bulls, and tether them to small thorn trees that grew in the field. The rest of us ambled over to watch the show. Children carrying jugs full of *agua fresca* or *pulque* followed.

After carefully inspecting the ground for ants, we sat with Joaquin and Ofelia on the long dried grass, in the shade of the hedge. Holding out our glasses for a refill as a jug passed by and drowsily shifting the weight from one elbow to the other, was the total of our physical effort that afternoon.

The appearance of the small black bulls as they grazed in preparation for quietly lying down to chew the cud, convinced us that the tranquil nature of San Lucas's mascot was a universal characteristic.

Then the young men rushed in and, several to each animal, tackled the little bulls until they fell on their sides. With their legs flailing in the air, a stout rope was tied tightly round their withers. And to make them buck, another was strapped round their hindquarters. With their peace disturbed, the bewildered animals were quickly stirred into anger.

Each taking his turn, young men leaped onto the backs of the bulls.

The show had begun.

Once astride, the aim of the youth seemed to be to further enrage the creature. Clutching onto the improvised pommel by way of the neck, they shouted and whipped its rump. The little black bulls obligingly bucked and snorted and kicked and bellowed.

But the bulls always won. Inevitably the cream of the Sánchez family's youth would be bucked off, to land on the ground with a deep thud.

There appeared to be no rules.

Quite soon, there were a lot of angry *toros* throwing increasingly drunken youths about the field.

The spectators roared encouragement and yelled with pleasure as the boys hung on. Amid great waves of laughter, the riders were egged on and on.

Soy de la opinión del pueblo	I am of the general opinion
qu'el mejor gusto del hombre	that for a man to have his fun
es, si te quise, no me acuerdo,	it's like this: If I loved you, I don't remember,

si te tuve no se donde,	if I had you I forgot where,
Y para mejor decirte	and if you really want to know
ni me acuerdo de tu nombre.	I don't even remember your name.

But as the afternoon passed, the young men began to drop off their mounts more and more frequently. Exhausted, they lolled around the edge of the field, quenching their thirst before falling into a stupefied sleep.

Gradually, the little black bulls returned to their own lives and wandered off to graze and chew the cud.

The sun began to sink low over the mountains, and in the company of our new friends we walked towards the technicolor sunset, in the direction of our homes.

Joaquin, like Richard, wore a pair of *huaraches*. Unaware that these sandals were only worn by *campesinos*, Richard had bought his in the market, mainly for their durability. Choice had been limited, the other option being engraved patent leather boots. These, with their fine pointed toes and high heels, were more for decorative wearing, for standing around in a display of machismo.

It transpired that Richard and the Green Architect had a political gesture in common.

Walking back towards Las Brujas, we began to describe were we lived. After a slight hiatus, Ofelia began to laugh. She explained that only last week her husband had plucked up enough courage to walk through the orchards and visit the barrio that traditionally had not welcomed strangers.

He had put on his sandals and thought about all the men he employed at a fair rate. Some must live in San Miguel. Until five years ago, no white person had crossed the invisible boundary of the place.

With the spirit of an explorer, Joaquin walked the back way into Las Brujas. It was the afternoon and there were few people around, but those he met, well aware of who he was, greeted him with formal friendliness. On his way up the lane towards the fountain and wash place, he passed by La Casita Azul. He noticed the door was padlocked.

He felt elated; at last he thought, the people in this barrio were emerging from hundreds of years of listless apathy, and had found the energy to limewash the fronts of their houses using traditional pigments.

I had to admit that my inspiration had been a museum further north.

The rumour that the inhabitants of this barrio still kill strangers who wander into their territory is still popular enough to deter most white people from even thinking of putting a toe onto Calle Emiliano Zapata. So why did Don Cándido encourage one of his client's sons to buy a house in this place of political subversives?

We parted company with Joaquin and Ofelia where the lane left the road, and they promised to visit us. They were to become good friends, although on that day of San Lucas we could not imagine how good.

For the Indians, San Lucas is the patron saint of *los accidentes,* those killed by accidents or violence. He also watches over those who have been murdered or drowned.

This saint is the Catholic face of the Mayan and Aztec female deity of water and rivers, Chalchiunhlicue. It is to her, rather than San Lucas, that people pray during a woman's labour and the baby's birth.

En una jaula de plata	In his cage of silver
se quejaba un pajarito	moaned a little bird
y en el quejido relata	and plaintively sang
de un modo muy exquisito:	in his exquisite way
Dicen que el amor no mata	They say love does not kill,
pero lastima un poquito.	but it does hurt a little."

*

It wasn't long before we had a visit from Joaquin. It was the standard fine warm afternoon we now took for granted when he burst through the coffee bushes at the end of our garden, to be greeted by our neighbours who were investigating their ripeness.

By the time we caught sight of him he was on his hands and knees looking into the shallow excavations that *los duendes* had dug, as they searched for the *caritás* that we were eager to buy.

We were very pleased to see the Green Architect, so we stopped work

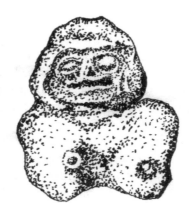

and made some coffee. Dolores, thinking herself the queen of diplomacy, vanished at the first hint of a visitor from the outside world.

Joaquin stepped into our living room with an eye accustomed to the way we lived. He understood the white and ochre walls and the horizontal blue stripe that divided the colours. He did not see it as an apology for gold-embossed wallpaper not sticking to the adobe. The books on the shelves were for reading, and the pictures now piling up on the table were to illustrate another.

His recognition and his enthusiasm were heartwarming.

He looked carefully at the *tromp l'oeil* painted furniture. This not only comprised the bed, but included a large table. I'd painted its top with a tree of life, from drawings made of the frescos in the ex-convento.

He also admired the corner cupboard that had been painted to resemble an elaborately carved stone doorway. Dolores, sure that it was built with the sole purpose of housing a saint, was horrified when its real function was revealed and we hung our clothes inside.

By now there was also a curly bench and an armchair made from an avocado tree that had fallen across the garden.

Speaking with delight about trees, the importance of labour-intensive projects, and the value of the adobe blocks, he eagerly looked around our home.

As the natural accessory to *huaraches,* Joaquin carried a sisal bag over his shoulder, on one side of which had been swiftly painted a pouncing jaguar. We both carried similar bags, so there was no surprise when he drew a Nikon camera out of his. Nodding our somewhat amused agreement, he began to photograph the entire contents of our home from every angle and every aspect. He was a light, agile person, and we just sat and watched as he leapt about in the rafters, taking pictures from the view usually reserved for scorpions.

When the light became too low, we sat and talked. While Richard emphasised the importance of a hand-made way of working, unsullied by machinery, Joaquin knew the longer it took a mason to chip away with a hammer and chisel to make a double flight of sweeping stairs, the more perfect the result. It had taken the mason weeks and weeks to carve his way to the front door. Local labour, local materials. We finished the Jamaica, the coffee and the tea.

Richard and Joaquin talked and talked. If they had conversed all night they would not have run out of things on which to agree.

It had grown dark, so we walked with the Green Architect to what we now knew to be the safety of the end of the lane, where Las Brujas met with the outside world. As we parted, Joaquin suggested that we have an exhibition of our furniture and prints in La Casita Azul. He assured us that his clients would be very interested. 'Post-Modern,' he muttered, as he turned to walk up the hill.

So we returned home very excited by the idea of an exhibition. It seemed then a simple matter of designing and printing the invitations and sweeping out the house.

Three or four turkeys were gobbling at our gate.

'Good night,' we said, even though we knew them not to be Dolores and her comadres.

'And if you go on disapproving like this, we might change the name of our house to…La Casa Pasada Moderna.'

Huaraches is not only the name for a type of sandal, but also for a delicious snack that is often made and eaten by the side of the road.

The oval tortillas are made with *huitlacoche,* the blue *masa* that is discoloured by a fungus encouraged to grow on maize. These toasted tortillas are the size of a giant's sandal, and onto this edible platter are arranged various ingredients, which may include beans, chicken stewed with tomatoes and *epazote* – a pungent herb native to Mexico – coriander, finely chopped onions or nopal salad. Over the top is sprinkled grated cheese.

The whole will be handed to you in a fold of coarse paper.

*

André Breton, also known as the father of Surrealism, realising the seat of his philosophy must be in Mexico, took up the kind invitation of Diego Rivera and his wife, Frida Kahlo, to come and stay in their twin homes in Coyoacan, a leafy suburb of Mexico's *distrito federal*.

A resounding cultural exchange was anticipated.

The great master duly arrived. Hardly having time to recover from his long journey, he was entertained to one of the artists' lavish, but formal meals.

Even Diego and Frida had the usual range of dusky-skinned servants to invisibly hover about, waiting to satisfy every whim of their masters and guests alike. It was the native qualities of his hostess that had impressed the avant-garde artist.

He was bowled over not only by her self-conscious beauty, but by her exquisite indigenous costume. The indigenous theme was consistent throughout both their homes, he felt.

After dinner, they retired to a sitting room where Breton's gaze fell upon a set of armchairs, the like of which he was not familiar with. They were made from wood, with a seat and back stretched with hide. It was a style popular all over the country, especially now that furniture was becoming more fashionable, albeit in cruder forms in everybody's home.

The guest found them very comfortable and mentioned this to his host. And how in keeping they were with the prehispanic ambience of his lovely home.

Diego was too polite to point out that chairs were introduced by the Spanish, along with that other four-legged seat, the horse. But the mural painter did tell the Surrealist that he too could have a set made by the local carpenter.

The next morning, the guest was up early, making precise isometric drawings so that there could be no misunderstanding with the furniture maker. These he presented to a rather confused artisan who, while he assured our friend that he had made a set of chairs for the plump painter up the road, said that this order was slightly different.

'Exactly as the drawings,' said André, thinking that he had made himself perfectly clear.

A week later, six chairs were delivered to the Rivera household ready for packing and shipping to Europe. They had been constructed with a great deal of thought and care, and in faithful reproduction of the isometrically-projected drawings. Unable to stand on their own, as two of the legs were much shorter than the others as per the illustration, they had been left propped against the wall of the hallway.

It is said that the man who had thought up the Surrealist movement, unable to see the funny side, fled in terror from a culture that has never segregated fantasy from reality.

The chairs that caused the debacle are known as *butaques*.

ELEVEN

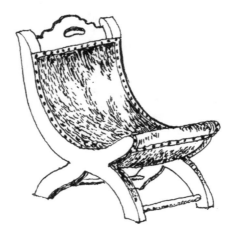

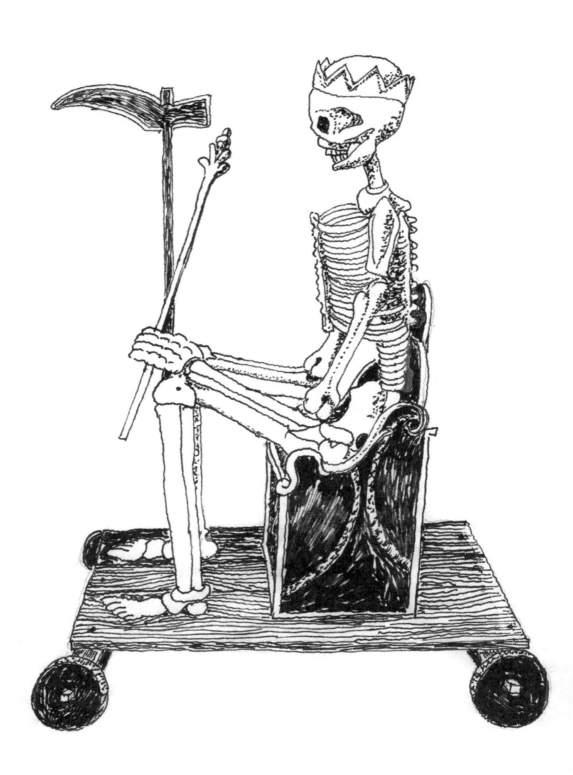

LOS DIAS DE MUERTOS

A COLLISION WITH
THE STIFF UPPER LIP

October 27th. A vigorous spring-cleaning was taking place. Wafts of cleaning fluid fumes floated into our living room on the cooling breeze. My nostrils were alerted by the smell of extra strong bleach as the washing lines became fully occupied. The lower slopes of the mountains were dressed overall with the whitest laundry. I had waited all morning for a vacant spot at the washing place. That was until Dolores noticed me hovering, and moved me and my sodium hydroxide sodden linen straight onto the next available scrubbing stone. Every woman was washing everything they could lay their hands on. The sound of this intense business was very invigorating, and soon I was as excited as everyone else. I, too, was caught up in the preparations for the Days of the Dead.

Listening to my freshly-pegged washing flapping in the breeze, I cleaned the kitchen. Sprinkling the floors with water, I swept all the shards cut from the lino blocks out of the door. Into the garden were brushed the insects, along with the other strange detritus that mysteriously accumulates in the home.

Standing in the doorway, I showed off my decorative brushstrokes to Richard and Dolores, before we left to walk over the mountain to the Town on the Hill, in time for the annual Day of the Dead market the next morning.

By way of the paths that led to the Aztec temple, we hopped over the rocks and irrigation runnels until we joined the precolumbian road that led steeply up behind the ruins. Until only a few years ago, this was the only way to reach the Village in the Valley, and also the only way out. It was down this magnificent paved military highway that Cortés had sent his men to rout the warriors of the military academy, before proceeding onwards to sack Moctezuma at Tenochtitlan.

Now it was reduced to a track, and its cobbles were dangerously higgledy-piggledy where the mules had kicked them about. It zigzagged up to the pass and then petered out, leaving us to follow a track through the woods before we came out onto the grassy plateau on the ridge. From here we could see the Town on the Hill.

It was nearly dark by the time we reached the *zócalo* and the Hotel Jardin.

The woman in reception must have remembered us from our previous visit (we had stayed here before we took the wrong bus to the spa town and ended up in Las Brujas), as she applied her look of disdain with definite familiarity.

Eyeing us with unnerving contempt, she leaned over the desk and peered at the spot where she thought the rest of our luggage should be. The huaraches, the sisel bag and the wicker basket did not impress her. But at that moment the proprietor stepped out of his office. He asked us if we lived in La Casita Azul in San Miguel. News of the white strangers who were not Protestants had luckily travelled further than we imagined.

Under duress, the grumpy woman smiled an expressionless smile and led the way up the staircase to the first floor.

The door she had been instructed to unlock for us revealed a room that, until quite recently, must been sumptuous. It was still large and square, with an ornamental plaster frieze continuing uninterrupted round the perimeter of the ceiling. (Frequently these rooms from a bygone age have been divided into four or five cells, each with the depressing proportions of a lift shaft.)

The statuary fly-blown light bulb hung naked from frayed wire, which disappeared into a magnificent central ceiling rose. Patches of less faded wallpaper indicated where monumental furniture had once stood. Where there had once been a magnificent wardrobe, now stood a warping plywood cabin, the advertised 'en suite'.

Not so very long ago, I would have longed to see the original furnishing and fittings of this room. Now I joined Richard in the simple appreciation of hot running water.

Making full use of the modern plumbing, we decided that there was no shower better than one you have paid for with money.

We opened the window and stepped out onto the balcony, which overlooked the main square. A slight breeze played in a sensuous way on our fresh, clean skins. Enjoying everything, we looked down and watched the frenetic preparations for the market the next morning. The busy scene was lit by strings of electric light bulbs that looped through the trees and around the bandstand. The smaller children were already being bedded in boxes, down underneath the stalls.

Delicious smells rose up from the brightly-lit food stalls below us.

Refreshed, we left the room. Leaning over the internal balustrade, we were level with the giant chandeliers that hung over and lit the large central courtyard. Originally, this must have been the 'Jardin', or garden, of the hotel's name, but it had been paved over and was now full of shiny cars. An elegant double staircase swept in symmetrically opposing curves down to a fountain, full of water lilies and black carp.

We wandered out in the direction of the food stalls, and chose the one selling *chalupas poblanas*. We sat down in front of plates crowded with small tortillas stuffed with chopped pork and marrowbone filling. We tucked into the food through the rising steam, our eyes watering from the piquant green sauce.

Waves of shrill, squabbling black birds were flocking into the square. They were fighting for a place in the leaves of the canopies. The branches were by now laid low with the weight of the nightly migration.

Having eaten, we returned to the hotel for an early night. We wanted to take full advantage of the smooth white bed linen. For us, it had been a stiff walk.

OCTOBER 28TH

An extremely unpleasant screeching sound woke us the next morning. We hurriedly dressed to remove ourselves from the ear-piercing noise. Opening our door, we saw the owner of the hotel turning the key into another door nearby. As this swung open he bent over, as if in a deep bow, and the occupants, a magnificent peacock and his mate, emerged. The proprietor straightened up, leaving a dish of grain on the floor.

The peacock gave an improbable hop, and landing heavily on the balustrade, he slowly and tantalisingly fanned out his tail into a huge arc and juddered. Strutting into a broad shaft of light, he turned on the banister rail until his feathers caught in the sunshine and their iridescence shimmered. Down below, the peahen nervously pecked at the grain.

The dining room was full of morning sunshine, diffused by the heavy

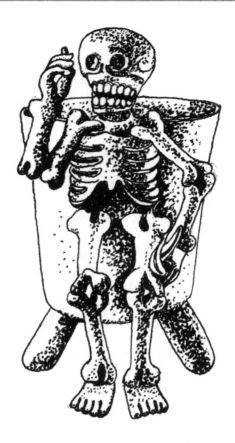

crocheted curtains. On the tables, gleaming glasses refracted the light, leaving fragments of rainbows on the stiff white cloths. The polished cutlery had been laid correctly for every place setting. Even with the electroplating removed by years of rubbing, the golden gleam of the base metal of the knives and forks and spoons shone valiantly through.

The *mozo*, or waiter, wearing the profession's usual black and white, put a symbolic helpful hand out towards our table and smiled as I tentatively lowered myself onto the dainty gilt chair. Every item on the menu could be read, as it were, from the small portions displayed on the *mozo*'s costume. Spreading the monogrammed napkins on our knees, we ordered the full breakfast – *el desayuno*.

Scrambled eggs, peas, tomatoes, pickled chillies, onions, avocado pear, soft white cheese and chorizo sausage came on one plate. A basket of warm tortillas was placed close at hand, as were tall glasses of freshly-squeezed orange juice. Large bowls of fruit salad were placed on our table, along with coffee, hot milk and a sufficient number of sticky buns.

So we were well set up for the day by the time we settled the modest bill, and made our formal departure. Don Peacock was still displaying on the cast iron railings, so we just waved in his direction as we headed out into the maelstrom.

The whole town was full of people buying and selling. The *zócalo* was crammed with stalls piled with essential accoutrements for the Days of the Dead. Everything necessary for the *ofrenda*, the offering for the family shrine, was on view.

La calavera is an optimistic word, meaning not only skull, but taking the masculine form, it describes a madcap, a reckless fellow. *Las calaveras* are the ornate sugar skulls, ranging from small to life-size, that were piled in diminishing pyramids on many of the stalls. Others just as decorative were made from moulded chocolate. Skeletons were stamped out from metallic paper. There were those that popped out from edible coffins, and jumping jacks that performed drunken dances. There were whole parties of humans dressed only in their bones, drinking and dancing, playing snooker, getting married, or riding bicycles, overloading buses, waving bottles, plucking guitars, or playing the marimba. Every skeleton was enjoying itself. The whole market had an exuberant atmosphere, as if everyone knew the party was going to be good. The dead were going to be celebrated in style.

We sat on a municipal bench, trying to overcome the temptation to buy something of everything. Strings of *papel picados* gently floated on the breeze above our heads, while in front of our eyes delicate *alfeniques* – sugar paste animals – were being arranged in groups of a kind. Lambs, dogs, donkeys and bulls in different postures filled the stall. There were groups of sugar baskets and *los muertitos*, tiny dead human figures.

There were little scenes in clay of the *Last Supper* being enacted by skeletons. Tree of life candlesticks depicted a cast of bony characters. Miniature scenes of light-hearted ribaldry, incarcerated in tiny glass boxes, needed serious scrutiny, before the joke became apparent.

Florists, deep inside their stacks of flowers, were doing brisk trade. The familiar smell of marigolds was thick in the air

Cempasûchil, from the *Tagetes* species, is at this time of year called *la flor de muerto*. Selling just as furiously was *il mano de león* ('lion's paw'): Celosia argenta, belonging to the *Amaranthaceae* family, looked like a giant, luscious, velvety cockscomb.

Why is death such a taboo subject in our culture?

I know that it can be argued that we have seen reason and dismissed the possibility of an afterlife, while the Catholics are still deluded, imagining they have somewhere to go after death. But this doesn't entirely answer my query.

My father was able to talk about sex until the cows came home, but mention death and he would come up with cascades of euphemisms.

'Macabre', I've heard these Mexican revelries described as. They are not.

I was reminded of lying in hospital in England when a bevy of starched nurses rustled into the ward and swept all the bed curtains closed.

What was it? Something 'not nice' was the whispered answer.

The elderly woman from the other end of the ward had died.

The woman to whom I had spoken the day before had died alone. She had been discovered by an orderly in the course of his duties. She was unceremoniously removed from the ward, lifted onto a tray and slid into a refrigerator. With the same undercover secrecy with which a bedpan is removed, her body had been wheeled out.

This was our way of death. It left me feeling sad and bewildered.

In the market, we filled the basket with decorations and weighed down the bag with more carpentry tools. Carrying huge yellow and magenta bunches of the prerequisite flowers, we set off on the return journey down the mountain.

Dolores had brought in the dry sheets and they lay folded on the bed.

OCTOBER 29TH

Tons of firewood was still being delivered to the bakery just up the lane. Salvador or his son Arsacio led a string of laden mules past La Casita Azul every day for a whole week. There had been no time for the usual stop, but the men had waved cheerfully. By now the wood was stacked perilously high against the walls of the bakery. The Day of the Dead bread is traditionally baked by the men, who were by now having to work day and night to produce enough to last until the final day of *Los Dias de Muertos*, on the 2nd of November.

Pan de muerto is a sweet, leavened bread, enriched with eggs and flavoured with oranges and aniseed. These little spherical loaves are surmounted by a smaller ball and decorated with the crossed femur shapes of the Jolly Roger. These represent the ancestors and the four parts of the Aztec universe. In the spaces between, tears of dough are affixed, symbolising the grief of the living for those who have died. Glazed with beaten egg and sugar, they glint temptingly in the candlelight.

OCTOBER 30TH

Before the Spanish arrived and began their wholesale conversion of the native population to Catholicism, the indigenous people had an extremely vivid picture of death and the afterlife.

In Nahuatl literature there are many references to life as 'the dream'. They wrote about 'the beyond', 'the land of the dead', 'the place of the fleshless', as a region of mystery.

Ritual was of paramount importance to the Aztecs, and an enormous amount of time and effort were expended in ceremonial activities. Among these religious celebrations were the rites concerned with the dead and gods of death:

— Mictlantecihuatl was the great feast of the dead. It is the day when the adult dead are commemorated.
— Miccailhuitontli was the little feast of the dead, the day children were remembered.
— Mictlantecuhtli was the god of death. His body partly a skeleton, and with his face covered by a bony mask, he sat among owls and spiders. With his wife, Mictlantecihuatl, he reigned over the underworld.
— Coatlicue, the earth mother, was the goddess of life and death. Her face is formed from the heads of two fanged snakes, and round her waist hangs a skirt of rattlesnakes. As a goddess of death she wears a necklace of hearts, hands and skulls.

One of the great intellectual problems that the Spanish friars found difficult to solve was how to present Christianity as an entirely different religion in areas where the two theologies were so similar. Both had made a cult of death and the afterlife. Both had skulls as well-established images in their iconography.

But before the end of the sixteenth century, the feasts of Mictlantecihuatl and Mictlantecuhtli had coincided with 'The Day of the Faithful Departed', which is All Saints' Day in the Catholic calendar.

Here syncretism worked hand in glove.

Before the arrival of the Spanish, flowers, food, paper ornaments, incense fumes and music were being offered to the dead. *Tamales* stuffed with green vegetables and *mazamorra* – a maize gruel – were put out as las ofrendas for dead relatives, before being given to the living, a practice that continues to this day.

The sweeping and cleaning that I had so enjoyed has prehispanic origins. So has the ritual renewing of kitchen pots and pans.

No wonder the friars thought it prudent to present an unoccupied cross to the pagans.

LA OFRENDA Y LOS NINOS LIMBOS
(THE OFFERING AND THE BABIES IN LIMBO.)

Everybody was either indoors or in their yards, constructing *la ofrenda*.

Our bookcase had been rearranged to accommodate the decorations that we had bought in the market. I had removed the photographs of our families, because they were still alive, and replaced them with a small lithograph of Santa Lucia holding out a pair of clear blue eyes on a tray, as she calmly held a palm frond in the other arm. This has always been a favourite picture of mine. Identical prints can be found across Catholic Europe. To balance the symmetry, I stood the patron saint of carpenters holding his son in his arms. In front of these, was the small clay scene of the skeletons' feast, and either side of these were placed several sugar lambs, a sugar donkey, an edible skull and a pop-up coffin. We pinned the *papeles picados* so that they hung in loops from the rafters.

The whole thing looked like a mantelpiece.

Dolores was worried that the souls of our dead would never find us. If it was too great a journey for our living relatives to travel, it was certainly too much to expect the dead to find La Casita Azul. She invited us to join her and her family at their shrine.

It was some time after dark when we finally we arrived at Dolores' yard and handed her some candles, a few chunks of copal resin, and a bag of pomegranates. A couple of dim light bulbs hung from the trees, and a big cauldron steamed over a wood fire. From the shadows of the dark garden, several men and women we knew stepped forward and greeted us. And as we looked more closely, we saw that place was full of people. Each one of us was given a bowl of hot tripe and cow's hoof soup.

When we had finished eating this meal (a meal that was much more delicious than our modern preconceptions would allow us to believe), Dolores took the bowls and ushered us into her room. This is where she slept, her *petate* was rolled into a tube and neatly propped up in the darkest corner.

As our eyes became accustomed to the localised pools of beeswax candlelight, we began to take in this extraordinary faerie scene.

The day-to-day household shrine had been moved to a sidewall, where the Virgin of Guadalupe stood as usual behind dozens of guttering candles. This is the shrine that Dolores keeps lit throughout the year.

In the Madonna's usual spot had been constructed *la ofrenda*.

A heavily starched white cloth had been spread over a high shrine table. The cotton was so stiff it hardly needed the support of the furniture that lay beneath it. Tied to the two front legs was a tall arch of supple branches, decorated with a lot more foliage, to which brightly-coloured paper flowers had been attached. Along the back wall and up into the rafters had been stretched a length of sky-blue, builders' polythene sheeting. Under these heavens, hung the strings of cut-out paper flags. *Papeles recortados* of kneeling angels had been pinned up at the back, as well as the front of this shrine.

Flowers in jars, and fruit in neatly piled pyramids, were symmetrically displayed, along with the new *alfeniques* and *calaveras*. Candles burnt in new holders, while copal smouldered in new burners. Standing on the floor, on each side of the new *petate* were large buckets of the golden and magenta flowers of the Day of the Dead.

Tiny toys, a knitted doll, a painted rattle, and a crocheted bonnet lay between two piles of freshly washed and meticulously ironed white infant's clothes.

At the back, in the most convoluted baroque frame, we could just make out a faded black and white photograph.

We peered in closer and saw a young couple, hardly more than children, posed in front of the photographer's painted landscape.

Their faces appeared to be blank with shock as they sat side by side. Resting on their knees, they tenderly held a tiny white coffin, tied with satin bows. Inside the white lace lining and turned towards the camera, nestling in a white broderie-anglaise christening gown, was the body of a newborn infant.

Neither of us could recognise the man, but the girl was Dolores.

It was a spellbinding scene.

The copal fumes had become very thick in the room, and by the time we turned and left a fiddle player outside was playing go-faster, cheerful tunes.

We followed the path of glowing marigold petals that showed us the way through the yard. Here, it met the thicker trail in the lane. This would lead out of Las Brujas to join the track that led to the cemetery

The moon was rising in the trees and the relatives were growing merrier.

In silence, Dolores walked with us to our gate. As we hugged each other goodnight she left in our hands two *calaveras*. On each forehead, our names had been piped in green and pink icing.

Dolores was smiling and we noticed a spring in her step as she returned home.

Following the iridescence and distinctive smell of the *cempasûchil* petals, the souls of the dead would be able to find their way home.

That night was for *los niños limbos*, when the souls of infants in limbo visit. These are the babies who have died before being baptised.

In each of the seven barrios the bells of the churches were ringing, as if to hurry the visiting dead.

Returning home, we saw our bookshelves as a meaningless pastiche. Carefully, we placed Dolores' skulls either side of the *Last Supper*, reinstated the family photos, and hoped that nobody had noticed that we had tried to imitate *la ofrenda*.

OCTOBER 31ST

The next morning, we bought not only a basketful of *pan de muertos*, but also some small salt loaves that were in the form of human figures, bulls, lambs and flaming hearts. The dough had spread in the baking and given them a prehistoric look. They had been adorned copiously with tears, buttons, bows, and, where appropriate, flaring flames. Each little decoration had been dyed scarlet with cochineal.

Prudently, we bought more candles. In all the shops, supplies were running low.

We dawdled down the hill, thinking that we would at least come across the woman who everyday had stood at the end of the lane cooking and selling tacos. There was no sign of the wayside grill. We passed nobody on the road, and the Calle Emiliano Zapata was just as deserted.

Everywhere was quiet, nobody could be seen going about their daily business.

The collective preparations for the fiesta were a fully absorbing occupation.

There was something in the air. While I couldn't exactly pinpoint the feeling, it became too difficult to ignore.

It took some time before we could admit that neither of us felt like working. Even though nobody would have minded if we had carried on, it became too irksome to do so. So we wandered around in a desultory way.

Not that we had been at all excluded, but neither were we involved. Dolores would have been only too pleased if we were to spend the next few days sitting in her yard, where she could keep the usual eye on us and make sure that we did not become lonely. But while we were worried that we might intrude on her privacy, she was still anxious that with no souls to visit us, we would be sad.

We sat in our garden trying to concentrate enough to read. Out of the corner of my eye I saw that Dolores was fully aware from our aimless movements that she had been quite right, we had become very sad. Anyway, I'm sure she thought reading books to be a pastime for the miserable. We divided the *pan de muertos* and candles into three piles.

It was well before dark that, together with one bundle of candles and a bag of bread, we were at the gate of Dolores' yard. And she welcomed us in so warmly that our English hearts were almost overcome.

The curtain that usually closed the entrance to the bed and shrine room had been removed, leaving the copal smoke to disperse more easily. Our little loaves were added to the piles of food on *la ofrenda*, and the candles put on those neatly stacked beneath.

The photograph in the Florentine frame from the night before had gone. In its place was pinned the new embroidery of Christ that I'd seen being finished a couple of days before. From under a crown of thorns, he was pointing with an index finger to the bleeding fiery heart on his white tunic. Tears sewn in silver thread glittered as they flowed from his rheumy eyes.

It was a relief not to be confronted with pictures of the dead children in this family. At the same time, I began to feel the greater responsibility of being *la madrina de fotografía*.

Toy trucks, small dolls, wheeled horses, doll's tea sets, and little mugs and bowls were all arranged between piles of tamales and sweets. Big bottles of fizzy pop stood on each corner of the table.

At dusk, the eerie singing began. All at the same time, from every yard, ethereal sounds wove and rose into the trees. The music was thin and heartrending. It seemed to come from nowhere I knew. It was as if these were passionate songs in defiance of the repressive conquistadors.

A moment later, the bells of seven barrios rang out, rockets burst all over the sky and the heavy fumes of incense drifted in layers of smoke through the orchards.

This was the day the souls of children – *los angelitos* – visited.

November 1st

The bells had rung all night and were still ringing when, in the early morning, Dolores appeared out of the lingering copal smoke. She was carrying some *tamales* and a dish of preserved fruit. She seemed breathlessly busy. *Los angelitos* would be gone by noon, and everything had to be ready for *las ánimas*, the souls of adults, who were expected to arrive soon afterwards.

But she lingered with us on the veranda, and while we all picked at the crystallised fruit she talked of her dead. While she didn't know many people who actually saw their dead loved ones, the feeling that they were with you was so strong and powerful, it soothed the grief and lifted your heart.

Being souls, they cannot eat the food or take the gifts, but they greatly appreciate the offerings. What is left, is shared with family and friends.

Dolores then darted off to reassemble the shrine to welcome the new influx of adult souls. We had never seen our friend so invigorated.

Even if we had been in the mood, it didn't feel right to ignore all that was going on around us and try and work. So we packed the *tamales,* the preserved fruit and a bottle of water in a bag, and set off up the mountain. We hoped to get beyond the mirador and escape the incessant striking of the seven bells. Until we were out of earshot of the ringing, I could not think coherently.

Up and up we scrambled, along the little tracks that must have led somewhere. Higher and higher into the Chinese landscape that had been our initial impression of the Village in the Valley. We did not meet a single sheep or goat, so we assumed that even the shepherds were at home with their animals corralled.

We rested in a field full of flowers and watched them being pollinated by the butterflies and bees. Out and over the seven barrios spread the most spectacular sunlit vista of lush vibrant greens. Birds sang and the warm air was occasionally stirred by a breeze. Noises from the faraway barrios were very faint, but reassuringly familiar.

It was like a dream. Like a perfect dream, as we lay back and watched the buzzards wheel about against the celestial blue sky.

But at the same time there was sadness about us. You cannot live for fifty years and not have something that saddens you. Richard must have been thinking of his mother, who had died when he was young. Maybe I was thinking of mine, who had expired before her time, too.

And that is when I learnt to feel happy and sad at the same time.

If this was 'the dream', what was England? But I could no longer see that part of my life at all clearly.

By the time it was dusk, we had returned. Las Brujas was shrouded in dense copal fumes, and the sounds were muffled by this fog.

As we walked up the lane from the fountain, every doorway was wide open. Every home had opened its doors so that their shrines were visible. In each, a magnificent *ofrenda* glowed in warm yellow candlelight. And each opening was an invitation to linger and look. There was quiet singing to the rhythm of the tortilla patting. Dark figures loomed up as silhouettes against the light, before vanishing in the shadows.

For a moment as we passed one doorway, we caught a glimpse of a tableau of young girls dressed in white satin, with wings of white feathers that seemed to spring from their shoulder blades. They knelt, a symmetrical host of angels, before and up the sides of their *ofrenda*.

Not only were Dolores and her family in the yard, but several other relatives were milling around, waiting to be introduced to us as we came through the gate. New candles and more copal had been lit, and we added our contribution to the quickly growing piles around the room. A cluster of framed photographs lined the back wall of the shrine.

I had been introduced as *la madrina de fotografía*. I was the photographer whose pictures would sooner or later end up on the back wall of *la ofrenda* on the Day of the Dead. Now I began to feel the weight of the other part of my responsibilities.

Pulque, mezcal, beer and cigarettes had replaced the toys. There were also piles of chillied *tamales*, bread and chocolate. A new machete and a gun lay beside a chair, on which was a pile of new and neatly folded clothes. An embroidered blouse and a shawl were ready for a woman, and a tall white hat for a man.

By the time the fiddle player struck up the tune for the eerie songs, everybody was totally engaged in this extraordinary ritual. It was as tender as it was beautiful. But we had not known the dead when they were alive.

Although we had been invited, we felt like intruders. So we kept to the shadows of the yard before sloping away.

The church bells valiantly continued to toll, and rockets continued to decorate the sky. The moon shone through chinks in the roof tiles, sprinkling the room with little shards of white ghostly light.

We thought of Dolores, her stillborn child, her vanished husband, and all the other sad things we did not know about her.

We thought of all the sad things she did not know about us, all the

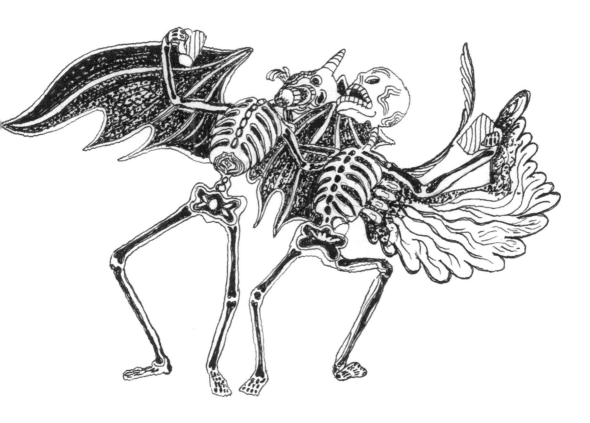

sadness we did not know about each other.

But we did feel this wonderful feeling of collective grief. It was not embarrassing, it was not coy, it did not gush all over the place, nor did it masquerade with a stiff upper lip. It drank and it laughed.

It was perfectly acceptable to be sad.

November 2nd

We spent the afternoon sitting on the veranda drinking tea, and eating bread and honey while we watched the grand exodus. Everyone in the barrio leading every available mule and donkey passed by.

It looked as if whole homes were on the move. Not only food and drink, but firewood and kitchens, chairs and bedding, vases, flowers candles and framed photographs, were piled high on the backs of the animals.

We waved until the last stragglers headed towards the road. They waved back, beckoning and insistently pointing in the direction of *el camposanto*, the cemetery.

Almost alone in the barrio, its emptiness and quiet made us feel uneasy.

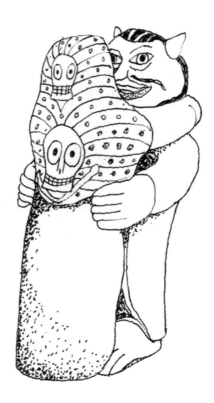

As night fell, we took the rest of our candles and followed the iridescent petal path along the lanes and tracks that took us through the field of San Lucas. Pausing at the shrine, we lit and threaded a candle through the iron gates, to add to the mass already flickering at the feet of the patron saint of *los accidentes*. Then we climbed up the hill to the avenue of red cedars that led to the cemetery.

The vigil was in full swing. The mules and donkeys, now unburdened, were nonchalantly grazing where they had been tethered outside the stone walls of the graveyard.

In a field beyond, a fairground with its mechanical music pulsating in time to the flashing lights, failed to mask neither the noise of the generators nor the excited screams of terror and delight that pierced the night.

Stalls had sprung up, and in clouds of steam food was being cooked and sold. Drinks and sticky sweets, as well as a range of skeleton toys.

The *cempasûchil* path led right up to the arched entrance of the cemetery. The great rusted iron gates had been lifted wide open for the occasion. We stepped nervously over the threshold.

Families had set up their one-night homes, settling themselves round their family graves. Deep inside the banks of flowers, fires had been lit, cauldrons bubbled and bowls were filled with hot stew. Jugs of *pulque* and bottles of mezcal circulated through the celebrating masses. Some people sat, while others slept out this all-night vigil. We picked our way through the monumental sepulchres and baroque mausoleums. From professionally carved vaults to home-made tombs, each was surrounded by a group of people busy with family life.

Steam and smoke rose above the blooms, and mingled with the layers of incense that drifted amongst the trees. Clusters of winged angels joined children and young men in skeleton costumes, as they playfully chased each other over and around the monumental masonry.

All this was lit by the soft light of thousands of candles and hundreds of fires. Beneath the strident and competitive tunes being blasted out by the big wheel and the carrousel, the jubilant yelling and laughing, rose the subdued hubbub of the chanting of incantations.

We lit the last of our candles and stuck them into the ground. And from the periphery we sat and watched this exuberant, mysterious celebration.

How slow is the repressed, undisclosed grief in our culture to disperse, and let us thoroughly enjoy the memory of our dead family and friends.

TWELVE

EMILIANO ZAPATA

THE MAN WHO KNEW HORSES

Don Basilio was a regular visitor. Mounted on his magnificent black stallion, he was the only person able to tower high enough on his horse while in the lane and greet us over the high retaining wall of the garden.

Without dismounting, he and Richard would have long conversations about trees and different types of woods. Sometimes he would bring a branch of a strange tree, often from the tropical south of the country. He labelled each specimen in meticulous handwriting.

His passion was for horses. He never left his stallion out of the conversation, and would talk quietly and gently to it. As he spoke, he would absent-mindedly caress its smooth dark neck. Or he would lean over to cup the soft sensual muzzle in his hand. We saw the rapport he had with this beautiful creature. The reciprocated pleasure was tangible.

His departure was always sudden, as if he was slightly embarrassed by this show of intimacy. Don Basilio would pull the bridle taught, turn around and ride off, waving an arm held high in the air.

He was different, being a taller man than was usual here. His clothes were much repaired and threadbare, but the threads that were still there hung together, archaeological specimens of expensive quality. They still looked as if once, long ago, they had been made and fitted for him.

There was a mystery surrounding the horseman.

He lived alongside the stallion, in a hut at the foot of the mountains, just outside town.

He was a very popular figure, and we too enjoyed his company. It was always a special day for us when he rode into Las Brujas.

For several days Richard had been making toy rifles. The first was made at the request of Sánchez, for his grandson Marco Antonio.

Then, swift on the heels of this well boasted triumph, a bunch of small boys from the barrio asked for others, just the same. They clamoured round the workshop door, jumping up and down enthusiastically to check up on the progress through the window, as Richard tried to keep up with the orders.

By the time a dozen or so of these wooden weapons had been distributed, our garden became a pantomime battlefield. Every bush bristled with nascent revolutionaries. *Los duendes* lay spreadeagled on the ground for the brief moment of their feigned bloody deaths.

We of course were mystified. In our ignorance we wondered what had prompted this sudden outbreak of violence manqué.

A few days later, on the morning of 20th November, Don Basilio rode up to La Casita Azul with unusually dignified solemnity. Pulling in the reigns, his horse came to a halt, and he called out for Richard.

The stallion was dressed in its best tackle. The elaborately tooled leather bas relief, illustrating triumphal revolutionary battle, gleamed with polish.

We were more surprised to see Don Basilio, who was wearing the traditional clothes of the *campesino*, and was dressed in white cotton trousers and shirt with a red woven belt, *la faja*, round his waist. Lifting his tall straw hat from his head and with a sweeping gesture of his arm, he cried, '*Tierra y libertad*'.

Land and Liberty. It was Emiliano Zapata Day.

The old revolutionary tied the reigns round an overhanging branch; I brought some mugs of Jamaica to drink, before we settled on the wall.

We drank the toast of the day, *tierra y libertad*, and listened to our friend. This elderly man quietly recounted the horrifying tales of the revolution. Bloody scenes as the fighting troops swung backwards and forwards through the towns and villages, losing and gaining ground.

He had seen small children dead in the streets. In 1915, he must have been a small child himself.

Emiliano Zapata is still the peasants' hero. We were still mystified, looking at Don Basilio's unsullied hands you could see he had never been a *campesino.* He unhitched the reins and, reiterating the words of his hero, firmly pronounced, 'It is better to die on your feet, than live on your knees.' Before he rode off, he urged us to come to the horse race that afternoon, in the fields just beyond the shrine of San Lucas.

Emiliano Zapata had achieved sobering changes to the so far unchallenged powers and corruption of the Catholic Church. He was possibly the only idealistic revolutionary, many of the others being in it for the glory, the excitement or the self-enhancement.

Zapata was murdered in cold blood by one of the opponent Carranza's generals in 1919. He is still revered and emulated today. Land reform owed much to his ideas. His phrase *tierra y libertad* became a rallying cry. After the revolution, massive tracts of hacienda land that had been worked by the peasants under slave-like conditions were seized by the state. This was redistributed to the communities who divided it among the *campesinos.* This was to become the *ejidos* system. Because the land was owned by the state, it could not be sold. It was worked as in prehispanic times, by the indigenous people for their own benefit.

It was only recently that President Carlos Salinas changed the law and allowed the sale of *ejidos* land. This made the indigenous *campesinos* very fearful that the land would be taken from them in lieu of their endemic debts. People were very vulnerable to speculators, as we saw in the Village in the Valley which was being speedily 'discovered' by the rich, who had doubts about bringing up their children in the seriously noxious atmosphere of the capital.

Sánchez became very depressed. As he tried to point out to those who saw no further than the lump sum of cash they might receive, once their land is gone, they have nothing.

Mexico City was crowded with families who, having sold 'their' land, had quickly come to the end of the paltry selling price, and were now bulking out the gutters, holding out the thin hands that had so shocked us on our arrival in the country.

Land and Liberty. Now it was turning into a memory, it couldn't be more true.

*

It took us some time to work our way up the hill on that morning of Emiliano Zapata Day. We had to weave our way through the congestion of the market.

We were quite hot and tired by the time we reached the *zócalo.* Here, we usually sat down with our heavy baskets and ate some lunch in the shade of the trees, before making the return journey home through the orchards. Instead of the usual tranquillity, the square was overflowing with people bristling with excitement.

Men and boys proudly mounted on their mules or donkeys, all resplendent in their traditional clothes, with the symbolic blood-red sash of the faja a shocking contrast to the white of the newly-bleached trousers and shirts. Out had come the tall-crowned straw hats to top every grandfather, father and son. Each rider sat as still and silent as a statue.

Head and shoulders above the rest, was one of the last veterans, one of the few left with a personal memory of the revolution. Serious and poised high up on the back of his gleaming black stallion, sat Don Basilio.

Men shouldered arms, while boys shouldered sticks, as they listened to the proclamation from the municipal palace balcony. While *il Presidente* wore the sky blue bandera of office, a hundred imitation Zapatas echoed this with ribbons of cartridges in a repeated pattern, diagonally across each chest.

The cry went up in unison:

'*TIERRA Y LIBERTAD!*'

Everybody roared the refrain, as a hundred straw hats were spun high into the air.

Only the boys from Las Brujas sported real wooden muskets. And we felt a real pride to be included on this day of remembrance.

In a small way we began to realise that we were no longer seen as the complete strangers that had arrived by mistake only six months before.

As the equestrian celebrators began to disperse, we reverted to our routine and sauntered towards the little row of food stalls set up outside the walls of the convent.

Each stall was furnished with a single wooden bench, so you can sit at the table. Each table was covered with a plastic wipe-down cloth. Each cloth was printed with the eye-achingly brilliant tropical scenes that we had grown so familiar with during the wet season.

Choosing an idealised snake-infested rainforest, we sat with a beer while we waited for the dish of *chiles rellenos* (sweet peppers stuffed with cheese or meat, fried with squash flowers in the lightest of omelettes) to be served.

The aroma of the chillies and the meat and the cheese rose up and whirled through our nostrils, flooded our tastebuds, until wild horses could not have torn us away from the stall set up in the shade of the *ex-convento* wall.

After this we carried our shopping back, as usual, through the mango groves. And as we did every week, we enjoyed the dappled light and the sound of rushing water, as the irrigation channels were in full, if miniature, spate.

The barrio was quiet, so we realised that a general exodus had already taken place.

*

THE HORSE RACE

This was the annual horse race between the Village in the Valley and another small town, higher in the mountains.

So as quickly as possible, we threw ourselves into what we quaintly referred to as our 'best clothes'. Failing to possess a mirror bigger than an envelope, we had to rely on each other's critique as to the final appearance.

Despite the rosy glow we felt about each other, and in this instance the need for a rapid departure, neither of us mentioned that the time had come to invest in some new garments. Now was not the moment to discuss the matter, but very soon we would have to admit our 'best clothes' were beyond mending. The backside of my dress was so thin it had split in several places, and the subsequent stitching did not improve the shape. Richard's trousers had been repaired with patches to the knees and seat. But this was the best we could do on this occasion. Putting on our straw sun hats, we locked our home, rushed out of the gate and down the lane to join the holiday crowds.

We soon caught up and joined the throng heading in the direction of the race course, which was just beyond the shrine to San Lucas, as Don Basilio had directed. Surrounded by the mountains, in a flat bowl of the valley, a straight track had been recently ploughed. About four hundred yards long and thirty feet wide, it was in the centre of the field.

The band was arranging its self in the shade among the trees, on a wooded knoll just above the finishing post. They were still talking and comparing practise notes.

The Zapatas of the morning had been joined by their mothers, wives, sisters and daughters. The women, full-skirted, were busily spreading themselves out on the grass, in related groups that extended one into another. Roughly circular areas were claimed with great baskets of food, and then staked out with the more sedentary grandmothers. A companionable pair to each settlement.

From neighbouring villages and towns, dozens of pedlars had appeared with huge wicker baskets, their contents hidden under cloth covers. Each was held in the crook of the strong arms of a vendor waiting for the crowd to build up. Each waited until the curiosity grew. They waited with dumb insolence, until the bodies of the crowd were pressing hard against him and his basket. And they waited for the magic moment when, with a flick of the wrist, a dramatic flourish of an embroidered napkin, all was revealed.

Almost everything you hadn't realised you might need, want or momentarily desire, was on offer that afternoon. As long as it could fit into a basket or be tied to a stick, it was available. The seduction to impulse buy had been raised to new heights.

In the sunshine, in the midst of the collective excitement, it was strangely difficult to resist buying. Buying for the mysterious act of just buying. Wanton buying with an added frisson brought on by the delicious guilt of not needing anything.

In the end, I came away with a toy helicopter made from coloured paper and plastic cups. Attached to a stick by a yard of string, it screamed when whirred round in circles above our heads. At this height, it quickly became a hazard in the already congested airways.

Ice-cream carts leaking melting ice were being pushed and pulled up and down the uneven pasture, relentlessly selling, selling, selling, racing against the time when the fluid mass ran completely out of control. But it was still early in the afternoon, and the frozen barrel was still being turned hopefully among solid blocks of ice.

Gigantic bunches of floating gas-filled balloons were being gradually dispersed among insistent children. Toys pinned to tall poles lurched

tantalisingly among forests of small, outstretched pointing fingers.

We sat on the grass. We had been lucky to find a patch between several familiar families, for it was in the shade on the incline near the finishing line. From this position we could see the escaped balloons as they rose hundreds of feet into the cloudless sky, away from sad but stoical infants below. Agile children, nipping through the masses, were delivering plates of broad beans and chillies.

The sun beat down and the straw hat vendor, his wares stacked a yard high on his head, sauntered through the milling crowds, hoping for the heat to become unbearable. He could spot a distant squint, a bead of sweat on a brow with eyesight as keen as that of a peregrine falcon.

Horses, mules and donkeys were tethered to every available tree, fence or branch along the perimeter of the field. Those with a Mexican $ sign painted in whitewash on their flanks were for sale. Here, bunches of serious men, their heads bowed, congregated in little groups discussing particular animals.

The hopeful seller spoke of the unique wonders of his animal, the distress at the impending loss of such a faithful friend, and the amazing luck of the buyer if such a deal should take place.

All the while the prosaic business of leg lifting, hoof picking and the feeling of limbs and withers went on. Then came the rolling back of lips, the peering into mouths and the close inspection of eyes and, with a flick of the tail, nether quarters.

This was followed by the denigration, the accusation and disbelief as the other side of the story was put forward to balance the scales. The prospective buyer would point out that it was only his good nature, and an unusual lapse of common sense, that would allow him to make such a gesture and take the animal off his hands.

Then came the compromise and the final agreement, before the rolls of notes were begrudgingly worked out from tight back pockets. With a final pat on the dusty shoulders of the past and present owners, and another pat on the animal's dusty flank, the creature would change hands, before the buyer and seller each turned away to hide the look of satisfaction on their faces.

It is probably a global phenomenon, that good, honest family men, hardworking and God-fearing to boot, are transformed into a card-carrying spivs at the first hint of a deal involving a horse. The trading continued for most of the afternoon.

Gradually, the hubbub subsided as the spectators settled down to their picnics, and the voices of conversation were interspersed with chewing, swallowing and drinking. The rum and mezcal had come out of the baskets, along with jars and jugs of *pulque*. The bottles were passing freely between the different groups, until we were aware that it was two vast family outings that filled the field. Our town and the other from higher up the mountain were waiting for starter's orders

Although the sun was hot, the site was open and airy. The magnificent mountains encircled the view.

The tote men and the tipsters began to shout and wave the cards above their heads.

There was a wonderfully happy holiday feeling in the air. The band had struck up and the music was in full flight.

The excitement, the anticipation became palpable.

So now we were nearly down to the nitty gritty. In the distance, at the starting post, horses and men were in a milling whirl of confusion. From our far viewpoint, it seemed that the tight congestion would never ease. But suddenly, in mid-melody, the band stopped. The breeze rustled the leaves and we all held our breaths.

A shot rang out.

And at the clear sound of the starting pistol, the first race, the first pair of horses was unleashed to gallop up the bare earth.

The spectators watched, mesmerised, as the pair of horses pounded up the course.

The ploughed track ended just beyond the finishing line with an exhausting incline, which effectively brought the horses to a standstill.

We watched as the great beasts thundered to a halt just beneath the band. And the seismic reverberations stopped. The crowd roared with delight until the band took over again.

There were numerous heats, the horses racing two by two.

The jockeys were the finest young horsemen from each of the two competing towns. Barefoot and bare chested, they rode bareback, with their knees strapped into the rope girth tied tightly round the horse.

Scores of hearts must have fluttered as these wild boys, in the prime of their youth, their bodies seemingly defying gravity, rose up from their mounts and flew above their animals, as they switched its flanks and shouted themselves hoarse to will their steeds to win

It was a wonderful sight, on a perfect afternoon.

During the last of the heats, one of the hoses reached the finishing line lame. Immediately half a dozen men, leaping as if from nowhere and with the concern fathers might have for a young child, surrounded the shocked creature.

Swiftly, a dressing of maguey leaves sliced lengthways, the sap side facing in, was tied around the affected limb. Then the horse was helped, almost carried away, to rest in the shade of the trees. Here the men, gentle as lambs, lovingly stroked and quietly reassured the frightened beast with lullaby whispering.

The onlookers returned to their pitches and the first of the quarterfinals began.

And so the afternoon pleasantly drifted on. The sound of galloping hooves alternating with rousing tunes played by the band.

The intervals of music not only entertained us during the time it took to line up each new pair of competitors, it also expanded the interval between races, so that a good deal of betting was able to take place.

By this time, we were feeling the pleasant effects of the bottles that continued to pass by. As we lay on the warm radiating earth, we listened to the enveloping sousaphone-led melodies. If we'd had the energy to get up and make a bet, we would have been in grave danger of making another and another and another.

Instead, we sat up and watched the frenetic waving and enticing as the tote men bellowed for custom, the tipsters sold their secrets. All sorts of people that we were acquainted with were waving and shouting their odds. Among them, we recognised one or two of the black-hatted conspirators that hung around on our corner.

But the most surprising was spotted by Richard.

'There's the doctor. He's got a day job then.'

So we laughed because his nickname in the town was 'killer of the well'.

With the bets laid, the band slid into silence.

The next racing pair was under starters orders, and the shot rang out, sharp into the relaxed afternoon. This pair of riders were ready to give their all. Their fleeting progress up the track was marked with a crescendo of cheers. Up the field nearer and nearer, until we felt the vibrations beneath us grow stronger and stronger and stronger.

Just as we were planning to turn our heads to the finishing post, a slight deviation in the expected rhythm alarmed us enough to make an instinctive lunge backwards. There was a static confused moment before the onlookers realised that something was wrong.

When I remember what happened, it is as if my memory will only play it back in slow motion. Every minute detail is vividly recalled.

One horse was veering to the left. To the left, where small children and tots stood in front of taller children, who in their turn stood in front of their mothers and fathers and aunts and uncles, and the rest of the clan. The crowd that had been arranged for the best viewing took a hopeless tangled step back.

The horse was careering to the left, while the jockey was desperately trying to the control the listing beast. The boy, his veins growing as thick and as gnarled and as proud as those on the neck of an old, old man, pulled and pulled on the wild beast's mane. He pulled until, letting out a desperate cry, we saw that all his strength, from his back, from his legs, from his arms, was spent. It was as if it had run out through has fingertips like quicksilver. It was gone. The child rider screamed as the brute drew back its lips and let out a terrible whinny.

Then it plunged headlong into the family assembly.

Through the tightly-packed spectators strode the tall, imposing figure of the man who had the power over horses, whose greatest love was equestrian.

Don Basilio could be seen purposefully stepping over the small children with the ringside view, and arriving at the front at the precise moment the horse left the track and ploughed towards the crowd.

Don Basilio took a final, confident stride out onto the track. He spread out his arms as if inviting an embrace.

It was all too late. There was a mad gleam in the eyes of the terrified horse, as Don Basilio's bulk stopped the full force of its momentum. His body alone, took the full impact.

A single mighty thud rang out. A single thud that in the following silence seemed to echo all round the mountains and back again.

The jockey was propelled from his mount and flew through the air in a perfect arc.

The riderless horse ran off without direction or intent, pursued by an enraged posse of yelling men.

Everyone backed away. And a low gasp, like the whispering sound of the breeze in the trees, rose and quickly subsided.

Now the crumpled body of Don Basilio could be seen lying motionless on the grass. Blood was already seeping through onto his white shirt. It perfectly matched his red *faja*.

For a breathtaking moment everything was still, as if petrified. The only sound was the sobbing of the boy jockey, as he lay where he had been ignominiously thrown, face down on the ploughed earth, next to the spot where Don Basilio's new hat had rolled and fallen to rest.

Then the pandemonium began. The doctor arrived, still clutching the board declaring his odds on the next race. The tournament was temporarily suspended while the broken form of Don Basilio was gently loaded onto the doctor's jeep, and gingerly driven over the lumpy ground to his clinic in the centre of the town.

While the man who knew about horses still drew breath, the race could go on.

'Back within the hour,' the doctor promised the race officials, who had arrived at the scene and wanted to know what to do.

We joined the many that had packed up and began to make for home.

The black stallion was still tethered to the tree where Don Basilio had so recently tied him. He was whinnying quietly as we passed on our way out through the gate.

We joined a subdued crowd heading home.

*

That night as we lay in bed, we could here the thumping bass rhythm of the salsa band playing in the *zócalo*. We hadn't the heart to go to the Emiliano Zapata Day Municipal Dance.

It wasn't until quite late the next afternoon that we walked to the town to learn the news. It was by chance that we met the doctor. He was on his way to the wake of Don Basilio, so we walked along with him.

The doctor seemed rather reticent about the accident, rather implying that the old man had been a bit of a fool and nearly scuppered the finals. It turned out that the Village in the Valley had not won this year.

Keeping quiet, we went along with what turned out to be a vociferously held popular belief, Don Basilio was A HERO.

Even before his dramatic death, our hero had been held in the highest esteem. By the time we turned through the gate behind the grocer's shop (popping in to buy our quota of candles), the courtyard was full of dark-besuited town dignitaries, sitting under a flowering canopy of creepers and vines.

Every one was describing, from his point of view, the horrific accident. Each gesticulating in ways that gave good reason to encourage the development of ham acting. Overdramatic it may have looked, but then overdramatic it had been. Every impassioned wave of the arm, every theatrical thumping of the heart, had been genuine. Richard was immediately offered a drink of *colonche* (a concoction brewed from prickly pears and cinnamon), as he was drawn into conversation by a group of men.

In the kitchen, several women were already cooking on the braziers in one corner of the courtyard. Two or three charcoal grills were already radiating intense heat, and huge pots were being heaved onto or off the flames to be cooked, tasted or stirred.

The black stallion stood patiently tethered to a jacaranda tree, feeding from a nosebag.

From an opening onto the courtyard came the drone of women chanting the rosary. They kneeled round the edge of the small space in the centre of which, among banks of chrysanthemums, was the coffin, raised on a pair of trestles.

Lit by a hundred candles and deep in the flowers was the body of Don Basilio.

I was ushered into the room with the women.

Peering over the dense mass of petals, I could see by the flickering candlelight, the body of our friend, snugly tucked into the padded white satin lining. He had been dressed in his meticulously pressed baggy church suit and a freshly starched shirt. His shiny shoes pressed against the bottom end. It was a tight fit. But Don Basilio looked comfortably at ease in the confines of the small space. Only his fob watch was missing from his waistcoat pocket. His big hands, hands that were not those of a *campesino*, rested across his wide chest.

He looked the same kind and generous man we had all known. His face in repose, without its natural animation, revealed the serious man he had been.

On the outside of the tin coffin, following the latest trends, had been glued long-staple fun-fur. It was stuck neatly onto the metal box in wide stripes of red, green and white, the colours of the revolution. The colours of La Patria. You could have stroked it.

On the wall above his head hung the regulation image of *Nuestra Señora del Sagrado Corazón* – Our Lady of the Sacred Heart. In the printed image, she smiles down on the infant Christ on her lap, stretching out for the heart that is for eternity held high by his mother, tantalisingly just out of his reach.

At the foot of one of the last witnesses of the revolution, a brown, faded photograph had been thoughtfully, if hastily, pinned. It was a portrait of our hero's hero, Emiliano Zapata. Underneath the portrait were printed the immortal words, 'It is better to die on your feet than live on your knees.'

More buckets of flowers were standing round the walls, and the floor was covered in rush *patates* to slightly protect the worn knees of the women preparing to keen their laments throughout the night.

I knelt with them, trying to follow their chanting with my imitative mumbling.

The perfume of incense, the scent of chrysthamums, and the smell of burning candles, all mixed together and with the combined smoke, filled the air until it became dense with the ritual of death. My eyes watered and my chest tightened as I mumbled along with the droning words of God and the moaning of grief.

The multitude of candles was no competition for the sun, as it dropped low in the sky and poured its rays through the wide open doors and onto the tableau of Don Basilio's wake. But as darkness closed in, the intensity of their brilliance filled the room and overflowed warmly right across the yard.

Still new to genuflection, my knees quickly rebelled. My back ached and the blood, unable to flow round the bends in my legs, soon reminded me of this. The numbness, unattended, turned into excruciatingly painful pins and needles.

As my copy-cat rosaries became more confused, I noticed that my neighbour in prayer (having arrived more recently than I) was completing her fourth round of beads and was preparing to go. I levered myself upright and, taking a last reverent look at the body of Don Basilio, hobbled out of the parlour of mourning women.

I felt very sad. But I also felt very sad that I had never before had such an opportunity to say goodbye to a dead friend.

Out in the yard, away from the oppressive fug of burning copal resin, the air was fresh. The wake was beginning to become a celebration for Don Basilio, who was already being fitted for the mantel of legendary hero.

Food was being served, the food of true horsemen, a feast of beef, pork, cow udder, chillies and bitter oranges: Zacatecas stew.

A violinist had arrived. We listened to his cheerful andante fiddle playing, as we sat talking, eating and drinking well into the night.

It had been difficult to trace Don Basilio's relatives, but finally a niece had been located and arrived with her sack of candles at midnight. She looked rather bewildered to have been brought to the wake of an uncle I do not believe she had ever met. But she was well embraced and gently took possession of the fat gold watch and chain, before joining the company of friendly strangers, who looked as if they had settled in for the night. There was no shortage of mourners to keep watch over the hero until his burial the next morning.

As we left the funeral festivities, the doctor once again hurried up to walk beside us. Last night at the dance, a young hot-blooded man had been challenged to the point that he had shot his best friend dead, so the physician was on his way to yet another wake.

As our paths diverged, he hesitated, so that we stopped in our tracks. Gently taking our arms, he explained, in halting English, that assassination is of no interest to the police. Murder was a family matter.

He thought the protagonist of last night's debacle would be well on the way to the United States by now, even if he had to swim the Rio Grande. The grieving family would be left to take their own revenge, with the prospect of generations of escalating vendettas.

The doctor then became his old self and complained that he saw his involvement in this lunacy in terms of how many trips he had to make, driving his jeep over the mountain, taking dying patients to the nearest hospital. Quite often the journey is pointless. It kills them.

'Every fiesta nowadays seems to end with an assassination,' he grumbled.

He then scurried into the ink black woods. We heard him stumbling over the rocks in the road swearing to himself. The 'killer of the well' disappeared into the darkness.

It was a strangely eerie night and we were very pleased to be home. Trying to dismiss the idea that the doctor's words had been a veiled warning, we put our anxiety down to the late hour, as well as the tragic and shocking events of the last couple of days.

The next morning was unseasonably wet. It was a bedraggled assembly that we joined outside the grocer's shop. Every layer of clothes was quickly absorbing the unpleasant drizzle. This added suitable external misery to the bleary-eyed gathering. The black stallion, held by its halter, led the funeral procession. The fun-fur covered coffin, its matching lid clipped firmly down, was quickly sodden. It looked dead, as if it had been drowned.

The red, green and white box was being carried on the bowed shoulders of the first of many relays of six young men. The Adonises of the races now came to wait their turn to carry the coffin of the man who knew about horses. And in this way to pay their last respects.

Everyone was silent, their hats pulled hard down, shuffling slowly behind. We followed the cortege to the edge of the town.

The only dry body was that of our dead friend.

We stood and watched the phalanx of men, accompanied by the customary chanting and often doused candles. A single drummer kept the pace. All but his legs were hidden from view by a waterproof sheet of Sunset Boulevard, as he beat out the snail slow dirge of respect and grief.

It was a moving sight as the rain-soaked procession slowly wound its way up the hillside to the cemetery.

THIRTEEN

NAVIDAD CHRISTMAS
SEVERAL NATIVITY SCENES

There was hardly time to draw breath between the last feast of Guadalupe and the first of the *posadas* that lead up to Christmas.

Only four days in which to turn my mind back and resume the work in hand. I found it difficult to even remember what chapters of the book had been illustrated. My mind remained congested with the real-life pictures that had spread themselves like a layer of compost, burying the images I had carefully culled from the stories.

Dolores sat calmly embroidering a new tortilla cloth with a picture of a large turkey.

She watched me as I read and drew, rubbed out lines, scrumpled up grimy paper and threw it in the direction of the fireplace before starting again. After I had gone through this pointless cycle several times, my friend sensibly suggested that I brought out my sewing instead.

We were to get ready for Christmas.

If the nature of these preparations were a mystery, a visit to the market the next day offered a partial explanation. Everything essential for the Christmas festival was spread out on stalls or piled in the road. There was a lot of jostling as people made their choices. Fresh and damp from the southern mountains were great bundles of flowering bromeliads, sacks and sacks of luxuriant moss, bundles of ferns and massive swathes of the grey-green *Tillandsia usneoides*, the epiphyte belonging to the Pineapple family that we know as Spanish moss. As it was unpacked, a familiar delicious smell, quite foreign here, rose from the vegetation. It was the sweet aroma of wet rotting woods. Out of nostalgia for England, I would have liked to plunge my face in the soft damp greenery.

Wooden models of stables large and small, elaborate or simple, were precariously balanced in huge stacks. Wild orchids segregated into genus were laid out on the many stalls along with the boxes of baubles and tinsel.

Glitter glued shooting stars (flying right or left, a massive comet, or minuscule spark from the Milky Way) were classified and stacked under batches of paired angels' wings whose white feathers curled slightly each time they caught the breeze. Bunches of golden halos in all hat sizes hung sparkling in the sunshine.

But most prolific of all the Christmas goods, were the multitudes of painted clay figures that lay in neat groups of size and kind.

Here was the wherewithall to make the *belen*, the Christmas crib. Most people were casting a supremely critical eye over the goods, for they were merely adding to their collection. In full view of these educated critics, we had to start ours from scratch.

We bought tiny figures, and the smallest stable. After we had chosen our minute infant and crib, we selected a Mary, a Joseph, and an Angel Gabriel. Then we picked out Three Kings, some chickens, and a bird on a nopal cactus, various farmyard animals and a pair of flamingos. Not everything was to scale. To these, we added some colourful botanical matter.

All this became the centrepiece for the bookcase. Just in time, Dolores pointed out that the manger and baby make their appearance at midnight on Christmas Eve. So these were put aside until then.

The *Posadas* take place each night of the nine days before Christmas. Now we were being told that nine symbolised the months of pregnancy, rather than the nine levels of pre-Christian eternity.

On each of these evenings, when Joseph and Mary knocked on the door of the *posada*, the inn, they would be rebuffed. Twice they would be turned away. Only on the third attempt was the stable offered to them.

On each of the nine evenings the story was re-enacted.

Most yards were again transformed. This time each was a Nativity Scene. Boxes of the most beautiful figurines, collected over the years were brought out and carefully unwrapped before being placed on the new deep pile moss carpet that had been laid on the earth. Lichen and epiphytes, bromeliads and orchids were balanced, tied or draped in the overhanging trees amongst the tinsel.

Dolores' Christmas scene filled her yard and faced out towards the road. We leaned over the wall to admire her display, as she attended to the dozens of candles she lit every day at dusk.

I had begun to think of Dolores' onerous day and night candle duties as not far removed from the circus clown who can keep a whole canteen's worth of plates spinning on the tops of sticks throughout the entire show.

Felice's yard had been turned into a similarly breathtaking tableau, as had many others in the barrio.

*

The first *posada* was on the 16th of December. This was to be at the house of Felice's cousin near the fountain. When we enquired, it was suggested eight o'clock would be a good time to arrive.

As the sun began to sink behind the mountains we sat on our wall with a basket full of pomegranates. This would be our contribution to hospitality we would never be able to return. With the dusk, the bats began to speed in zigzags through the air and the sound of cicadas took over the quietness.

Then we turned into the yard of Felice's cousin.

Knocking loudly on the door, we were refused entry twice. As expected, on the third more urgent attempt the entrance was opened wide, and everyone was warmly welcomed into the mysterious interior.

The house consisted of one large high room. This had been entirely filled with a nearly full-scale nativity scene.

The Angel Gabriel stood behind the holy family, while the shepherds clustered round the sides with their animals. The Three Kings genuflected near a space where the infant Christ would be. Their beasts, a camel, an elephant and an Arab stallion had been slightly scaled down, but each papier-mâché model was resplendent in their vividly painted and elaborate decorations.

Behind them, on a mossy hillside, were models of farms and mills. In this agricultural landscape, small shepherds were tending correspondingly diminutive sheep and goats. Pinned to the back wall was a simple painting of the mountains, against a night sky full of silver stars and the curly tailed comet. A small stream had been picked up from the fountain outside and diverted by way of bent corrugated iron sheeting into the house. This entered the room through a small window high in the wall, at the top of the hillside scene, and ran through the whole stage set as a bubbling brook. It flowed through the mills and irrigated the fields and orchards, continued over aqueducts and under bridges until it splashed into a huge earthenware cooking pot, in which floated purple water hyacinths. It then gently lapped over the brim into a gutter which took it through a neat hole in the adobe wall and out into the lane.

Each of us was handed a bowl of steaming food.

Later, full of the delicious stewed turkey and clutching our mugs of *atole*, we followed the rest of the party into the yard for the ritual breaking of the *piñata*. Dozens of *duendes* jumped about, hardly able to contain their excitement.

It is said that the *piñata* originated in China. Marco Polo brought it back with him to Italy in the thirteenth century, where the Bourbon Kings of Naples and Sicily adopted it. Filled with jewels and precious stones, it quickly it became a traditional part of their fiestas.

Soon it appeared in Spain. It was neatly converted it into a serious Christian symbol, and from there taken to the New World.

In Mexico it was originally part of the celebrations for the first Sunday in Lent, but by 1587 it had become an established part of the *navidad posadas*.

The body of a *piñata* is a round-bellied vessel, rather like a large bean-pot. This is filled with small treats. Decorated with brightly coloured paper and metallic card, it represents the devil hiding behind an attractive mask. The most traditional *piñatas* are stars with seven points from which paper streamers hang. Each of these cones represents one of the seven deadly sins.

Our *piñata* had been slung over the yard between a couple of trees. Ropes had been tied to the two holes in the neck of the pot. The other ends were held by two men who were already perched in crotches of the trees ready to tease and provoke the young protagonists each of whom hoped to be the one to break the *piñata*.

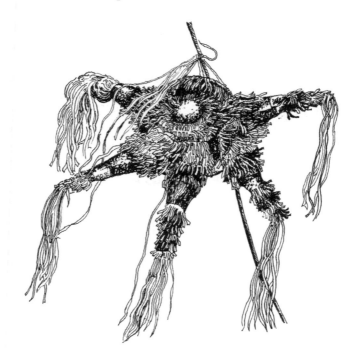

Each child waited in turn to be blindfolded, spun round, and the stout stick put in its hand. Blind faith will surely destroy the evil spirits.

Disorientated, they flayed the air as the *piñata,* now as the Star of Bethlehem, flew backwards and forwards above their heads.

Finally, when every child had taken their turn, and the whole company weak with laughter, the ropes were lowered enough to allow the last aggressor to smash the brittle clay to smithereens.

Enough goodies poured onto the ground to satisfy all in the ensuing scrum. As the crock is broken, sweets, fruit and nuts fall as if from heaven onto the ground below. The demon is destroyed with another vivid show of the triumph of good over evil.

*

We awoke the next morning slightly sad. It was a mild empty feeling that I recognised from my distant past schooldays as being homesick. It seemed so ridiculous; I did not mention it.

The evening before had been unexpectedly poignant. The extraordinary images that we had seen were still bouncing around our heads. I had been bewitched by the nativity scene and spellbound by the *piñata* game. Richard was unusually subdued.

We were still sitting on the veranda lingering over breakfast, when Dolores made her morning visit. She was quick to remark on our gloom and told us that we were missing our children.

As we told her yet again that they were grown up and had their own lives to lead, we realised that she was right.

'Yes,' said Dolores as she saw the penny just starting to drop, and revolved her eyeballs heavenwards. Her lessons in how to be human were starting to take effect.

Christmas is a treacherous time of year for repressed emotions.

*

For more than six months Las Brujas had been our home and apart from the first couple of weeks, when we were wandering about on buses for somewhere to live, we'd seen little of *La República*. Remembering the invitation from the writer in Oaxaca, we decide to go south.

In the teeth of the bewildering fact that not a single member of our families was planning to visit us, Dolores thought that this was a good idea. But we were to be back by *el día de los Santos Reyes*, the Day of the Three Kings, on Twelfth Night. She would be making the cake.

We paid our rent without mentioning our planned trip.

A couple of days later we packed a bag, tucked the writer's card in our wallet, locked the door of our home, gave Dolores the key and walked through the orchards to catch the first of several buses that would take us south to Oaxaca.

The route took us up above the snow line and down to the fertile plains, through treeless orange desserts, before winding about the sixty kilometres of cactus forests. We marvelled at the landscape through almost transparent windows, from the breathtaking sunrise to the glamorous sunset.

At nights we stayed in hostels near the bus stop.

Just when you thought your bladder would burst, or that thirst or hunger were making themselves obvious, the bus would shudder to a halt. Here, all immediate bodily needs would be satisfied. Off would go some of the passengers, making room for the food and drink vendors to insinuate themselves among those waiting to be served.

Tacos and *quesadillas*, chillied mangoes and bags of fruit salad, sweet and savoury *tamale*s were tantalising paraded up and down the bus, just above nose level of the seated passengers.

But coming from the land of marmite and peanut butter sandwiches accompanied by an apple, it was the pyramids of jellies and blancmanges in little transparent cups that took my imagination and memory back to children's parties. Swooshing through the space above our heads on tin trays, they looked much more appetising than they were.

The same food was available for those who had stepped off the bus. Here, it was possible to add to your comforts by lighting a cigarette, or heading for the privy queue. I would recommend that someone stay with your luggage.

Oaxaca was kind to us and without difficulty we rented a room in a dilapidated old colonial house, opposite the Alameda. We tip-toed by the muttering witch in her wicker rocking chair, through a clump of sickly monstera plants, up the cracked marble staircase, where we arrived on the balcony from which led our room. Here, we caught sight of ourselves in the dark glass of a great gilt-framed mirror.

We were surprised by a sight we had not even glimpsed for a good six months, our own reflections. I had chosen to remember myself as looking younger. Richard just laughed, and we turned into the room. It was fortunate to have been re-introduced to ourselves in an old flaking reflection, not a cruel modern one.

We continued to enjoy the restful feeling of anonymity we had cultivated on the bus ride.

Still quaking from the movement of the journey we found ourselves in the beautiful *zócalo* of Oaxaca. We stood under the huge Indian fig trees whose branches supported the thousands of white bulbs that lit the festive scene. The grand central bandstand raised its jelly mould roof on the thinnest of cast iron pillars.

We sat that first evening basking in the electric light, eating tacos and ice creams, and enjoying the armchair height of the municipal benches.

A brass band with no fewer than eight sousaphones rendered the whole of *Aida* in a single passionate hour.

Oaxaca is a most cultured and elegant city. Many of its mint-green buildings, their elaborate facades carved from *cantera verde*, the local stone, date from the sixteenth century. Walking along the wide pavements, there was the chance of an occasional illicit glimpse of the courtyard interiors.

As we strolled around enjoying the city and savouring the conveniences available in a municipality that expected and catered for strangers, we drank coffee or glasses of fruit juice, and wrote postcards we had bought from a revolving stand. We found the state map shop and the university bookshop, and we wandered in and out of art galleries curated by discreet girls or young men, who were not in the least bit concerned by your ethnic or religious roots. We were able to browse in craft co-operatives and sort through beautiful indigenous clothing.

It was being unrecognised, being strangers among strangers, that gave us a feeling of freedom and thrilled us most.

The next evening we telephoned the writer. He was called Luis, and his wife, Cristina. They invited us to visit them the next evening and suggested that we might like to accompany them to a party their friends were giving. We calculated it to be the sixth *posada*.

The friends of our acquaintances lived in a magnificent old colonial palace within the historic centre of the city. We entered the building through huge portals that opened onto a plant filled courtyard paved with white marble. It was dramatically lit by gentle floodlights, the sources of which were invisible to the casual glance. Not one, but several large *piñatas* hung between the potted trees. There were of a secular nature being in the shapes of animals and birds rather that stars.

Inside the palace the marble continued up a pair of staircases that curved symmetrically up to a wide balcony. Vast scenes from heaven, or possibly merely views of Europe covered the walls and ceiling and were framed in gilt stucco in an exuberant rococo style.

Musicians dressed in tuxedos, their hair slicked down with pomade, played a medley of inoffensive classical music from a rostrum framed by a hedge of trembling potted palms. Three giant Venetian glass chandeliers hung from the high ceilings, while at the far end of the hall a long and mighty table supported an almost pictorial display of food.

The fruit and puddings looked as they had been the still life on which Mrs Beaton had set her original engravers to work to illustrate the whole chapter on table decoration and desserts.

Shoals of decorated fish leaped across a foreground behind which was arranged a landscape of vegetables and salads. The meats and pies struck me as more architectural and stood amongst the dishes of sauces and pickles.

The wine waiters, immaculately dressed in their white jackets and bowties skilfully wove through the guests, trays balanced on one hand raised above the heads refilling every glass the moment it became almost empty. The 'Cubas' flowed.

Many of the women were dressed in handmade Indian costumes. Some wore *huipils* embroidered with feathers, or minutely woven in brilliant coloured thread. Others were displaying the traditional clothes of the women from the Juchitan, a skirt and blouse entirely covered with stitched flowers. These clothes would have been collected from all over the country to be bought and worn as party dresses by women of mainly Spanish descent.

This fashion had been originally instigated by Frida Kahlo.

We were almost overwhelmed by the magnificence of this spectacular wealth, so it was with high expectations that we began our search among all the antiquities, for the Nativity Scene. When we finally tracked it down, it was resting on the outstretched palm of our hostess' hand. The tiny figures were stuck onto a piece of green card and had been stamped from plastic.

I didn't know which way my emotions would take me, but to laugh or to cry was totally out of the question. My English nature rose to the occasion: I smiled.

Coming from Las Brujas, I had expected a great *son et lumière* spectacle with mechanical angels flying through the palace.

Only a few people joined in the *posada*. Our party comprised mainly children who had been coerced by their parents. The rest were parents whose were anxious in case we were mugged on the way round the block.

So it was a nervous little party that stood outside the closed entrance doors, rattling off the words and going hurriedly through the motions until at the third plea, the doors were opened ajar. Quickly, we all slid in to be plied with more Cubas, the apéritif to the pending feast.

The waiters momentarily clustered round the buffet before they spun away to circulate themselves as if without effort with laden plates to feed the throng of guests. We ate and drank, talked, laughed and danced until the early hours, when some people sent for their chauffeurs and made ready to depart.

Thanking our host and hostess for the most splendid evening, they replied without irony and thanked us. They explained that because we had danced so had the others. Luis said that people usually sit around and talk, but this had been fantastic.

As we parted company, he and Cristine invited us to eat with them on Christmas Eve.

Our lodgings were just round the corner. We stole past the sleeping witch and shoes in hand, padded up the stairs.

Christmas crib not withstanding, it had been a wonderful party.

*

By the time we had taken a turn round the market, ducked under a thousand *piñatas*, disentangled the strings of artificial flowers that had become caught up in our hair, floundered through the sea of toys and decorations, we came up for air in a space. It was a small space with its walls lined with bottles of mezcal, each of which had been decorated on its side with a blue Agave and its name hand-painted in flowing lines. We bought a litre bottle and a string of dried gusano worms, the grubs that are traditionally used to flavour mezcal.

Following our noses, we wandered on towards a smell of roasting cocoa beans. Finding the source, we sat at a nearby fruit drinks bar and breathed in the delicious almost addictive aroma of chocolate.

Finding a juice bar, we climbed onto a high stool beneath the horseshoe shaped bar. Its marble counter was at eye level. This was covered with not only the glass jars of fruit, but vases of green herbs, dishes of eggs (both hens and quails), jars of grain, but a plethora of unrecognisable ingredients.

It would be possible to pound all the ingredients in a *molcajete* with a *tejolote*, but the electric blender is the tool of the trade for every fresh fruit drinks stall. An electric orange squeezer is the other essential piece of equipment.

We ordered our drinks, which were made, before our eyes.

A drink made from beetroot juice is said to help alleviate tinnitus and toothache, headaches and helps the blood clot. Mixed with orange juice makes it even more delicious.

On the other hand, *nopales* – prickly pear cactus – pulped together with fresh parsley is as unpalatable as the muddy bottom of a slow flowing river sucked up through a straw.

On the way out of the frenetically busy market we bought a bag of medium sized grasshoppers that are very popular in these parts.

Returning to the tranquillity of our room where we poured ourselves a mezcal to ease the path of, the grasshoppers, *los chapulines*, down our throats.

Grasshoppers are caught either in the early morning or in the evening. (Not in the heat of the day when they are able to move much faster.)

The insects are caught in the rainy season, during the months of May to October, when the vegetation is damp. Our elderly neighbour, Maria, remembered as a young girl being kept fully occupied darting round the tiny fields, *las milpas,* capturing the leaping *chapulines.* These were rare

uncharoned moments during the courtship with her late husband. She repeated the onomatopoeic phrase *es brincan* ('he springs') as she smiled with fond memories of catching the chirruping insects leaping through the air, defensively displaying their brightly coloured under-wings. 'We put them in the front pocket of my best embroidered apron,' she chuckled.

Ideally two people are needed for this operation, one to sweep the top of the plants with their arm, while the other scoops the sleepy grasshoppers up into an apron or skirt, or drops them into a narrow-necked bottle.

Once captured, the insects are starved for twenty-four hours and left to defecate. This prevents them from tasting bitter. They are then blanched in boiling water before being fried in lard until they are slightly crisp.

They are served with a sprinkling of chillied salt and a squeeze of lime juice.

I admit that they could be labelled 'an acquired taste' by many, but for me they are a delicacy and excellent accompaniment to a glass of mezcal.

It was well into the afternoon by the time we returned to the *zócalo*. Dozens of trestle tables had been erected under the trees. These extended in long lines around three sides of the square. While ostentatiously armed but jovial policemen kept crowds of curious bystanders at bay, the sculpture exhibition was being installed.

By dusk and illuminated by white floodlights, in the wake of judges, *el Presidente* and a bunch of local civic dignitaries, and under the superfluous control of the paramilitia, a deep queue of the general public was allowed to file slowly by the panoramic display of entries for *la noche de los rábanos*. Every year especially cultivated radishes are cut, peeled, nicked, flounced and manipulated into red, pink and white sculptures.

There were dancers, their skirts billowing in the air next to prehispanic figures leaping under huge feather headdresses. Baskets of fruit and birds in flight were on show under swathes of flowers. Fierce looking Aztec Gods contrasted with a range of sycophantic saints. A walled cemetery illustrated the festive atmosphere on the Day of the Dead. Some scenes had been inspired by pre-Columbian myth, others by Bible stories. A miniature bandstand with a *banda* in full swing had won a prize, as had a touching Christmas crib, whose cast looked as if it were about to be mown down by a hatchet of a shooting star.

But my favourite came complete with two Marys, Roman soldiers, a nine runged ladder, three nails, and vinegar sponge on a pole, gaming dice and a crowing cockerel. Against a pink and white hill full of pink and white flowers, was a tender tableau of Our Lord crucified. All had been made from radishes.

*

With its peppery flavour and its attractive appearance, the radish is one of the most refreshing and decorative of salads. Eaten with a little salt before a meal it will clean the palate and stimulate the appetite. Even though the radish is 90% water, it contains as much potassium as bananas, is a good source of vitamin C and has trace elements of magnesium.

While the colours of radishes range from white and pinks to red, purples and black, the crisp interior, by contrast, is usually white. Its size also varies, from the small round specimens that are popular in salads, to the apocryphal 100 lb giants that in China may be pickled to eat, or grown for their seeds, which are crushed to extract the inedible oil suitable for bio fuel.

Radishes were grown in eastern China more than 2000 years ago, before the 'Silk Road' had become the important link to the West, so it is likely that this vegetable was independently farmed in both Eurasia and eastern Asia, and records show that radishes were grown in many Mediterranean countries as early as the fifth and sixth centuries BC.

In the fifth century BC, Herodotus claimed to have deciphered grocery accounts inscribed on the walls of an Egyptian tomb, proving that 4000 years ago radishes were cultivated as part of the diet of slaves. They were found in the tombs of the pharaohs, along with other food for sustaining the dead on their journey to the underworld.

In ancient Greece, the radish was so revered that gold replicas were offered to Apollo, the god of (among many other things) medicine

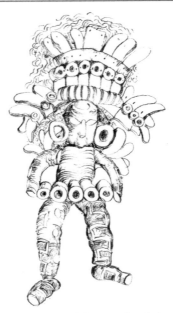

Dioscorides (40-90 AD), a Greek military physician, used the extracted oil medicinally, as it was thought to cure a wide range of unpleasant conditions.

In complete contrast to its status as a sacred symbol, there are comic accounts of its reputation as a punishment for adultery, when a specimen of the small spherical variety was inserted into the rectum of the guilty party.

Nearly fifty years before its reintroduction into England, the radish was already known in the Americas. Mendicant friars, at pains to show the Amerindians the benefits of the traditional European kitchen garden, had landed in the New World bringing with them not only the Bible and the onerous task of converting the aboriginal population to Christianity, but the quickly germinating seeds of the radish.

Early in the conquest, the brutal programme of conversion swung into its monstrous action. Once the friars had replaced the indigenous religions and their rituals with Christianity, Catholic ceremonies and customs could be established. The last meal of the fast of Advent is on the 23rd of December, when Spanish *bacalao*, salted dried cod, is traditionally eaten.

The season of Advent superimposed neatly onto the month-long Aztec fast, which also culminated near the winter solstice with the festival of *Atemoztli*, which in Nahuatl means 'falling water'. This ritual was to ask the god Tlaloc to send rain to prepare the earth for the rebirth of the agricultural cycle at the beginning of the year.

Tlaloc means 'he who makes things sprout', and is pictured as a man in a net of clouds and a cloak of dew, a crown of heron feathers, sandals made from spume while he holds up the serpent bolts of lightening and shakes the rattles that make thunder. He was believed to live on the tops of green mountains with his wife Chalchiuhtlicue, the goddess of seas and oceans, who was also associated with ceremonies performed during childbirth.

As a sign that Tlaloc was satisfied with the sacrifices and devotions made in his honour – models of the mountains where rain clouds form were made from a paste of corn and amaranth seeds – he would gather the clouds that give gentle rain, rather than invoking violent storms that would damage the crops. Water was the Aztec symbol for birth, so the syncretism was no giant leap of faith.

Right at the end of the sixteenth century, in *Henry IV,* part 2, Shakespeare's Falstaff describes the puny physique of Justice Shallow as 'for all the world like a fork'd radish, with a head fantastically carved upon it with a knife'. So perhaps the sculpting of radishes had already become a tradition by the mid-seventeenth century, when the monks began to encourage the indigenous farmers of Oaxaca to continue their tradition of making miniature scenes, not from corn and amaranth paste, but by transforming turnips, radishes and carrots into religious tableaux. The stalls in the markets began to sell these carved vegetable models to decorate the festive tables.

It was the red-skinned radish, with its glowing white interior flesh, that came to be grown, not only for its colour and sculptural qualities but, by selective cultivation, its colossal size. In 1897, the municipality of Oaxaca city took over this tradition and turned it into a competition. It is now on community land that the radishes are grown.

At eight o'clock on the chilly Saturday before Christmas, we arrived at the experimental farm. As the mist lifted, it revealed a large area divided by string into rectangles about ten by fifty feet. A handpainted billboard by the footpath explained that the expected crop of ten tons was reserved for the competitors of the 'night of the radishes'. The variety grown being a hybrid of the monster 'Bartender' and the fast-growing 'Champion', thereby crossing size and colour with expeditious growth to produce the prerequisite red monsters.

Each plot was numbered and labelled with the name of the competitor. Dozens of people muffled in jerseys and coats were digging up their allotted vegetables. Radishes of up to four feet were being gently lifted from the soft damp earth. Curling and bewhiskered, contorted and gnarled, these were the suggestive shaped roots piling up ready to be transformed into works of art for the great *noche de los rábanos* fiesta on the 23rd of December.

By the time the sun was breaking through, evaporating the mist and dew, the participants had discarded their woollies and were stacking the harvest into the backs of trucks, cars and carts, before clambering aboard for the journey home to begin turning their imaginative plans and ideas into reality. There were only three days before the grand judging.

Before nine o'clock on the morning of the 23rd, the stalls that had been erected

overnight around the perimeter of the city square had been numbered
and labelled with the name of the approved entrant. By ten, most had
found their designated table, and were unpacking the boxes of component
parts. Under the branches of the huge Indian fig trees, and against the
backdrop of the blancmange mould bandstand, began the great assembling
of extraordinary and individual creations.

We passed some tables where children were producing a wonderful
variety of monsters and reptilian beasts (to be adjudicated separately
from the adults). Slowly, we walked around listening to a quiet hubbub of
murmuring voices that hardly rose above the gentle splashing sounds of the
fountains. The usually dry air was already becoming humid with the task
of keeping the radishes damp and crisp. And when the sunshine caught
the sprays of water, fleeting rainbows were formed.

At four o'clock, the competitors were standing by their creations and
the judges moved in.

There were still the old favourites on display. A crucifix complete with a
mournful Christ was next to a miniature cemetery filled with lively people
dancing among the gravestones and sharing their fiesta with the dead.
Spread over two tables, an elaborate *belen* – the nativity scene – displaying
not only the holy family and accompanying angels, but mounted on a
camel, a horse and an elephant rode the three kings, while beneath them
were sheep; shepherds also headed towards the vegetable stable. All nestled
in damp moss under a suspended pink comet.

There was a replica bandstand housing a tiny orchestra. A model of the government building vied with an exquisite miniature, depicting the baroque church of Santo Domingo,

Three cyclists were pedalling their way up a mountain, a bucking stallion at a rodeo, a baby being born, a befeathered Aztec dancer, every harrowing detail of the Road to Calvary took up an entire table next to a huge leaping grasshopper. All had been carved and constructed from the red and white government root.

The creators now waited with growing tension for the judgement.

The first prize went to the most intricate assembly, depicting the numerous and varied handcrafts of Oaxaca state. There were weavers making carpets, a women plied a back strap loom tied round a tree trunk, some leather workers were up to their elbows in vats, while others hung out skin to dry. Potters threw and turned great bowls on a foot wheel.

Behind the miniature artisans, and accompanied by a band playing the full compliment of brass instruments, young people were dancing under the trees. Every figure was dressed in traditional costumes correct in every detail, down to their lace collars and embroidered skirts. It was breathtaking. A huge red rosette was now pinned to the table where the winners of not only a substantial monetary prize, but great kudos, stood unable to stop smiling.

As dusk fell, the lights were switched on and illuminated not only the exhibits, but the town *belen*, the bandstand and the trees that were adorned with strings of tiny bulbs that spiralled around every trunk and branch in the *zócalo*. The streetsellers were carrying baskets filled with *alegría*, the small cakes made from amaranth seeds and honey whose name means 'joy'.

At the end of the evening, when smell of compost began to float in the air, the sky filled with great spheres of sparks. Walls of pyrotechnical rain fell in sheets from the roof of the cathedral, as if harking back to the festival of *Atemoztli* and the promise from Tlaloc, the god of falling water to secure a good start to the agricultural year.

And to the rousing music of the town band the huge Catherine wheel on a tower began to rotate under its own rocket power, to spell out *Noches de los Rábanos* in flames of red. The odour of rotting vegetables had changed to one of spent cordite.

Never underestimate the qualities of the radish; it is a delicious gem of a vegetable.

*

The centre of Oaxaca was packed with crowds of people. Tourists outnumbered the café chairs on the *zócalo* and sat in each other's laps. Dozens of stalls had sprung up around the cathedral, while other traders spread their wares on the steps and pavements. Hawkers and beggars seemed even more insistent than usual.

The state marimba band played at break neck speed and drew a large audience, whose static bulk jammed the gardens as far out as the portales.

Sucked in by the slowly moving flow of people, we were taken in the direction of the cathedral. Here, the large raised terrace of the atrium had been kept clear.

A group of *locos*, mad cross-dressing giants, danced on their stilts, twice as tall as the crowds beneath. Their long print dresses swirling with the music, barely out of earshot of the frenetic marimba players of the town band.

Flocks of young boys and girls were dressed as angels, the volume of their wings and halos diluting the human density of the phalanx which continued to move with the momentum of a glacier towards the Holy Mass.

As we were pressed up the steps and into the fairy-light and candle lit interior, I turned to look back at the wide queue snaking round the trees of the Alameda and disappearing out of sight down Calle Independencia.

Many of those who patiently waited were cradling an infant Christ. They were arriving in a variety of cribs, mangers, tin trays of mossy knolls, or plain hand-held. Each was moulded in the regulation pose with their knees slightly draw up and the right hand signalling the blessing.

The family ahead of us had a magnificent clockwork model in a casket. Lifting the lid set off the mechanism and the Christ child rose slightly from his cot as he raised his right arm in benediction. The demonstration of this novelty was drawing quite a crowd.

In every size possible, the Jesuses were being brought to be blessed before they were placed among the waiting cast of the Christmas crib at home.

As the populace inched into the cathedral through one vast entrance, so those already purified were extruded, their blessed infants in their arms, from its twin doorway a little to the right.

It was growing late, so we escaped the long journey up to the altar and back again, by scrambling out before we were pushed too far in.

We passed a stall, enveloped in a cloud of spicy smelling smoke, selling traditional Christmas fritters. Syrupy and spicy, hot and greasy, we sat down and ordered a dish full of these delicious *buñuelos* coated in the regulation viscous sauce.

Still sticky, we climbed into a taxi that swiftly removed us from this maelstrom and drove up the hill to the quiet streets at the top of the town to where Luis and Cristina lived.

We were welcomed and introduced to the four other guests. It surprised me how quickly we felt at ease.

By contrast, I suddenly remembered Don Cándido. Only now, when he was so far away and with so little reason to be in my thoughts, did I realise that he was the slight but constant anxiety that had penetrated my psyche.

Richard and I began to enjoy an evening without feeling as if we were stepping on eggshells, it was possible to stand, move around, sit, accept a drink, an *antojito* and talk and laugh at the same time.

Tall windows opened onto a balcony, from where you could see the lights of the city below. From here, later on in the evening, we were able to watch the municipal pyrotechnics we'd seen being assembled.

There was a familiarity about the way Luis and Cristina lived. It was not only the shelves full of books or the paintings on the walls without religious connotation that made us feel at ease. Nor was it the flowers in vases in the centre of a table that was not a shrine. It was neither a marble palace lit by a rank of chandeliers, nor an adobe shrine with a *petate* rolled up in a corner.

A feeling of well-being pervaded me as I sank deeper into the womb of the first sofa I'd sat in since leaving England.

Everyone was curious as we described our lives in Las Brujas. We invited the assembled party to the exhibition planned for February. To our surprise they accepted with enthusiasm.

It was a warm evening and we insisted on walking back to our lodgings. It was downhill all the way.

The streets were wide and empty. We remembered Luis' words when we had first met at the Guadalupe feast:

'Look out for yourselves.'

While I still didn't understand his warning, I realised that it wasn't only the soft furnishings and our hosts' taste in art that had been so enjoyable that night, but a relaxing familiarity. But at the same time, I was thinking tenderly of our friends in Las Brujas.

As we turned the key in the door of our decaying lodging house, we strained our ears to listen for the silence that would indicate that all was well on the other side.

FOURTEEN

GUATEMALA

A SHORT SHARP VISIT

W e were travelling in the Mixteca, north of Oaxaca City, certain of the direction as indicated by our map, and confident that soon some form of public transport would pass by and take us along the road over the mountain, to the magnificent ex-convento at Teposcolula.

From the shade of a tree, we waved vigorously when a bus came into view. It slowed down just enough for us to see the driver solemnly wag his finger to indicate that we could not board. Immediately his signals were contradicted by a stout woman who leaned out of the door, and learning that we wanted to visit what we called 'the church' reached out to us, and with the power of her Herculean arms hoisted us into the moving vehicle. Children were directed to bunch up even closer to make room for us.

Looking around we quickly realized that this was a privately-hired charabanc, overflowing with one extended family. The combination of the brilliant floral prints of their stylish clothes together with the yawing of the bus, gave us the feeling that we had been caught up between the pages of a seed catalogue on a blustery day. There was the general exuberance of a party heading towards a fiesta. 'San Jeronimo, to bless our church,' and everybody nodded and smiled at the white strangers.

It was New Year's Day, the celebration of the Circumcision of Our Lord.

And that is how we came to be standing after the mass with a group of people, blessing the new bell-tower and the barbed-wire fence of the recently rebuilt church of San Jeronimo Gusanillo, instead of spending the day gazing at the sixteenth-century architecture of San Pedro y San Pablo at Teposcolula.

After the mass and the blessing, the slightly larger than life San Jeronimo was lifted down from his cabinet above the altar, sponged with a damp cloth, his Bible wedged securely in the crook of his arm, and then lifted onto the shoulders of the first relay of strong men, who carried their solid wooden saint at the head of the procession that would circumscribe the village.

We placed ourselves with the stragglers and, unable to join in, listened to the strange melodic chanting of the melancholic song. Candles melted in the sun faster than they could burn.

Stumbling in the heat, over and along the fissured track, I noticed that the perimeter hedge of prickly pear cactuses were velvety white. As I peered closer to make sure that this was not a trick of the blinding light, it became clear that the racquet-shaped cladodes – the flattened shoots – of the *Opuntia*, otherwise known as the prickly pear cactus, were covered with large blotches of white boucle fluff.

Having completed the circuit and witnessed the return of the saint, we waited for further instructions.

'*Vamanos,*' ordered the stout lady and we followed her back to the charabanc. '*La Comida,*' – lunch – she explained sternly, as more and more people crushed onto the only available transport, before it rolled under the arch of paper flowers and lurched down the mountain track to the place from where we had set out.

By invitation, along with the entire party, we followed the stout lady into her house, to be directed to a table in the shade of a tree where two teachers, their children, a doctor, his wife and their elderly uncle were already seated. Only the uncle still lived in the ranchito of San Jeronimo.

We slaked our thirsts from the large jug of cool ambrosial fruit drink placed in the middle of the table. In the smiling hiatus that followed the introductions, my curiosity overcame me.

'Why are your prickly pear cactus covered in white fluff?'

Astonished that we did not know and surprised that we were interested, he began to elaborate.

On the arid mountainside the uncle kept a small herd of goats and a couple of mules, and harvested cochineal, the scale insect that we had noticed infesting the cactus fortification.

He described not only with words (he soon saw that we found his dialect

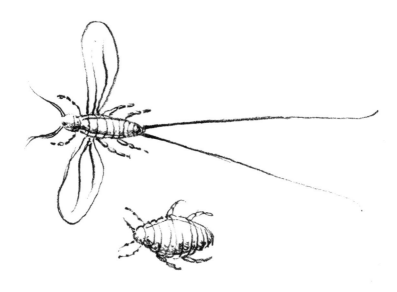

incomprehensible), but also – and much more clearly – by expressive mime. With his whole body he demonstrated how newly-hatched nymphs crawl out from underneath the mother and begin to colonize both sides of the cladodes, before plunging their proboscis into the flesh of the host *Opunitia* cactus. This was graphically demonstrated as a tube sucking up nourishment from the plump pads. After this, a flaying of arms mimed the extrusion and spinning of the waxy white fluff that not only baffles their predators, but prevents desiccation.

We watched, gripped, as the *campesino* simulated cutting and weaving leaves into roofs to deflect the rain in the wet season. Crouching, he showed us how he lit the fire and fanned the flames alive to warm the air, and protect his *nocheztli* – the cochineal bug – from the bitter cold nights of winter.

Only the males develop into a pupa and metamorphose into flying insects. This was made clear by our mimic emerging from a make-believe cocoon before bending his arms at the elbow to indicate wings in flight. The males have no alimentary system; their short but hectic life lasts about a week. They produce no carminic acid, the sole purpose of their existence being to fertilize the immobile females. This scene ended with the imago – the final stage of an insect's metamorphosis – subsiding in death, while his audience applauded with enthusiasm. Only when we were silent did he continue.

With three fingers raised and the word *meses* – month – being uttered, he signalled how the three-month-old females are gently brushed (traditionally

with the tail of a deer) from the cactus pads, while the eggs and nymphs are carefully collected to be placed back on the cladodes. With the nimblest of gestures he spread out the imaginary silvery creatures to dry in the sun.

Next, he knelt and piled the dried insects onto the stone *metate* and showed us how with the *metlapil*, the small stone rolling pin, how the women crush the dead insects until the blood red carmenic acid flows.

The uncle's entertainment came to an end just as the huge plates of delicious steaming food arrived.

Nocheztli is its Nauhatl name. *Nochli* refers to the Nopal, the prickly pear cactus and *eztli* means blood: 'The blood of the cactus.'

The next day, heading home, we changed buses in a small town, Nochixlán, its Nahautl name meaning 'place of cactus blood'. In

prehispanic times, this town had been an important trading post dealing with *nocheztli* from the surrounding area, then the centre for its abundant production.

It was from this area that the Aztec nobility demanded, among other tributes, extortionate quantities of *nocheztli*.

Cochineal appears to have been introduced into Mexico from Peru about 1200 years ago, and was cultivated by the Nahautl-speaking Toltecs, who ruled the area that is now Mexico State. In about 1200 AD, they were conquered by the Aztecs, who came to power and began to demand huge tributes. Oaxaca, with its ideal climate, became the great centre for cultivating the precious dye, much of which was sent to meet the demands of the Aztec emperors. One of the ways aristocratic women displayed their wealth was with the wide smile of teeth dyed blood red.

Not long after their arrival, the conquistadors noticed the wonderfully intense red clothes that people wore. Just think of a cardinal and you realize the symbolic importance of the colour red. Just as in prehispanic Mexico, the colour of blood also indicated power.

The red dyes available in Europe at the time were far less intense. Cochineal was precious to the Aztecs, and quickly became so to the Spanish as well. Along with gold and silver, it was the most valuable commodity to be exported from the Americas.

Tlapanochestli is one of the few farms left in Mexico that still cultivates cochineal. It is in the Zapotec region, south of Oaxaca. Here, in polytunnels and greenhouses, the cladodes of the *Opuntia*, sponged clean and with their spines removed, are planted in serried ranks, each plump pad standing upright in the sandy soil ready to host the *Dactylopious coccus*. About fifteen fertilised eggs are placed in a tiny 'crib' (a woven rush tube about a centimetre or two in diameter and about four long) which is then attached to the 'racquets' of the cactus. Aside from being protected more efficiently from the vagaries of the climate, they are then left to develop in a similar

way to those at San Jeronimo. The dye is also processed on the farm.

Cochineal is one of the most vibrant and precious natural dyes and is used the world over. Depending on the mordant – the dye fixative – employed, its colour ranges from purple, through bright red to orange.

Today, very little cochineal is produced in Mexico, with 80% of the dye now coming from its original source, Peru, where family-run farms cultivate the scale insect in conditions that are less blighted by parasites and disease than in Mexico.

Although its bitter taste repels many of the insects' predators, cochineal has many culinary uses. In Mexico, bright red dough still accentuates the details on the prehispanic shaped effigies of bread, which are baked specially to place on the shrines that are designed to tempt the deceased home for the celebration of Day of the Dead.

The dye was not only used to enliven the subdued natural colours of jellies, trifles and other children's party treats, but also of sausages, pies, shrimps, dried fish, jam, sweets and tinned cherries. Medicines, both tinctures and ointments, were made to look attractively pink by the addition of cochineal, while lipstick and rouge were also imbrued with 'cactus blood'.

But in the 1870s the invention of a synthetic aniline dye known impertinently as Cochineal Red A, made from coal tar, began to supersede cochineal, and by the early twentieth century had almost entirely replaced it.

*

Our visas were at their end. The immigration office in Mexico had refused to renew them again. We had talked about this with Sánchez, who had said that we would have to leave the country for a short time.

How long is short? It was thought that two hours would do the trick.

But the suggestion that we go to the United States did not interest us one bit. Quite in the wrong direction as we planned to go south.

That is why we found ourselves in the back of a Volkswagon combi van heading towards Guatemala. We had met the driver in the southern state of Chiapas. He was a young man escaping the rigours of a Canadian winter. Our initial impression that he had an excitable nature proved to be an underestimation of his character.

As we reached the border, he broke out into an alarming sweat. This was accompanied by a bout of involuntary shaking that came on as we entered the immigration office. But the customs officials stamped us into their country, and waved us away with a dismissive gesture. So far so good.

Our chauffeur sped round the corner into a petrol station and collapsed. He lay over the steering wheel like a rag doll. We filled the vehicle with fuel and negotiated an exchange of currency to pay for it, as had been the arrangement.

Turning round, we were relieved to see that the young man had recovered enough to be standing by the van, rummaging through his luggage.

Several slugs from the retrieved bottle of tequila and we were away. This time it was our turn to sweat.

In many of the villages we stopped, and children flocked round the van waiting for the Canadian to emerge from his travelling home. Seconds later, he would jump out through the fringed curtains that hung over the side doors to be revealed in his true colours as a conjuror.

Roses popped out of his ear and a pocket watch was pulled from an unsuspecting boy's mouth. A string of silk flags was swiftly drawn from the bonnet of a baby. Our driver swallowed a sword. He blew flames from his mouth and pulled a rabbit from his armpit while the children watched in stunned amazement. He blew up long thin balloons and bent them into the shape of dogs, lambs and bulls, helmets, shields and swords, all of which he threw into the audience as a dramatic parting gesture. Then, slamming the doors shut, leaping into the driver's seat, and waving out of the window, we roared off on the continuing journey.

In the wing mirrors we could see the sparring and laughing that was left behind at the roadside.

'I come this way every year,' said the Canadian, whetting his whistle.

We had arranged to travel to Lake Atitlan, where the conjuror planned to stay with friends. The countryside we drove through was spectacular. The neatly terraced mountainsides were being worked by *campesinos* wearing the brilliantly coloured costumes of their village, as they bent double over their mattocks or leant over almost horizontal to push their weight behind wooden ploughs.

Fuelled by Dutch courage, each magic show was more bewitching than the last.

As the emptiness of the bottle became more complete, my agitation became more acute. I followed the map; although it didn't make the road any shorter, it gave me something else to calculate other than how drunk our driver was becoming.

At last we reached the shores of the lake.

'One more minute,' cried the Canadian, 'one more minute.' And the van turned a corner and braked to a halt.

We had stopped just in front of a smouldering heap. Wisps of smoke from the remains of a house gently floated up into the charred branches of overhanging trees. Nearby was a burnt-out American jeep.

For a second it was very quiet, while we watched the Canadian draw in a mighty breath. The next second he leapt out of the driver's seat and in a crescendo of screams ran blindly into the adjacent woods.

We sat and waited. After a few minutes the yelling faded away. We gathered up our belongings and walked back into the village to find a place to stay.

So our holiday began.

*

The thirteen villages around the lake exist by farming and fishing. The lake had once been full of small fish and crabs that it was possible to catch in the shallower water from little canoes.

To encourage rich men to fish for sport, a larger predatory beast, the black bass, had been introduced to the lake. As it swims much deeper, it is much more difficult to catch. Meanwhile, it consumed most of the native water life.

We walked round the lake by the road, or by the water's edge. Sometimes we swam in the warm shallows. People weaving in the villages were friendly, and showed us their work. Each village wore a different pattern, different colours. By the end of the first day we were enchanted by what we were seeing.

Soon we noticed that some people were dressed in stripes that had been embroidered all over with little birds. Brief sideways glances at these

costumes enthralled us. We only dared to glimpse as the men and women wearing these clothes passed us in the lanes or in the market. With great excitement we kept a lookout for this material, which looked as rich as the ornithological section from an illuminated medieval bestiary.

The woman who owned our *posada* told us to take a boat across the *caldera,* the lake formed in the crater of an extinct volcano, to Santiago.

The small motor boat left from a small wooden jetty and the journey took an hour. The lake was glassy still, and as the early morning mist lifted the cones of the two volcanoes that rose behind Santiago were perfectly reflected in the water.

We were the only strangers on the boat and as we alighted on the shore, a dozen little children rushed up and hung onto any part of us that was not being held by another. Weighed down in this manner made the walk up the shingles very heavy work.

By the time we reached the gravel road we were exhausted. But the frantic behaviour of these children, their clamouring for nothing in particular but to touch part of us, some part of Richard in particular, began to strike us as odd.

Sitting down, we began to search for the pointless little things that we carried around to give to children in the hope they would think we were at least friendly. But these children wanted none of that. They stuck like limpets, and when we got to our feet hung like millstones round our necks.

Their language was a series of passionate noises. As we looked closer we saw that their eyes were entirely without expression. It was as if they were dead.

Under their weight, we began to drag our way up the hill towards the church. A woman came out of a cottage and shouted at them to leave us alone. Instantly they let go and scuttled away like rats.

We plodded on in the sunshine. The atrium outside the church was bare earth, on which no tree or bush grew. The doors of *il templo* were wide open.

Once inside, our noses drew in the smell of fresh pine needles, the carpet that our feet were bruising. But it took a moment before our eyes could distinguish anything of the interior. To the right of the altar, a hundred candles lit the most beautiful and touching nativity scene. The nearly life-sized wooden figures were dressed in the clothes of this village and five or six infants lay on the straw in front of the holy parents. Around was the usual accompaniment of shepherds and kings, animals, angels and shooting stars. Dangling by strings from the roof were hundreds of oranges glowing in the low light. And among these oranges hung a dozen feathered birds in flight.

As we stood there in amazement, a small boy emerged from behind a curtain and held out a collecting box. Richard dropped in some coins.

Without responding to our smiles, he turned towards the Christmas stable and pulling back little levers released the brakes of each clockwork mechanism.

The birds began to sedately flap their wings and sing as sweetly as the dawn chorus. The boy vanished.

At the end of this wonderful concert we turned towards the light streaming in through the doorway. As we did, three large, distinct crucifix shapes loomed out against the darkness of the walls. These had been made from scores of small white crosses, cut from paper and pinned straight onto the bare adobe blocks of the nave.

On the first cross, carefully written on the smaller crosses, were the names of the wounded. The next displayed those who had disappeared. On the last, those who had been murdered.

As our eyes opened wider, we could just make out some of the names and dates.

On the crispest, whitest most recent additions, we learnt that four weeks before, on the night of the 2nd of December, an unarmed group of

villagers had approached the occupying military base, demanding to know the whereabouts of a missing person.

The answer came in the form of a volley of automatic gunfire.

The result was fourteen villagers dead and twenty-eight wounded. Among these were young children. The hairs on the back of my neck stood on end. An icy chill flooded through my body. Taking each other's arm, we stumbled out into the heat of the treeless atrium.

Under the shade of the *portales* sat a group of women. They were selling clothes. We moved towards them mainly from a need to be near living people. There were piles of trousers and huipils – a traditional garment worn by indigenous women – all covered with minute embroidered birds. Some of these were over-sewn with vivid flowers. There were skirt lengths of *ikat* – a dyed woven fabric – with brilliantly coloured stripes full of glittering thread.

Yesterday, I would have been simply delighted with such an opportunity to peer so closely at all this exquisite work. Now, we just felt our thoughts to be revoltingly trivial. We bought something from each stall, and then sat in the sun hoping that our bodies would soon warm up.

The women were friendly and we began to talk. They were selling the clothes to earn money so that their children would have enough time to go to school. Education, they all fervently agreed, was the only way forward. Usually they went to the more touristic places to sell their clothes. Yes, tourism had trailed off recently, today it was very quiet.

The sun had risen quite high by the time the mothers began to pack up their wares.

We made our warmest farewell to these extraordinarily brave and stalwart women, and carrying our souvenirs we returned to the jetty and sat silently waiting for the boat.

The return journey was slightly choppy. As we approached the far side, we noticed our wash slapping against a black rubber dinghy tied up and half hidden in the rushes. In it, dressed resplendently in brand new army combat gear, lay a young boy. It was as if he had been lulled to sleep by the gentle waves. He clutched his submachine gun to his chest as if it were a soft toy.

Within the hour we were sitting, still silent, on the first of many buses that would slowly take us back home to Las Brujas, with new visas, we hoped.

FIFTEEN

EL DÍA DE LOS SANTOS REYES

A PLETHORA OF THREE KINGS

Mexico City is like a hub as far as the transport system is concerned. Rather than trying to travel round the circumference of the wheel, and avoid one of the most massive cities in the world, we took the option that the spokes offered.

With a day or two to spare before the rendezvous with Dolores, our bus from the south pulled into one of the vast bus stations. To go west meant crossing the greater part of the City. As it was quite late in the afternoon, we went to find a hotel near the *zócalo*, where we could enjoy its flat floor and modern plumbing.

That craving was soon satisfied and by dusk we had left our room, hoping to melt into the great evening *paseo* – the throng of people out for a stroll – and savour the anonymity we sometimes missed in Las Brujas.

Several amplified bands belted their music out across the *zócalo*, which was otherwise packed with Indians and Mestizos from other parts of the country, selling hand-made toys and clothes. The Christmas fair would finish with the arrival of the Magi bearing their gifts: the day of Epiphany, of the Three Kings, or Twelfth Night, as it's variously known. That is the traditional day all gifts are exchanged.

The traders continued to replenish their stock by painting and sewing more, as they sat by their goods, displayed on cloths spread out on the paving.

Here, you could buy the most awkward relative something quite lovely and quite useless. Something they would have never seen before, and which, after the initial gasp of pleasure, would be relegated to a drawer.

Nevertheless, an enthusiastic man, painting whole landscapes onto the tail sides of tiny obsolete coins, caught our attention. Three for the price of two made the offer irresistible.

Even though I had no idea who would appreciate a view a half an inch across depicting the Yucatán with flamingos in full flight, it was mesmerising.

We wandered off in the direction of the Alameda Central, the oldest park in Mexico, imagining a sedate walk among the trees before sitting on a bench to watch the fountain playing. Instead, our spirits were immediately lifted to new heights as we were met by a huge, loud and colourful jamboree.

Lining both flanks of the park, facing the road, dozens of small, travelling theatre booths had been erected. In each was displayed a wildly different interpretation of the Magi. All the tableaux were individual stages for the Three Kings, and in each was the regulation camel, elephant and stallion, life-size and made from papier mâché.

There were tropical scenes set in jungles, with parrots and biblical serpents slithering down lianas. Among the sand dunes of the desert in the Holy Land, the Star of Bethlehem shone over the distant village.

A frozen cavern in Greenland sported an additional cast member, by way of a Santa Claus, ducking with the others under the stalactites of icicles. I noticed that Mickey Mouses and Bambis were also successfully elbowing their way into the tradition.

Religion and pantomime appeared as the perfect match, all the way down both sides of the Alameda.

In each kiosk were three dashing young men, dressed magnificently as Caspar, Melchior and Balthasar. Their lively eyes looked out from shiny masks of thick grease paint. Each trio comprised a face in white, another in black, and a third left a more natural colour. Wigs of nylon curls in ethnically-appropriate colours cushioned great bulbous crowns.

Flashing the perfect white teeth of youth (or maybe skilful orthodontics), they all smiled and waved to the passing families, hoping to entice them into their theatre to be photographed with them, against their sparkling and individual backdrops.

Jewelled crowns and caskets were stuck all over with precious stones, tiaras and swords were similarly decorated, as were the plentiful props.

Each scene was brilliantly floodlit. Outside and below stood the photographer with the Polaroid camera. Either side of him was a technician. One to warm the photograph under his armpit and accelerate its development, the other to staple the family picture into a small frame and take the money.

People spent a long time on the serious matter of choosing a booth. Then they had to pick out the relevant queue from the tangle that was snaking back through the gardens. Patiently, everyone waited. When they finally returned to the particular setting that tickled their fancy, the families were hoisted up onto the stage by the strong arm of a king. Children were lifted onto a beast, before being lent an appropriate accessory. Then, literally in a flash, they were passed back down to wait for the results.

Walking back towards the hotel, we scrutinised our portrait. There we were, sat on our chosen animals among the grinning kings. With our faces set stern and nervous, our expressions resembled the participants of the wedding photographs I'd criticised in the photographer's window in the Town on the Hill.

We looked as miserable as sin. Never believe what you see in a photograph.

*

The next morning we set off to catch the last of the buses that would take us to the *colectivo* stop for the Village in the Valley. Anticipating delays and the subsequent waiting, Richard bought a newspaper.

On the front page was a photograph of about half a dozen Three Kings, looking studiedly glum as they sat round the table of a café.

'Three Kings Threaten to Strike,' said the headline.

The council had announced that they planned to double the rents for the pitches on the Alameda next year. I idly imagined that the argument this was unfair was being promoted by a collective called something like the 'Federated Union of Three Kings and Auxiliary Workers'. It was.

'For nigh on two thousand years,' their statement in the paper read, 'we have been distributing gifts to every child in this land, entirely free of charge. If you raise the rent, we fear that we will not be able to afford to continue this tradition, which we do now, only out of the goodness of our hearts.'

The Municipality had capitulated immediately.

Only then did I realise how difficult it was going to be when we did return to England.

Early that afternoon we arrived home. It was more beautiful than we had remembered. The orchards seemed greener and more pleasantly shaded than when we left. It was as if we had rediscovered a wonderful treasure, the value of which we had not altogether appreciated until that day.

Nothing had changed. The barrio was still alight with dozens of *belens* – nativity scenes.

Nothing had happened while we were away, Dolores informed us. But we noticed that our floors had been swept and the infant Christ in his clay crib was now a central part of our Nativity Scene.

Richard unlocked the doors of his workshop and in a moment the men's club reopened. Dolores and I could hear the guffaws of laughter from the veranda, where we continued our sewing as if there had been no interruption.

That night, the quiet calm of the barrio was once again shattered by a spate of gunfire. We lay in bed listening to the now familiar sound of bullets whistling over the roof.

We had not thought of this alarming and mysterious aspect of Las Brujas since we left for our holiday. Habituated, we thought no more about this disturbance than if it were an owl screeching, dogs fighting or the hullabaloo of a drunken husband being told to sleep off the effects under a tree.

We were pleased to be back in our own bed. The next morning we awoke and gave no more thought to the shooting practise. It was *el día de los Santos Reyes* – the Day of the Three Kings.

In the afternoon, the Green Architect and his wife, Joaquin and Ofelia, visited. They too were on their way to the Three Kings' cake party. We were really pleased to see them. It felt as if a certain reality was invading our lives.

Briefly, we discussed the date of our exhibition, for which I was to design the invitation. It was planned for a Saturday in February.

*

In all the months we had been living in the Village in the Valley, our only connection with the outside world – apart from physically taking ourselves there on public transport – was the postal box rented from the nearest *correo* or post office, which was over the mountains in the Town on the Hill.

In the Village in the Valley, the single telephone still lay dormant among the ribbons and threads of the haberdashery and fancy goods shop on the *zócalo*. It was waiting for a landline to reach this outpost.

But just before the Guadalupe celebrations, we noticed a table and chair set out on the pavement in one of the streets occupied every week by the market. At the table sat a man in a brand new uniform, a bunch of keys jangling from his belt, and radiating an enthusiasm you could feel all the way up the road. He smiled with pride from under a hard peaked hat, on which shone the polished coat of arms of *La Patria*. On the table was a pair of scales, several folders containing stamps, and a cash box. Not every

office offered this facility, thus enabling you to actually post a letter. It was to be an important establishment.

In the building behind, several men were working hell for leather to finish *el correo*'s offices. Already a big safe had been installed against the back wall, while a fan was being wired up in the ceiling.

A few days later, a bank of about two hundred *apartados postales* was sat on a table ready to be individually rented. Ours was number ten, and we were issued with a key to unlock the little steel door that would allow us to collect any letters. Each door was a miniature version of the one that secured the safe. Each was identically emblazoned with the heraldic nopal cactus, eagle and snake, to match the official hat.

And soon after this, the postmaster moved his desk ten feet back into his new office. He was as pleased as Punch, and for the moment less corruptible.

When we asked if we might leave our key with him in case we mislaid it, he shuddered at the thought, pointing out that we must be the only people able to unlock our box and remove the contents. There must be no possibility for confusion.

'Quite right,' we agreed, and kept silent about the open backs into which this same postmaster would place the sorted mail. We'd just have to be careful with the key.

We quickly became accustomed to a facility that, in the first few weeks of its existence, had seemed like a supreme luxury. When our post arrived, the postmaster would send a runner to alert us. Quite often, this would be some innocent bystander who had loitered too near the office. It was a wonderful service, and we no longer felt entirely isolated from Europe.

Soon after the postal facility was established, I'd wrapped a *rebozo* (a finely-woven shawl that women wore to carry everything from potatoes to infants), in some paper to send to my daughter. Could it possibly reach her before Christmas? Also included was one of the thousands of small paperbacks that retell both popular and classic stories in comic strips. The original writing is always rendered down, in order to use as few words as possible. These are usually in dialogue form, rising in a bubble from the conversationalist's mouth. To retain the reader's attention, the pictures are very spicy, and often border on the pornographic. Pert plump breasts abound, even to illustrate sexually tame tales such as Robert Louis Stevenson's *Treasure Island*. Picaresque works in this form were extremely popular. *Don Quixote* was skilfully adapted with profuse illustrations in several volumes. Delving between the covers of the more adult publications was quite an education.

Folding what I had chosen to be one of the more amusing novelettes up in the shawl, I had presented the parcel to the postmaster. Ponderously, he turned the package over several times with the professional eye of an expert, before pulling at the string to demonstrate its lack of tension. Shaking his head, he began to explain that while my parcel was in his keeping, it would receive the care it deserved. If it were possible, he would like to deliver it in person to my daughter.

'Your *only* daughter?'

'Yes.' I just stopped myself from saying, 'but we are not Protestants'.

'Also a son,' I added lamely.

'Well,' he said, 'I shall demonstrate the conditions under which this gift would without doubt travel, once it leaves this office.'

And with a determination, a vigour bordering on violence, our official began to fling the parcel about the room. Time and time again, it was hurled through the air only to come to an abrupt halt as it hit a wall.

With this abuse, the wrapping quickly disintegrated. Out fell the *rebozo*. Our postmaster looked at the shawl and agreed it was a fine example of weaving. How much I had paid for it?

At this moment, the booklet fell out and landed on the floor. There followed a moment's uncomfortable silence, while the official searched through his papers. Picking up a pamphlet, he ran his finger down a long list covering several pages until he came to 'P'.

'Pornographic Material' was an item on the list. And in case I hadn't understood, he opened the comic book and pointed to a sequence I hadn't noticed.

A lady with a symbolically curvaceous form was showing off a pair of knickers, clearly not designed to exclude draughts.

I don't think the postmaster had read the book either, for he became briefly quite absorbed in looking for pages to illustrate his argument that sending this through the post would be to contravene the obscenity laws. He assured me he had only my daughter's welfare in mind, and offered to relieve me of this heinous literature.

He was a kind man. It was as if the drawings were in a language I had not grasped. He pointed out that I could not have known. My deep embarrassment was slightly eased.

Now the official had taken over the moral welfare of my daughter, he became responsible for the security of the *rebozo*. He would run down the road to find some cardboard and stronger string. I was to stand in the office and tell any customers that he'd be back soon.

'Don't let anybody in,' he added.

So I stood there, hot with shame, hoping that nobody would come by for a stamp, a letter, or anything at all, and see my red face.

'Mother caught trying to post tits and bums publication to only daughter.' I imagined the shocking tale being spread around the village at this very moment. Actually, no one would be interested. They were not Protestants.

Thinking that it might speed up the process of returning my complexion to its more usual pallor, I switched on the ceiling fan. With this, the neat piles of loose paper that constituted the filing system in this branch office took to the air. They rose and swirled round in the artificial turbulence.

I switched off the ceiling fan and watched the papers float to the floor in disarray.

At this moment the room grew dark. Across the doorway a stallion had drawn to a halt. Hanging down its flank was an exquisitely-tooled high-heeled boot, resting in a full leather illustrated stirrup. A thigh clad in leather rose skywards out of view.

The men from Monte Grande had arrived to collect their post. Dressed in their finest, they sat outside the post office in silence.

I tried to explain that the postmaster would be returning in a minute. They sat on their high mounts without answering. For them, the sight of a woman in the office was tantamount to the doors being slammed in their faces.

This stand off was only ended when the postmaster returned and fetched their letters. By this time, the papers were back on the desk in tidy piles. I had reshuffled them. They were now classified by size.

Everyone knew it was only pantomime. The parcel was repacked and posted.

The comic book had vanished, but I later heard that the shawl had arrived before the day of the Three Kings.

*

Being Twelfth Night and the day when children receive their Christmas presents, we had wrapped the last of the small toys brought from London and waited with Joaquin and Ofelia for the appropriate moment to cross the lane.

The four of us eased ourselves into the small part of the yard not overwhelmed by Dolores' Christmas nativity scene.

Other guests had already arrived to celebrate the day that Melchior, Casper and Balthazar arrived at the manger in Bethlehem with their gifts of gold, frankincense and myrrh. These included many members of Dolores' family.

We drank coffee and squash, and admired the three crowns of Three Kings bread – *rosca de los reyes* – that were placed equidistant down the length of a table. Each bejewelled crown was overlain with glazed fruit, including candied cactus, and lay gleaming through a brittle layer of crystallized sugar. Dolores' nephew approached the display with a machete that was sharp enough to shave a cat. With a cunning gleam in his eye he cut the *rosca de los reyes* into large wedges.

Within the spicy body of the cake had been hidden four tiny dolls, *muñecas*. These miniature babies are baked in the bread to symbolise hiding the infant Christ from King Herod's troops, on the day of *los Santos Inocentes*, the Holy Innocents.

With a nod and a wink, together with judicious cutting, Richard and I each received generous slices of the Three Kings bread. Watched with excitement by the other guests, we both retrieved a minute pink baby. Naked, it came complete with male genitals.

Joaquin and Ofelia each received a similarly endowed slice. The recipients of the dolls must now be responsible for the feast of Candlemas. *Candelaria*, on 2nd February, is the day of the purification of the Virgin Mary, when she presents the Christ child to the church.

Our anxiety was short-lived. That we should give the party was not part of Dolores' plan. So to our relief it was arranged that we donate money for the food. The subsequent festive occasion would take place at a cousin's farm in the mountains. Joaquin had already offered his contribution, Richard followed suit.

Everyone agreed that this year's celebrations promised to be good.

The three crowns may have been consumed, but *el día de los Santos Reyes* was just beginning. We left the yard with our stomachs full of cake, and very pleased with the arrangements. Joaquin and Ofelia left with us, but continued up the lane towards their home.

La Misa, la misa – the Mass – were the words left ringing in our ears, along with the church bell, as the sun sank behind the mountains.

As we turned to look back at the yard, a general exodus seemed to be taking place. A rush to be away from the constraint of Dolores' religious fervour? Maybe they were off to their own church. We called back that we would join our friend across the lane.

In the darker regions of many people's shrine room, hung an item of fancy dress. Each would have been splendidly altered and repaired, until little of the original fabric remained. Bits of exquisite brocade and silk velvet would have been patched or expanded with modern acetate material, recently bought from the market. Battered centurion armour was annually

beaten out and reshaped by the car repair shop.

These costumes are carefully and jealously guarded, before being passed down from one generation to the next. Once a person had secured a good part in *el día de los Santos Reyes* celebrations, a not inconsiderable amount was invested in the resplendent costume, and it would stay with that family.

Early on in the colonialisation of New Spain, the Spanish clergy found that this theatrical way of evangelising – a twist on the miracle plays that were performed in Europe – helped to overcome the problems brought on by of total lack of communication. Often, neither side could understand a word of each other's language.

So didactic plays were concocted. And with all the mechanisation and papier-mâché props available to the sixteenth and seventeenth century European theatre, they were performed in church. Dramatic trickery abounded.

Dolores had described to me an Ascension Day miracle, when by means of a cardboard cloud, its silver lining sparkling in the candlelight, a stout rope and some pulleys, Christ was seen rising all the way up into the dome of the church. Below flickered the cardboard fiery flames of hell. Even as she described the simple stage mechanics, we knew she believed without a doubt in the reality of the miracle. Yes, she had seen the Lord risen with her own eyes.

That evening, we walked up the hill to the *zócalo* and joined the fiesta that was underway in the atrium of the *ex-convento*.

We bought peanuts and pumpkinseeds in little paper cones. Eating them, we stood pressed up against the high wall that surrounds the church, well out of the way of *el Loco*, who was already dancing in a very excited way. They were keeping a keen eye open for someone to tease.

Out of the wide open doors came a long tongue of light, as if to tempt you in. The bells rang out, and the crowd stood expectantly still.

Like a demonstration of the wonders of pyrotechnical skills, and with the hiss of a giant serpent, the Star of Bethlehem whooshed down a wire that was fixed securely to a tall tree at the other end of town. All spinning and sparks, the comet hurtled through the night sky until it reached the end of the wire that had been tied to the bell tower. Here, it smashed into the crumbling fabric, and was extinguished by the force of the impact. The dying embers floated slowly to earth.

At this moment, our attention was arrested by the arrival of the Three Kings in full regalia of wigs and bulbous crowns, each holding a tasselled cushion on which rested an elaborate casket.

Through the gates, and onto the tongue of light, they entered the church, drawing us all in their wake.

Everyone watched in the comforting glow of the candlelight, as the wise men from the barrio placed their tinsel boxes in with the Nativity. There lay gold, representing kingship, frankincense a symbol of God, and myrrh, the dark reminder of pending death that we would all grieve for in the spring.

An accordion played slightly ahead of the choir, and rosaries sped past our inattentive ears. Young people drew circles and signed their names in the incandescence spraying from three-foot sparklers. Boys with feather wings, unable to live up to their angelic image, could not resist an opportunity for a kick or a punch, and a couple of dogs growled over a bitch on heat. At least one child was unable to resist the temptation to poke another in the bottom with a spent incendiary devise. The responses dragged their heels.

The newly-acquired mechanical angels in niches turned their bodies, and blessed the people with a right arm swivel that was not without patronage. As the congregation rested in the pews, hard up against the bodies of their neighbours, the building heated up. Babies slept or were suckled.

Our minds drifted off, like many others, into a peaceful daydream. Detached for a moment from the outside world, the priest droned on as if far away.

Sixteen

EL DIA DE LA CANDELARIA

AN OFFER WE HAD TO REFUSE

W ith great deliberation I began the onerous job of designing the invitation for the exhibition. When it was finished, Dolores thought it was unprofessional as it was drawn by hand. Even when I explained that it would be photocopied, she was not convinced. It should be typed. But I had no machine to do this. Finally, we had it reproduced on coloured card and went to deliver the bulk of them to Joaquin.

He was climbing into his Volkswagen. We accepted his invitation to join him before we had any idea where he was going. It was a beautiful evening, so we squeezed ourselves in beside a small machine and some tools that were already occupying the seats.

The Green Architect could definitely be referred to as hands-on. He was delighted to be taking us to *la fabrica*, where both roof and floor tiles were made.

The first stop was at one of his palaces in progress. Through gates in the already completed perimeter wall, we could see the builders swinging in hammocks, or sitting round the fire waiting for their supper. They lived on site until moving on to the next job. Joaquin brought the quiet swinging to a halt as he yelled through the wrought-iron bunches of grapes, hanging from the swirls that made up the gates.

Soon he was able to hand over the machine he had brought.

The man who received this piece of equipment observed it with disdain. It was a device for compressing adobe blocks using leverage. Although we had struggled to heave the machine as far as the gateway, the builder lifted it with ease. The exchange had been jovial, but we now knew that it was a man's skill and strength that made good adobe bricks. Not a machine.

Joaquin took it very well, and we were soon back in the car to be bounced over the hillside. Richard leaped in and out of the front seat to open and close the dilapidated gates in the hedges that marked the boundaries of the various *ejido* lands. We could see the glow of the firing long before we finally came down to a cooler, damp area where rushes grew. Huge trees were being fed into a fiery furnace at the base of the bottle-shaped kiln.

A solitary man worked here. With a single pick, a shovel and a wheelbarrow, he dug the red earth from the hill behind. He then wheeled it to a nearby pond, shaded by a *palapa* awning. Removing his *huaraches*, he puddled the clay, squelching endlessly until it was smooth and consistent.

This material was then pressed into moulds of varying shapes, before being carefully removed and laid out in the draught of an open shed to dry. There were square shapes and hexagonal shapes for the floor, and there were rows and rows of Roman tiles for roofs. All were nearly ready to be carefully stacked tight inside the kiln for the next firing.

It had become dark. We sat well back, away from the intense heat, and by the light of the glowing embers savoured the wild terrain.

With his mighty strength, the tilemaker shoved the massive tree trunk still protruding from the fire further into the flames. Then, picking up a jug of warmed and spicy *pulque*, together with four mugs, he came to sit with us.

We sipped the drink while we watched and listened to the night.

An owl screeched and another answered in response, as the sounds ricocheted throughout the hills.

Richard described how he heard that the Romans formed the tiles for their roofs, by moulding appropriately-sized sheets of clay over the bare thighs of a row of seated maidens. Joaquin laughed with amusement, while the other, more practical man, smiled and shook his head in disbelief.

We watched the fire until sprays of orange sparks and lashing tongues of flames sprung from the tall chimney.

Nothing more could be done, so we piled the remaining tools into a smaller corner of the back seat, so that all four of us could cram into the car. We took the return journey at a gentle pace.

It would take the kiln two days to cool before the Green Architect would be able to help with the unpacking and collect his hand-made tiles.

Early on the morning of 2nd of February, which is the day of Candlemas, we watched as Dolores and her niece Teresa loaded the mule with every bit of culinary equipment needed to cook the feast.

Surmounting the kitchen sat a little girl, Dolores' great niece. Sitting among the flounces of her new dress, she held in her arms the infant Christ, who only a few minutes ago had lain in his crib, the central player in the *belen*. Now he was dressed ready for the blessing at the mass.

Waving goodbye, they began the trek to the farm in the mountains. We had arranged to go to the church for mass, before climbing the ancient track behind the Aztec temple up to the farm. It was quiet, and we anticipated an uninterrupted day.

*

At about eleven o'clock I was surprised to see an acquaintance, who lived in a barrio near the centre of town, in the company of a younger man.

They sauntered up the lane and casually pushed open the gate, entering our garden in a very familiar manner. It annoyed me that they behaved in such a proprietorial way.

Wide smiles radiated from their smooth, clean-shaven faces as they settled themselves on the veranda. I called to Richard.

With hermetically-sealed formality, we were introduced to Don Rodrigo and his nephew, a 'designer' who had expressed an interest in the Englishman's furniture and his methods of construction.

Richard and the designer disappeared into the workshop.

I was left uneasily drinking coffee with the European-looking Don Rodrigo. Having asked if everything was well, he playfully chided me for not visiting him and offered to send numerous wealthy people to the exhibition.

Lamely, I showed him some proofs of the linocuts, but his eyes glanced off the prints to other parts of the room. They darted here and there, but without the satisfaction of finding what he was searching for.

It felt as if he was trying to elicit some information, but without me being aware what it was. To each of his enquiries, which ranged from our health, our happiness and our life in Las Brujas, I gave nothing but enthusiastically positive replies. And all the time his eyes roved round the room.

Richard and the designer returned from the workshop and our lame conversation petered out in mid-sentence.

Handing Don Rodrigo several invitations to the exhibition, and another for the designer, we made our formal farewells and watched with relief as they extracted themselves with alacrity. Our fixed grins quickly relaxed, as we saw the supercilious figures of the two men stride out of the village.

I felt that there had been something conspiratorial about the visit.

'What was it they wanted?' I asked, thinking that Richard might allay my fears.

'They wanted me to buy a large amount of cocaine.'

We both sat down.

Richard had thanked the designer for his kind thought, but he explained that it was not for him. It had been offered at an almost giveaway price, with the excuse that the bottom had fallen out of the market, now that Ecstasy was all the fashion.

The more we thought about the situation, the more depressing it appeared. Now they knew that we knew that they were not above a bit of dealing. It seemed that whether we'd bought it or not, they now knew that they could frighten us with their newly imposed power.

Had they chosen a time and a day when they knew the barrio would be nearly empty? Or was that a coincidence?

Questions rolled around our alarmed minds. Consciously, we decided not to fan the flames of pending paranoia, and not to keep asking ourselves 'What for?' 'What if?' or 'Why?'

But what we did realise was that Don Rodrigo could no longer be dismissed as a harmless acquaintance.

Living in Las Brujas we hardly needed to dose ourselves with cocaine.

*

The invitations had been sent or delivered and there were still a lot of things to finish.

The mass would be at noon, so we quickly dressed ourselves as respectably as possible. Stopping off to buy a bundle of candles from the general store, we joined the road and the throng that was heading towards the mass for the Purification of Our Lady and the presentation of the hundreds of Christ childs to be blessed. These were the same mannikins that had been lying at the feet of the holy parents since Christmas Eve. Dressed all over with velvet and satin, and decorated with golden braid, the baby had been transformed into a small boy. His two fingers were still raised in benediction, but golden sandals had been buckled to his feet and a matching jewelled crown was fixed to his head.

As we added ourselves to the milling crowd filling the atrium, we saw that every woman and every girl held a similar Holy Infant. While their sizes ranged from minuscule to life size, each was sat up in an elaborate plywood throne.

There were battalions of dolls dressed in the stylistic costumes of every saint known to the faith. So the whole gamut of Catholic idolatry waited patiently outside in the sunshine for the procession of the holy family to arrive. We could hear the accompanying lutes as they approached.

Once the holy family had arrived and been settled in above the altar, the full panoply of infant Christs was brought into the church. The crowds pressed into the cavernous interior for the blessing. Not only was there a multitude of more regular saints, but there were miniature doctors with tiny stethoscopes slung round their necks, Madonnas and Christ childs, and even Aztec dolls resplendent in sequins and feather headdresses. Buckets of water decorated with rose petals, as well as baskets of maize, waited to be consecrated along with the rest, at this ancient celebration of impending regeneration.

We had lingered far too long enjoying the shade of the trees, to even enter the doors of the church, so we sat on the ground with the rest of the overflow, listening to the intermittent music of the brass band that was playing in the choir loft. The congregation was still lolloping through the rosaries as we sloped out of the atrium to find Joaquin and Ofelia.

As we were early, we sat on a stone bench outside their house. We basked in the sunshine, trying not to think about our recent visitors. We hoped that its warmth would dispel our anxiety.

Together, we walked up along the wide grassy tracks, passing old ruined houses full of trees and flowering plants. Bees buzzed and birds sang. The small fields were immaculately cultivated.

The farm belonging to Dolores' family was at the end of a long lush valley. Behind, were the wooded mountains that rose steeply up to the Town on the Hill.

The view back over the *ejido* land and down to the town below was spectacular. In the quietness of the countryside the sounds rose clearly from the village. The distant hubbub of the people flocking out of *el templo* and the irregular tolling of the bell reached our ears as if in miniature.

A massive sabina tree grew at the place where the water sprung from the hillside. Here, a natural bathing pool had been made by damming the stream. It was already crowded with *los duendes* jumping and diving and splashing. We had never seen the children of Las Brujas having so much fun.

All around, the tiny plots were fed by an irrigation system that flowed from this spring.

A few cows grazed nearby. Some goats gambolled in a pen, while a row of mules and donkeys were already tethered to the fence.

Just further out from where the vegetables grew in neat rows, beyond the patches of shorn alfalfa, were the fruit trees. Covered in blossom, they were filling the air with gusts of petals that gently floated down onto the assembled party.

Several women including Dolores were crouched over a huge cazuela that was balanced on the three stones in the fire. Piles of tortillas had already been prepared and lay wrapped in the ubiquitous embroidered cloths.

The special drink of the day, *agua de Candelaria*, was immediately poured into mugs and handed to us. Its brilliant red colour derived from one of its main powerful ingredients: beetroot. This *agua fresca* was a welcome drink after our walk.

Behind the women, the one-roomed house was overflowing with shrines. Here sat a porcelain Christ child resplendent in a tailored jacket and knickerbockers, edged with fine lace. He came with all the regulation accessories, but these were not only old, but also exquisitely beautiful. They had been saved from long ago, when the family must have been more prosperous. The precious stones, now embedded in grime, were real.

This Infant of Prague sat on a golden throne, against a mossy bank resplendent with kneeling angels, their gilded wings gleaming.

Behind this was another shrine. This was dedicated to San Isidore. Ploughing with a pair of delicately carved oxen, he is the patron saint of farmers. It was surrounded by lines and lines of *papel picadas*, so old and frail they looked as if they would disintegrate if disturbed by anything more turbulent than a sharp intake of breath.

But it was perfectly still in the room, as if nothing there had moved for a long time. The steady flames of over a hundred candles lit the scene.

Back beyond the Christ child and the angels, further back from San Isidore at the edge of the light, something imperceptibly moved.

We peered into the gloaming. Right up against the back wall, lying on a small thin mattress were the bony forms of two people. So long had they been in the habit of lying in bed with each other that they moved in unison. They fitted together like a pair of spoons in a drawer. Their lips puckered over toothless mouths. The parts of them that appeared above the quilt had the colour and texture of pickled walnuts. An excellent camouflage.

'Good afternoon,' we muttered. A duet of mumbling came as the reply.

These two relatives were Dolores' aunt and uncle.

The banquet that was served was extraordinary. With our tastebuds somehow sharpened by the pure mountain air and our appetites peaking after the effort of climbing to this spot, the savouring of this dish was slow and exquisite. It was *pancita rellena*, literally 'stuffed belly'. It would be unflattering, although not altogether wrong, to describe this dish as haggis.

We ate sitting on logs that had been placed to form a circular bench round the fire. Now the cooking was over, this had been refuelled and fanned so that great flames leaped up and lit our faces.

Later, when the effects of the mezcal had mellowed our inhibited natures, we jumped up and joined in the dancing. Everyone clapped and laughed as we jolted round the field.

However crippled by arthritis, however misshapen these *camposinos* had become over the years of arduous work, they danced with wonderfully nimble steps to the intricate syncopated rhythms of the music, played by a squeeze box and a fiddle by two very old men.

We felt we were among friends. Although our fears had evaporated, they had left an indelible dark stain. The Saturday of our exhibition was looming with accelerating speed.

We were pleasantly surprised, and also slightly alarmed, when we counted up the number of people who had accepted our invitations. Most of Joaquin's had not fallen on stony ground, while ours, given to friends and neighbours in the barrio, had been received with a touch of bewilderment.

Both Felice and Dolores thought the invitation was a gift in itself, and put them away carefully in their dowry chests with the other treasures.

On the morning of the exhibition, Dolores didn't make her usual morning visit. Even though it was Saturday, no children came to use the swing, ask to dig in the garden, or show us their new masks.

Once we had swept the floor, cleaned the house, dusted and arranged the newly finished furniture, rearranged the bookshelves, washed ourselves, and dressed appropriately, all that was left to do was to make the Jamaica, which was put aside to cool in a large earthenware jug.

Richard had returned from the village with a sheet of crispy dried pork skin, called *chicharron*. And a bag of *salsa de jumiles*. (*Jumiles* are rather grey-looking insects.)

Now we were quite ready for the guests. There was nothing left to do but to sit on the wall and strain our ears to listen for any unusual noises that might mean someone was on their way. We began to feel very awkward.

Then we heard the sound of people heading from all directions towards La Casita Azul.

It was a relief to see Joaquin and his wife leading a rather bemused couple, teetering down the path through the mango orchards.

At the same time, we looked up the lane to see what appeared to be a cavalcade of shiny, four-wheel drive motors bump slowly towards our cottage. Through their darkened windows we could see only the shadows of the chauffeurs.

The Gonzales, the *mayordomos* of the Guadalupe fiesta, came with some guests. The writer and his wife, with whom we had dined at Christmas, had kept their promise and driven with their friends from Oaxaca.

El Presidente dropped by and embarrassed us by thanking us, in extremely flowery language, for taking such an interest in his little domain. It was his first social visit to the barrio. He must have been stunned to meet a government minister and his wife, who was an ophthalmic surgeon, passing the time of day in Las Brujas. Just as he must have wondered about the implications of these sorts of people planning to build their country homes near a barrio that had a reputation for repelling strangers.

It was very good to see Jaguar and his wife, and to be able to introduce them personally to someone who would become one of their best customers. It looked as if the Green Architect had persuaded most of his clients to come to our exhibition. All these people were dressed in a consciously casual style. Many, men and women alike, sported shorts, training shoes, and open-necked shirts, with sweaters draped over their shoulders.

While the more adventurous had walked, others came by car. The lane became crowded with people and vehicles. Several couples disembarked from limousines with darkened glass windows, and their uniformed chauffeurs were left behind to lean against the polished paintwork. They looked very uncomfortably alert, as they waited for the visit to be over.

A couple of men in dark suits, someone's bodyguards, took up their duty positions on the front wall.

Joaquin became the exhibition's curator and our agent, and the conversation flowed.

La Casita Azul was scrutinised as if it were a museum. A particularly enthusiastic lady looked at the hearth and told me this was how the Indians had lived a hundred years ago. I smiled and decided against telling her that we actually lived here.

I overheard the mention of bespoke furniture and realised that Richard's future, as far as work was concerned, could be assured. I felt warm and pleased and proud. And astonished to be basking in the reflected glory of my partner. How stealthily married life had caught up with me. How pleased I was.

Every one spoke in exceptionally complimentary ways as they thanked us.

By three o'clock the last of our guests had departed. Only the faint smell of petrol fumes hanging over the lane gave any clue to the unusual gathering. We sat down to watch the dust settle.

As if they had waited for the coast to clear, the men from Monte Grande arrived. Led by Salvador and Arsacio, they came to a halt at our gate. They were dressed in their most elegant and formal costumes. The leather boots displayed silver spurs, their holsters were loaded with jewelled pistols.

Magnificent tailored jackets with dozens of buttoned pockets were worn over white *guayabera* shirts, pleated and tucked. On their heads each wore the tall wide brimmed hat of the spaghetti western baddie.

Presenting their invitation to Richard, they asked for his permission to enter the garden before they rode up on their finely groomed horses and dismounted.

Shaking Richard's hand, they asked if they might shake mine.

Their mounts were so well trained that they stood exactly where they had been left. They were so still that I could read the stories of bravery engraved on the leather of the saddlery. These were the men I'd met at the post office. I recognised them by the decorations on their outfits and the comic strips tooled on their machete scabbards.

Apart from those we'd met delivering wood, the others graciously behaved as if we had never set eyes on each other before. It was clear that they preferred a woman to be in the home, not trying to run a government office.

We brought out the bottle of mezcal and some small glasses, and invited them to sit down. They enquired how many coffee bushes we had, and what fruit trees there were.

A great interest was shown in the two religious factions that they had heard made up our country. How much rent did we pay? After this, they had a short discussion in a language unknown to us and reported back that it was expensive.

But Richard showed them the workshop and the garden, and pointed out the furniture that he'd made from the curved wood that Salvador and Arsacio had brought down with the firewood.

Back in the house, and clearly not used to seeing everything so close up, they peered minutely not only at the furniture, the books and the prints, but at the tubes of ink, the blocks of lino and the piles of paper. Not a flicker of the surprise they must have felt was betrayed by their expressions.

With great formality they thanked us and we thanked them, before they remounted and prepared themselves for the four-hour return journey home, to the high hills of Monte Grande. The Elder, their spokesman, invited us to come and stay, promising to send horses and an escort.

Their visit had been a very great honour.

Then in the early evening the neighbours came, and it was at last time to sit down and be natural. The only piece of furniture that interested anyone was the swing, and while we talked, the children flew as high as the rafters.

We finished the bottle of mezcal and talked until it was dark. It was quite late when they departed by the light of the fireflies.

Don Cándido had not come, but that was no surprise to us. By Mexican etiquette this could only be interpreted as a snub. Richard then told me he had met him that morning. In rather frosty tones the news was relayed that our rent was to be doubled. Why? Because we'd taken and used the wood in the garden.

But he had suggested that we use it.

It seemed that he had meant we could burn it. Making it into furniture was not part of the offer.

In my confusion, the anxiety I felt about Don Cándido reared up like a painful peptic ulcer. In panic, I wondered if our friends from the mountains could help us. Richard thought they already knew all about the Olympic gold shot. He thought that everyone would be very aware of the situation. And, in the best possible sense, enjoying it. And so should we.

Reflecting on the visitors who came today, we realised we were hardly friendless.

It had been extraordinary.

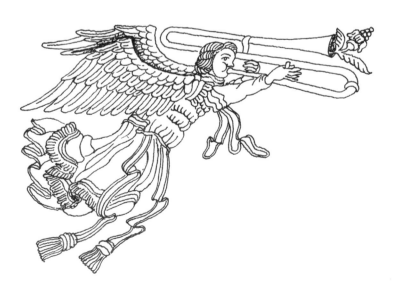

TRAVELS IN ITALY

PREAMBLE

The destination of many of my journeys, however circuitous, ended in Italy, to stay with the food writer Patience Gray and her companion Norman Mommens. I was married to Patience's son, Nick, and for many years these were family holidays. I always travelled with a pen, a drawing book and a bottle of black Quink. My in-laws, great 'makers' themselves, both inspired and encouraged me.

It was some years before they moved to the Salento, the tip of Italy's 'heel'. I brought my paints and canvas boards to their home, Masseria Spigolizzi. It was the surrounding landscape that I painted and continued thinking about when in England.

Sometime after Nick and I separated, Patience and Norman invited me to stay with them at Spigolizzi. The children were nearly grown up, so I returned by myself, now with bigger canvases and more paints. Together, Patience and I chose which of my illustrations were to go in her book, *Honey from a Weed*. The twenty-year accumulation of drawings made during my many visits were to be the basis of the illustrations. It had also been the places we visited together as well as the things she pointed out that inspired me.

I heard that she had died while I was staying in Oaxaca. We had been wandering around in the big wholesale market when, tucked away in a dark corner, among the piles and crates of goods, I spotted a public telephone. A shopkeeper stepped out of the shadows and was willing to dial my home number in England. He hovered, timing the call with his watch. But noticing how shaken I was by the news and hearing why, he gently invited me to sit down and catch my breath on one of the large sacks of *chapulines*, the delicious chillied grasshoppers.

Looking out across the market, the entire view was filled by heaps and swathes of brilliantly coloured fruit and vegetables. I felt it to be a rather appropriate place to hear this sad news. Patience died in 2005. I had known her for nearly half a century. I miss her sometimes acerbic letters, her encouragement and support. But most of all, I feel bereft of the amused and malicious look in her eye that reminded me that none of us is particularly exemplary.

SEVENTEEN

DINNER WITH THE COUNTESS

ON THE EDGE OF THE PAST

Two or three times a year I would visit Patience and Norman in Puglia, staying in the tower of Spigolizzi. With their encouragement, it was a perfect place to paint and draw. I have been visiting this extraordinary place for long enough to know well people who, like me, have grown up and grown older…

The buildings I drew have become more and more tumbled down. Before electricity came, the dark nights were only lit when there was a moon. Now, in the distance, the night landscape was looped all over with sparkling necklaces of the street lights of the villages.

Back in 1980, Francesco, an English teacher, was the translator into Italian of my book *Rustic Structures*, which had just been published locally. So I thought it perfectly appropriate when he invited me to dine in the family home of a colleague, Maria. We arranged that he would pick me up the next evening. I was waiting in my best dress when Francesco arrived to collect me. I was relieved that he, too, was smartly clad.

Beyond the decision to wear my 'tidies', I hadn't given much thought to the level of formality, so I was rather amazed when our journey ended with a drive of some hundred yards along a track through a field, before drawing

up in front of a baroque palace. Its size might have been described as slightly compact, but though rather dilapidated, you could see by its tumbled down grandeur that it had been built in times of confident optimism.

Maria came out to greet us before she led us through the archway of the massive central portico. Inside, we squeezed by a listing carriage, under a lop-sided chandelier, foggy in cobwebs, over the cobbled yard and out onto a terrace, on which a table had been laid for what appeared to be a formal banquet.

Where I had anticipated an open view from a garden, grew high walls of clipped hedges. They must have not only cast deep all-day shadows, but evoked a terrible gloom and a feeling that there might be no escape from this dark evergreen labyrinth.

We were early, so to fill the hiatus Maria suggested we wander through the rooms of her family home. She directed us up the sweeping stairs to the 'piano nobile'. Each door we pushed open revealed an abandoned past that seemed to have not been entered since the carriage lost its wheel and sank to the floor.

The echoes of our footsteps were muffled by thick layers of dust. Once elaborate and beautiful furniture seemed to be held together only by the glue of the veneer. Much of the wooden structures, eaten by termites, had been reduced to little cones of sawdust, and now lay on the threadbare carpet. Curtains hung in brittle swathes that were too frail to draw back and let in the light. We found ourselves speaking in hushed tones.

From carved frames, both oil paintings and sepia photographs, stared out, with the rather blank expressions of the long exposure, several generations of one of the saddest families I had ever been among.

So it was fitting that by the time we were invited to sit at the table, the fading light had helped to set a dark mood for the evening.

Ten of us each took our place in front of a startling array of family silver, eighteenth-century porcelain and troops of sparkling glasses that had been set out meticulously on the stiff white cloth. Taking my cue from the others, I flicked open the starched brocade swan, and placed the resulting table napkin on my lap.

Then I was introduced to the family.

The countess sat nearly centrally on the side of the table that overlooked the forbidding topiary. Francesco was offered a place directly opposite, close enough for match-making scrutiny. I sat next to him while the six daughters, each a beauty, placed themselves evenly round the board, carefully leaving the place of honour for the seventh and youngest sibling, their brother, the count. Neither man nor boy, the present incumbent of the family title snuggled up to his mother, stroked her breast and giggled with affection. He laughed out loud his love for the countess, touchingly oblivious that elsewhere subdued politeness reigned.

A meagre glow issued from a dozen economy bulbs that hung from loops of wire slung between the glass flowers of the chandelier.

Obsequious servants in threadbare livery, pushing humility to near satire, scurried anti-clockwise round the party, serving, refilling and replacing, as we embarked on this meal, *La Cena*, which was to be a feast of many courses:

1. *l'Aperitivo*

Our glasses had been filled with the driest of sparkling Prosecco, and small dishes of olives, nuts and little loops of biscuit – *taralli* – were scattered around the table. We drank a toast, to whom I wasn't sure. As I picked at the plump olives, the succulent nuts and herb-scented biscuits, the daughters talked of their work as teachers, doctors and lawyers. All but Maria lived in towns or cities to the north of Italy. We drank another toast.

2. *l'Antepasto*

Quickly the little dishes were cleared away as the *prosciutto crudo*, that had been cut so thinly it appeared only as a slight blush on the white plates, was served. A local astringent white wine filled the next glass. It went perfectly with the delicious ham. I began to lick my lips with pleasure.

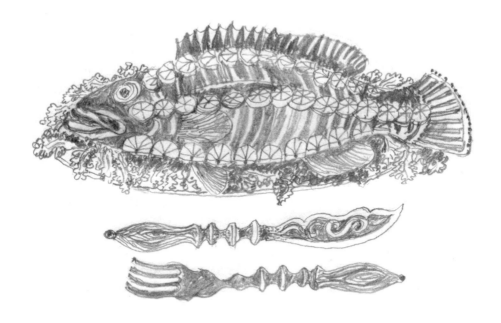

3. *Primi*

As if by sleight of hand, the plates of blushes were replaced by shallow bowls of freshly made *orecchietti* – 'little ears' – the pasta of this region. Each ear had been made under the pressure of a butter-knife and folded with a flourish over the thumb, before being dried on a tray This was served in a sauce of tomato and *cacioricotta*, which is a young, soft cheese. My appetite and appreciation were in full swing. Now the wine was the local red Primitivo.

4. *Secondi*

Only missing a fanfare, a gigantic oval dish, held shoulder high was to be gently lowered onto the table before we could see that it was a huge baked fish. Initially it was placed, maybe symbolically, before Francesco who, sensibly feigning incompetence, left the delicate job of serving to the cook. The dish was extraordinary, a mighty *cernia* – a dusky grouper – nearly thirty inches long lay among a decoration of edible flowers and leaves. A hardly visible aromatic steam rose into the still air. Soon the fillets were handed round. I drew in a mouth-watering breath and began to eat the firm flesh.

So we continued to talk of many interesting things, always punctuated by the count's happy laughter, until I noticed that I was the only one eating with such zest.

Looking around, I saw plates of hardly touched food being whisked away, back to the kitchen. I began to feel rather mystified, a bit uncomfortable as I realised I alone was finishing each plate of food. The daughters were merely rearranging each dish with a fork. The countess was engrossed in the welfare of her son. Francesco rather picked at his food.

5. *Contorni de verdura*

The vegetables in big dishes arrived at each end of the table. Once the lids were off, we helped ourselves to the slices of golden brown baked *finnochio* – sweet fennel. Now in step with the others, I repressed my exuberant appetite. With a pirouette, the vegetables were taken back to the kitchen.

The word *finnochio* is also slang for a homosexual or gay man.

6. *Insalata*

This stayed only briefly on the table before the green and red leaves rejoined the other dishes. The count was now sleeping in the arms of his mother.

7. *Formaggio* and *Frutta*

A soft ricotta cheese, with the imprints of the rush basket still very clear on its flanks, was arranged around the basket of fruits. Bunches of black grapes, peaches, purple figs and…

The basket was returned. The courses were now galloping by, as if to prevent us from actually being tempted to partake in this feast.

8. *Dolce*

While we talked – and barely even noticed by the six sisters – ten slices of the most ambrosial gateau were left to tempt us. This tiramisu was made with, among other ingredients, fingers of cake steeped in coffee, and built in layers with lemon-flavoured mascarpone cream cheese. Its perfect complement, an architectural sorbet, only made a fleeting visit, disappearing before it melted. I was unable to forgo the rare treat of tiramisu.

9 & 10. To finish the banquet…

Then came tiny cups of strong back coffee followed by a glass of Amaro Grappa, a bitter, syrupy herbal liqueur. The meal was coming to an end.

Above the count and countess had hung, in a heavy gilt frame undulating with the damp, an enlarged sepia photograph of a bewhiskered man in military dress. The picture leaned out at an angle from the wall in an oppressive way. It gave the impression that the late count, encrusted in medals, glared down with a steely authority that had not died with him. Only now did I understand that the toasts, the raising of glasses, had all been for this phantom at the feast.

We left with warm thanks.

As Francesco backed the car to turn round, the sound of hilarity caught our attention. A long trestle table and chairs had been set in the garden. Around it sat, along with their families, all the staff who had together produced our miraculous meal. Their serious working expressions had evaporated, revealing them to be warm-hearted families and friends enjoying a party.

As we drove off, we noticed a tray of coffees and the bottle of Amaro were being let down on a cord from the kitchen window, directly above the exuberant party. Now I understood this symbiotic arrangement between the classes.

Various pieces of olive pruning and gathering equipment:
a. olive sprig, blessed and in position; b. furcina and ruezzulu (rake and scraper); c. harvesting nets;
d. runcedda (billhook); e. sarracchiu (pruning saw); f. cernitrice (sloping grid to separate the drupes from
the leaves and twigs); g. mmile (terracotta water cooler); h. log of olive wood; i . la scala de 'mmunna
(ladder); j. new axe handle.

EIGHTEEN

OLIVE OIL

PRUNING & PRESSING IN PUGLIA

Stu munnu è fattu a scale, ci la scinne e ci la 'nchiana.
(The world is a ladder, some go up and some come down!)
Pugliese proverb

In Puglia, it was traditionally early spring when the olive trees were pruned. February and March used to be the general rule, although now it may be a year-round task. While *rimondare* (to clear or clean again) is Italian, *la 'mmunna* is the Pugliese word to describe the annual thinning of the olive trees that have been cared for by generations of *contadini*, whose well-being relies on the fecundity of the crop. As much as 40% of olive oil produced in Italy comes from this area of the country. Italy supplies 20% of the world's production.

La 'mmunna may sound like an incantation, an expression from the prehistoric casting of spells, but *'mmunnare* simply means 'to prune'.

There tend to be *anni si* – 'yes years' – when the yield of olives is abundant, which often alternate with *anni no*, that produce only a paltry crop.

It was back in 1987 when my friend Assunta first arranged for me to see *la 'mmunna* for myself. The *'mmunna* seems to be a rather private family affair, but the team readily agreed for me to watch and draw.

That year was a remarkable May, warm and dry. The little fields were overflowing with flowers. The olive trees that had not needed pruning this year were covered in clusters of small white flowers, while the leaves flickered silver in the breeze.

Throughout the day, there was a constant hum of bees that gave us all a feeling of well-being.

Although it was early when we arrived at the olive grove, the team of furese had already congregated among the trees. The tools of their ancient craft had been unloaded from a tiny truck called an *Ape*. These are the ubiquitous three-wheeled, scooter-based pickups that buzz across the terrain like their eponymous namesakes – *ape* means bee in Italian.

The *mannatu de scala* – 'hand of ladders' – were dealt out like a hand of cards, each to be leaned against a leafy tree and only needing to be secured to the highest springy branches.

The *sarracchiu* – little pruning saws – and a variety of *runcedda* – billhooks – are given a final sharpening as the various rakes, the furcine, are propped against the trunks, together with the *ruézzula*, ready to clean the ground under the trees after pruning.

Earthenware flasks, *'mmile*, propped up among the roots of the trees, are filled with water that will cool as the day grows hotter, while the *panareddhu*, the little basket of *marrena*, the midday snack, is hidden in the shadiest part of the *Ape*'s cab.

These men have worked together from their youth. Fathers, brothers and sons, uncles, nephews and cousins, made up the genealogy of the male members of an extended family.

Soon the *strincituar*, the pruning, begins. The tangle of branches is cleared and opened up, and the centre of the tree exposed to the sun and air.

One of the most experienced, if no longer so nimble, older men – *capua'mmunnaturi* – directs the operation from the ground, while the rest of the team climb up the tall ladders and cut out the dead or congested wood as instructed from below. Each twig and branch is named after its shape or potential use, and from beneath the trees, the name is sung out, as in 'the butterfly to your left', 'there is a coat hanger in front of you', 'a pot hook near your hand', or simply given the name of the tool it will become.

During the sawing and cutting, each part of the tree is searched for parasites. Both the olive fruit fly and the olive moth are great enemies of a bountiful harvest. Historically, young lads were sent out to poke into the holes made by the larvae with a sharp stick or wire, and the owner would pay a small reward for each one found.

Each year, the dead wood is cut away, so that over the decades the great

trunk gradually grows into the convoluted hollow tree that is a familiar sight in the old groves.

Heavy stones are placed at strategic points by or in the crotch of branches, to calm and reprimand trees that have produced too many barren suckers. Sometimes a branch is cut off, as a threat of further, more drastic amputations if the tree doesn't produce soon.

Extremely old trunks that may be more dead than alive are cut down to make way for new shoots to spring up. The prunings that fall to the ground are sorted into their potential various uses. Small twigs and leaves are swept into piles and burnt, leaving the ashes to be spread around each trunk to fertilize the earth.

Not until the tree has reshaped into either a calice or a candelabra, such that 'a swallow can fly through the branches at speed', as they say, does the team move on.

The Pugliese dialect has a multiplicity of origins, owing elements to each of the peoples who settled in the peninsular: Messapians, Greeks, Romans, Lombards, Normans, Turks, French, Spanish, even Arabs. It is very different from Italian.

Beginning his researches in 1922, Gerhard Rohlfs, a German linguist, spent years cycling round the lower part of the heel of Italy – the Salento – learning enough vocabulary to produce the several heavy tomes that are needed to translate these spoken words into a language comprehensible to Italians.

Words in the Pugliese dialect are quite often peppered with a bewildering number of m's and n's, perhaps reflecting a local habit of muttering and mumbling. Although the dialect is tending to disappear, along with the old ladies who used to bathe in the sea fully clad in their voluminous black frocks, it still survives, not least in the agricultural communities. Hanging on by its fingertips, it hasn't quite gone the way of other obsolete tongues and become the property of academe.

While the originally aural language has been written down and saved by the literate, it is still the spoken communication of the teams of pruners. A language in which the word for 'stupid' is *babbaluccu*, for 'little child' is *piccinneddhu*, and for 'fart' is the politely onomatopoeic *pìvutu*, must evoke some curiosity. (*ì—ivutu* is a corruption of the word *pirutu*, which means

flame). I cannot help but fall for the words *zoccula*, big mouse, and *zzozzu*, meaning dirty.

A cross between the buzzing of bees and an afternoon nap, the words are to my ears as calm and restful as a quite siesta swinging gently in a hammock.

In case you might have the impression that this Mediterranean climate is pleasant in winter, the dialect word for the painful condition of chilblains is *prudicheddhi*.

On Palm Sunday, an olive branch previously blessed at the Mass is fixed to the highest point of every God-fearing home, to jog the Lord's memory and keep the occupiers safe for another year.

When the pruning is done there will be sturdy new hooks for hanging up clothes, as well as pegs in the kitchens for pots and pans. The mattocks and rakes will have new handles, as will the axe used to chop a large pile of firewood ready for the cold and damp winter.

Like elements of the Pugliese dialect, the olive tree originated in the East. It was native to Asia Minor and spread from Iran, Syria and Palestine to the rest of the Mediterranean basin 6,000 years ago. It is one of the oldest cultivated trees.

It was the olive branch in the beak of the returning dove that was proof to Noah that the flood waters were at last receding.

Moses spared the men who cultivated olives from military conscription. In both the scriptures and classical writing, olive trees represented peace, while olive oil symbolised goodness and purity.

The winner of the Greek Olympic Games was crowned with a wreath of olive leaves. The Romans, who valued the beautiful honey-coloured olive wood with its strong black and brown grain, forbade its being burned by the hoi polloi, reserving it for the altars of the gods.

Olive groves said to have been planted in Pliny the Elder's lifetime, before the eruption of Vesuvius that engulfed both Pompeii and Herculaneum (and which contributed to Pliny's death as he attempted the rescue of a friend), are still bearing fruit nearly two thousand years later. Look carefully at these ancient trees, for they could have been planted even earlier, perhaps in the fifth century BC, when Pythagoras was teaching mathematics in the South of Italy.

After the pruning is finished, and the earth raked and weeded, broad beans are often planted in concentric circles around the trunks. This is a two-way arrangement: the spreading branches of the tree produce ideal dappled shade for the bright green beans to grow, while the leguminous roots enrich the orange soil with nitrogen. They are either ploughed back into the ground, or left to ripen to make a delicious dish.

In September as the fierce summer heat declines, after the beans have been picked and eaten, the groves are meticulously cleaned ready for harvesting. Nowadays, nets are often spread out on the ground, ready to catch the fruit, making the task less backbreaking, less arduous. This is described by a single dialect word – *ajere* – which means 'land cleaned and ready for the harvesting of the olive'.

The harvest begins in October and continues until the last olive is either plucked from the tree or gathered from the ground, which could be well into the New Year. It is usually a communal group activity, not a solitary task. Although a man might be perched in the tree shaking the branches, it is more often the women talking to each other who are on their hands and knees collecting the drupes.

While the impatient shake the trees or even beat the branches with a *cotulaturu* – a wooden flail – to bring down the crop onto the net more quickly, it is said that the best olives are those that have fallen naturally and then painstakingly picked up from the ground by nimble fingers.

In the evening, the overflowing baskets are tipped onto a *cernitrice*, a sloping grid through which any leaves or twigs fall, leaving the fruit to roll down freely into a crate.

*

The morning after the day I spent at *la'mmunna*, Assunta turned up in her tiny car just after breakfast for another mysterious tour.

We drove to her parent's smallholding, a place where the family still spends the summers. The car bounced straight through the gateway and abruptly stopped in the yard of swept earth. In a corner stood a particularly ancient tree; it was as wide as it was tall, gnarled and knotty, split and hollow, its sprouts of small branches covered in tiny cream blossom.

A faded curtain hung on a wire stretched across the open side of the trunk. Assunta smiled and explained that this had been her privy, where she had spent many hours reading and doing her homework. Pulling the fabric aside I could see not only the disused sanitary arrangements, a bucket with a wooden lid, but a series of little bookshelves. The tree is still burgeoning. Its erstwhile occupant is now a teacher.

Underneath the main piazza of the nearby town of Presicce is an underground olive oil press. Now restored, its ghost is part of the town's museum of local life. It is a collection from bygone times only recently past. It was possible to get tantalising glimpses of its subterranean workings through several grills and windows in the pavement. It would be open later in the day.

But Assunta had other ideas, and we set off through the lanes and tracks until we came to a collection of dilapidated buildings in the country. It

was hot as we left the car and began to walk round to the side, where the brambles were particularly vigorous. My friend tackled the tangled growth with a stout stick and, as if following the instructions of the Brothers Grimm, parted the thorny wall to reveal a flight of steps leading down into the dark.

A narrow staircase had been cut into the tufa rock, and down this, calling me to follow, plunged Assunta, her laughter echoing all around. Carefully, I descended, apprehensively feeling my way in the dark, down to a vast underground cavern. It took quite a few minutes before our eyes adjusted to the gloom. We could see only by the grey shafts of sunbeams that filtered through circular holes in the roof. It was damp and chilly.

We were in an abandoned subterranean oil mill, a *trappitu*, a grotto. Although it looked quite ready for the millers and their families to return, they had gone forever. These caverns had been a complete – if tiny – industrial complex. Those who worked the season lived incarcerated in these dank dungeons. For the men, there were sleeping holes with stone platforms, as well as stabling for the mules that turned the primitive machinery. The production of olive oil must be kept cool at all costs.

As we reached the bottom of the steps, we came upon the most impressive grinding mill. The vertical drive-shaft that once turned the huge millstone was embedded in the rock of the roof. The stone itself sat in a massive circular carved stone bath, round which it used to roll to crush the olives. Around this great stone cavity was a circular trench, worn in the surrounding rock floor by the hooves of the mules that for many years kept this machine rotating day and night.

Next to the mill was an oblong hole in the roof, through which a few pale plants had mistakenly grown, and beyond them we could see the sky. Through this aperture the olives would have been tipped straight from the back of the cart into the *trappitu* below.

The mill ground the olives into an oily paste, which was then placed onto *fiscoli* – flat, round coir mats. These were threaded onto the central posts of the press, making a tall column. The press was then slowly and arduously wound down by hand, until the oil ran away into an underground vat called the *ancilu*, a word signifying 'angels'. The olive also contains a

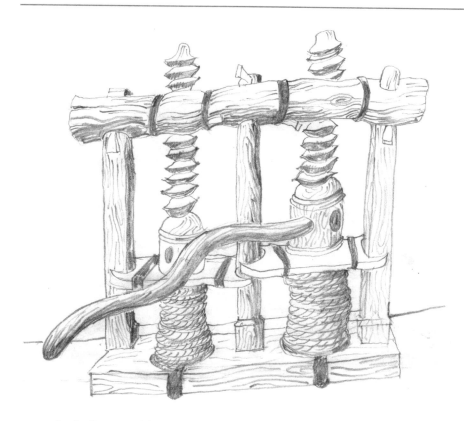

great deal of vegetable water, satina, from which the oil must be separated. As oil floats, this largely happens naturally, and the satina is allowed to drain into a lower underground vat, picturesquely called *'nfiernu*, 'hell'. It is also separated, as the cream is skimmed from milk, with a special plate.

In the comparative cool, this microcosm of sweated labour lived out the whole of the olive oil producing season, from soon after the *vendemmia* – the wine harvest in September – until all the olives are processed, possibly as late as May.

We climbed back up the steps. It had been claustrophobic even with just the two of us, and we were glad to be out in the sunshine.

Above ground were the abandoned buildings. A small house for the tally clerk had collapsed behind the derelict office. A slightly less modest dwelling, built for the manager, was set apart from a cluster of outbuildings that must have stored the necessary equipment needed to run this industry.

We poked our noses into the forsaken homes and waded through thickets of brambles, before we came across a tiny vaulted barn that had been built utilising an ancient, upended olive press too worn to be used.

Once it was prudent to send your grandmother to watch the process from beginning to end, her eagle eyes focused on the family's harvest. And

also to see that every quintale (100 kilos) of olives made at least the expected
15 litres of oil, and that your olives wouldn't be making someone else's oil.

Olives are nowadays taken to the local mill, where they are processed
mainly under the auspices of a single technocrat, who taps his instructions
into a computer controlling the stainless steel machinery that fills the
ecclesiastically-proportioned factory.

We were introduced to the proprietor who showed us round. He
enthusiastically described the various qualities of oil produced by his
family's mill.

It was a wonder to behold. I stood there bewildered by the multitude of
pressure gauges and the shiny pipework that joined one hygienic machine
to the next. Not even a single hiss of escaping steam broke the efficient
atmosphere.

Only mechanical means can be used for the production of 'extra virgin'
or 'virgin' oil, which is often described as issuing from the 'first cold pressing.
If your olives are rancid or badly fly-attacked you may be only able to make
lamp oil, even with the first cold pressing. Extra virgin refers to the low

acidity (less than 0.8%), not the cold pressing process.

The residue from that process can be mixed with water and heated to extract an inferior quality oil, olio di sanza, destined principally for industrial use or soap-making, but it is often treated chemically and sold for the kitchen as 'refined olive oil'.

But none of these secondary processes were visible in the Frantoio, an old olive mill poetically named *Le Macine di Athena*. From the mill here in Presicce, near the tip of the heel of Italy's boot, comes only the most excellent olive oil.

As we left, we were given a large bottle of *fiore del fiscoli*. This is the first oil that exudes naturally from the paste, before it is pressed or processed. It is so fragrant and so delicious it is traditionally kept for the family. On its label was a majestic portrait of Athena, an olive branch held high as she clutches a miniature mill to her breast.

Back in England, we broached the precious *fiore* and inhaled its delicate perfume before tasting the sumptuous olive oil. It certainly lived up to its reputation.

Nineteen

THE RECIPE

THE DISH THAT SAVED MY BACON

In the summer of 1959, between leaving a sheltered boarding school and the start of the term at a London college, I became an au pair to a family in Rome. I had a greater enthusiasm and knowledge of what I was to see in the museums, than experience or aptitude for child care.

At the beginning of July, I set off for Italy, to a land I was unaware I knew very little about. My knowledge had been entirely culled from my mother's art books.

I arrived in Rome. Before I had time to unpack my bags, and still swaying from the motion of the long train journey, I was introduced to my charges. The children eyed me with suspicion. Lucia was a rather disgruntled, hesitant-looking child of six, while her brother, three-year-old Gigi, was the son his sister should have been. From the waist up he had the appearance of a cherub that had been cut carefully from a Botticelli painting. Below, the allusion came to an abrupt halt. His legs were fixed by leg irons, a contraption in which he cheerfully clambered about.

Their mother, *La Dottoressa*, was a child psychiatrist, while the father, *Il Dottore*, a geneticist, was deeply involved in tracing the origins of the Etruscans. They had very full lives.

The saviour was *La Nonna*, the maternal grandmother whose name,

Crocifissa, immediately endeared me to her. She was to become my ally.

My brief was to speak English at all times, to entertain, and most importantly, to keep the children spotlessly clean.

We learned to communicate by a quickly-invented private sign language. The strong element of subversion was only noticed by Crocifissa, who every day helped me bathe away the day's grubbiness and dress my charges ready to be displayed in fresh crisp outfits at *la passeggiata* – the evening stroll.

In August we were all invited to a weekend party by some friends who lived on the coast. We were all very excited as we set off in a car, with a roof rack piled high with suitcases and a boot crammed with swimming and diving equipment.

We sped off north-west, to a tiny peninsular moored to the mainland by a triple isthmus. The little town was perched on the vertical cliff top, high above the rocks of the lacy edged sea. Turning into big sweeping gravel drive, we came to a halt at the portico of an enormous marble palace. *Il Dottore* pulled on the handbrake, which was more or less to be the last mechanical effort he made the whole weekend.

In a matter of seconds we were besieged by liveried servants. A genuflecting retainer opened the doors of the car as he proffered a white-gloved hand to help us out. Similarly clad porters bore down and carried away all our luggage, before the car was whisked out of sight.

At the top of the steps we were greeted by our hosts. Bereft of the obvious costume of a nanny, and feeling neither fish nor fowl, I was introduced as a friend, an artist, even though we all know I was to be the childminder.

The bedrooms were beautiful and airy, the views from the balconies breathtaking. The attention from the hired hands discrete and efficient.

Diaphanous curtains billowed into the rooms from the breeze gently coming in from the Mediterranean. My room was next to the children's,

and together we unpacked our suitcases (in my case a small rucksack) that had preceded us.

It was like a dream that belonged to someone else.

After greeting each other on the terrace, the party began.

Most people disappeared down the steep steps to the beach below. I just managed to peer over the brink.

In the distance, the guests could be seen, as if through the wrong end of a telescope, enjoying a diversity of water sports. The idea of trying to get back up from the beach with several children as well as Gigi's leg irons was too much for me. Besides, there was green grass and a swimming pool up here.

By the early evening everyone had dressed for dinner, and was sitting comfortably in the cushioned wicker chairs with their aperitifs, to enjoy being entertained in each other's company with the easy familiarity of old friends.

With some late arrivals came two more children. I was pleased to have four children to hide behind.

In general, Italians are good-looking, but this young, professional, well-educated and cultured group of friends were stunningly beautiful. *La Bella Figura* was displayed before my eyes. I enjoyed their company and warmed to their friendliness, although I was pleased to have another purpose, and keeping an eye on the children kept me at a comfortable distance.

Each evening dinner was served on the verandah, under a vine from which hung bunches of black grapes. A long marble table had been set with gleaming silver and glistening cut glass. Brilliant starched white table napkins were folded into castles or lilies, and stood by plates of the thinnest bone china, whose golden rims gleamed.

On all three sides was a perfectly manicured and green garden, beyond which sparkled the turquoise sea.

As the meal proceeded, servants dressed in black and white replenished the dishes and kept the debris at bay. The food was delicious. Everything was from the local market, bought and prepared on the day of capture or harvesting.

Pasta was freshly made each morning. The children and I had noticed it drying under muslin cloths, in the shade outside the kitchen next to the herb garden.

On the second evening *La Dottoressa* turned to me:

'Are you enjoying the food?'

And as I nodded with enthusiastic appreciation, I sensed, too late, the minefield that had been laid before me.

'We hear that in your country the food is bland.' And then she added, as if it was an afterthought:

'Perhaps you could give us a recipe; we could have an English evening.'

It was to be a duel, the chosen weapons, recipes.

I looked out at the calm sea. As the light of the sunset faded, the wide open landscape of the day was gradually reduced to the small area lit by half a dozen candelabra, hemmed in by the dark night.

It was 1959. In London, a pea soup was a very thick, acrid-smelling yellowy fog.

I remembered it as a land of brown food, meat marooned with over-cooked root vegetables in thick brown gravy. Many staple foods came out of tins, as did the reconstituted meat of spam and corned beef.

Stodgy puddings swam in custard, and seemed to still be influenced by nursery food, or possibly catering for those without their own teeth.

In cafes, the dark brown milky tea was poured directly into thick mugs from a tap low down on a huge urn whose shiny chrome plating was so reflective, so shiny, that you might be greeted by your own distorted reflection. This apparatus usually sat on top of a glass cabinet displaying substantial, lacklustre cakes.

Bowls of grubby sugar along with salt, pepper and bottles of sauce clustered in the centre of each table.

Books about European food had just begun to be published, but these foreign ways were still for many an anathema. People still remembered ration books, when food was regarded as sustenance.

'Yes,' I said.

Someone pulled out a notebook and pen to write down the ingredients and method of preparation. Everyone was listening and I noticed *La Dottoressa* smiled in a slightly triumphant way, as I began to recite the recipe:

One week before you wish to eat this dish, catch a dozen larks and feed them solely on bread.

After seven days, drown them in brandy.

Pluck and clean, before carefully removing their tongues and placing on a dish in the cool.

Take a peacock and carefully remove its plumage, taking care not to damage the feathers.

Keep them safely.

Cut off the head and neck, carefully draw back the skin up to the head and cut through the oesophagus.

Remove the inside, with which you can make a stock.

Finely chop up the liver, heart and gizzard.

Mix with wholemeal breadcrumbs that have been soaked in cream.

Rinse the empty neck in cold water and refill with the stuffing.

Draw the bird and set aside.

Pluck and clean:

A Guinea foul,
A Capon,
A Pheasant,
A Partridge,
A Quail,
and a Woodcock.

All of these should have been hung in the cool for a few days until their feathers part from their flesh without effort.

The woodcocks entrails must be kept in a cool larder.

Place the larks' tongues in the cavity left by the woodcock's organs and sew up the aperture.

With patience and a sharp pointed knife, tunnel from the neck end, and then from the backside, into each carcass, delicately cutting through the tendons and scraping away the flesh from the bones until the skeleton can be extricated from the body. Great care must be taken not to break open the skin. The bones will make an excellent stock.

Stuff the woodcock into the quail, the quail into the partridge, the partridge into the pheasant, the pheasant into the capon, and the capon into the guinea fowl. Each must be sown up with linen thread. As with a set of Russian dolls, fill the peacock with this assembly of birds.

Place this preparation on a roasting tray spread with butter, and cover the whole with greaseproof paper. Roast low down in a large oven at a medium temperature. After two hours place the neck and head by the birds. When the whole is nearly done, place the larks round the peacock.

Remove the greaseproof paper for the last half hour and allow to brown.

Remove from the oven and place on a large dish.

Let it rest for fifteen minutes.

Gild with gold leaf before redressing it with its own plumage in imitation of its original splendour.

Spread the woodcocks entrails on small pieces of toast and place round the edge of the plate, alternating with the larks.

The larks should be eaten while your head is under your table napkin so that the songbirds' last alcoholic breath can be savoured.

It will also hide your shame as you indulge in such profligacy.'

After a short pause, everyone began to laugh.

My case was rested.

I was relieved to see that *La Dottoressa*'s expression had changed, her smile had become kinder.

The enthusiast with the notebook had, to my relief, abandoned the idea of putting this improbable recipe into practice.

TWENTY

THE URANIUM SPIDER

A TALE OF RADIOACTIVE LETTUCES

I t was nearing the end of April 1986 when I set off for the south of Italy. After an English winter I had accepted a very welcome invitation to stay with Patience and Norman in Puglia.

I was not the only person to be jumpy after Ronald Reagan's bombing of Libya, and to be tense with worry about the course any recriminations would take. Still fearful, I flew to Rome on the first step of a journey to the southern tip of the heel of Italy. A few days in the Tolfa mountains, enjoying the beautiful clear air of a late spring, almost dispelled my anxiety about the ugly events taking place in another part of the world.

The night express leaves Rome at midnight to meander south, taking eight hours to trundle the 400 miles to Lecce, a principal city of the peninsular. After the sun had risen, each one of us – the six occupants of the couchette compartment – made it known with small purposeful movements that we all were awake. With little encouragement, the blind was flung up to reveal a brilliant day.

Once the bunk beds had been reinstated as seats, we rearranged ourselves to pass the remaining hour of the journey in conversation. We spoke of everyday life, and we listened to the familiar problems and triumphs, trials and tribulations of our families and friends. While nobody mentioned the worldwide worries and kept things on a domestic scale, life seemed manageable.

Tomorrow would be the first of May, a holiday when families celebrate Labour Day. There was a festive mood in the air, it felt as if everyone was hurrying towards their nearest, if not dearest. And when the train finally jolted to a stop at Lecce, it was a happy, friendly coach-load of acquaintances that helped each other out with their bags and boxes.

By eight o'clock on that morning, I had settled myself at a table outside the station café for breakfast and a coffee to wait for the local train that would take me to the tip of the Salentine peninsular and Spigolizzi. The dark cloud that I had been travelling under had evaporated, leaving me to enjoy the feeling excitement.

The local train pulled into the platform ready to start its journey south to Galiano de Capo for Capo Santo Maria di Leuca on the coast. To the end of a land where the atmosphere is often laden with water sucked up from this place where three seas meet: it is here that the Adriatic, the Ionion and the Mediterranean join forces.

Like everyone else I settled myself on the slatted seats, drawing my bags and parcels close.

We would be stopping at every station, to be greeted with formality by the stationmaster dressed in his slightly theatrical uniform studded with various glinting buttons and badges. With dramatic gestures he would oversee the correct exchange of mail and packages. This gave the passengers time to admire the garden, fill up their bottles with water from the fountain, pass on messages, and gossip with friends. There was then time to watch the points being changed and to read the date and time of arrival or departure, written in extremely neat handwriting on a blackboard fixed outside the waiting room. And then to lean out of the window and make sure that the single track baton had been received by the hand of the driver, before the green flag was unfurled and waved by the master himself. The hoot of the engine heralded a chorus of farewells, and once again we were off.

There are many stations on this country line, and each individual name rolls pleasantly off the tongue. Reading down the timetable, pinned inside its mildewed cabinet on each platform, may sound like doggerel, but to me it was poetry:

Novoli, Magliano, Copertino,
Nardo and Galatone
from where the branch line continues onto
the tiny Venetian port of Gallipoli.

The countryside appeared unusually plush and green, and full of brilliantly coloured flowers glowing in the sunshine. A profusion of scarlet poppies, blue vetch, and white crown daisies piled up in the landscape, and was easily identified as we rolled by.

But in spite of the spring lushness, this was unmistakably Puglia. Groves of convoluted olive trees that had been planted in ancient times still fanned out across the flat landscape, and grey-green prickly pear cactii grew up against the honey-coloured drystone walls, marking the periphery of the tiny fields we passed.

The train pulled into the little towns of Tuglie, Parabita, Matino, before stopping at Caserano.

Here, an elderly woman dressed in black and laden with capacious bundles hauled her ample body up through the door, and sat down on the nearest seat, opposite mine. Quite out of breath, she began rummaging in one of her holdalls, and, after deciding against her crochet, pulled out and unfolded a large newspaper. Flapping the pages into some sort of submission, she found the horoscope inside. This left me with a view entirely consisting of the front and back pages, conveniently stretched out before my eyes by the strong arms of a farming grandmother:

GREAT NUCLEAR TRAGEDY IN NORTHERN EUROPE

This headline nearly filled the entire front page.

Before I could even start to pick up one or two of the smaller words, the woman flipped the paper shut, folded the pages, and exchanged it for her minute hook and white cotton thread attached to a length of fine lace edging. While she seemed at odds with the forecast of her day, she was certainly not concerned about a tragedy in Northern Europe. With a speed that blurred the movements of her hands, she continued her work.

I began to feel sick.

In rapid succession we drew into the stations of Taurisano, Gemini and Aquarica di Capo. At each stop, I watched as if in slow motion the same meticulous rituals which, performed earlier that morning, had so enthralled me.

The next stop would be Presicce for Salve, where I would alight to leave the few remaining passengers to travel on to the end of the line at Gagliano de Capo and from there to Capo Santa Maria di Leuca.

With the usual screeching and clanking the train came to a stop, and I stepped down onto the tracks in the blazing sunshine, to be greeted by my hosts. Soon, we were driving away from the little town, south towards the last escarpment before the seas on which stands the ancient, massively built, stone farmhouse that is the home of my friends. Here, a pleasant breeze made the weather perfect. I moved with my baggage into a pink tower, from the top of which was the full view of the tip of the heel of Italy.

Lunch was taken in the dappled light under a fig tree, and I listened to the slight noises of nature, and basked in the peace. The noise and rush of the journey began to fade from my memory. It was just wonderful to be there again.

I hadn't the courage to mention the headline I had glimpsed in the train. So when the subject was referred to over coffee, I realised to my dismay that I had not dreamt it. It was difficult to acknowledge that I hadn't imagined the crisis.

'I heard in the bar that there has been a terrible nuclear accident in the Ukraine, and a great radioactive cloud is being blown towards Scandinavia.'

It did sound far away, and the main concerns were whether it was an accident and not the starting shot of a nuclear war.

A feeling of unease had come to haunt us.

*

The next day was the first of May. In the tower, I arranged my brushes and paints on the table before going out to choose a view for this year's picture.

I walked along the ridge among the *Cistus,* whose crinkly flowers were in bloom on their dried sticks of bushes. I was deep in banks of serapes and orchids, seasquill, asphodel and feathery fennel. Red and black beetles clung to the stems, while swallowtail butterflies fluttered about at eye level, as I waded about through ripe grasses up to my armpits. The almond and fig trees that grew among the olives were swishing and rustling in the breeze. Two black kites were hovering over the brink of the escarpment, while below people were working in their fields, bent double, up to their elbows in the red earth.

Late that evening, great clouds began to amass on the northern horizon, sending a chilling wind that forced us inside to eat.

As the storm brewed, night fell early, as if to display the lightning to its best advantage. First came the big drops of rain that slapped down as if with defiance on the ground. Then thunder rolled about the skies, until only seconds parted the lightning and the sound effects. The billowing clouds looked like an unfamiliar mountain range towering up from the flat landscape. Illuminating forks of lightning flashed an intermittent monochrome light over the landscape. As the raindrops accelerated to become a deluge, the electric forks broadened into sheets of theatrical lightning. Bouncing off the roofs, torrents of water gushed down the traditional gullies and drains into the great underground cisterns, where it would be kept cool and clear. It was the much welcomed water to top up supplies before the hot dry summer ahead.

The dawn broke, but as the storm continued there was little reassuring light. The thunder that rolled round and round felt like a bombardment. With each lightning strike appeared a glimpse of a ghostly landscape wrapped around with swirling mist.

After two days the storm gradually abated, and on the third, our bodies stiff and chilled, we stepped out into the wet and blustery weather and went to the village. It was market day and rumours were gathering speed. Everyone we met was strangely subdued. A sinister gloom pervaded the square. We went into the crowded bar for a glass of wine and a place to open the newspaper out of the wind.

Today, few people were scouring their horoscope for a sign of good fortune. Maps with concentric rings spinning out from a place in Russia no one had ever heard of covered the pages of every newspaper.

Not even the man who had walked home from Siberia after the Second World War recognised the name. Some were saying 36 dead, others 3600. Where? How? Why?

The circles encompassed the entirety of Europe. The whole leg of Italy, including the heel, was well within its perimeter. Out in the street, we joined the crowds looking up into the sky. The clouds were still rushing overhead at a speed that seemed to increase the general alarm.

What was it? Nobody knew, for nobody had seen it. Neither had a single person heard nor smelt the danger that had rippled out from far, far away to reach us on the first of May. It must be a bad omen, someone argued. But it's already here and you could feel the fear. 'Is worse to come?' 'Worse than what?'

Deeper into the damp newspapers we delved, only to come up gasping in the half-light of half-truths. The barman's authoritative explanation made good sense to his assembled audience. 'The rain has washed the poison from the Russian clouds deep into our earth.' The crowd gradually departed to broadcast this opinion as news over the entire peninsular.

The name Chernobyl had entered our psyche, a bewildering mythic hell that was the centre of all the invisible concentric circles.

The cloud had passed and we were left in a limbo of confusion.

*

Lecce is a town not only of Roman remains, but also of exuberant baroque architecture. Honey-coloured stone carvings decorate every building. Swags of robust, gravity-defying cherubim swoop from the walls and doorways. Swirls of acanthus and curlicues of olive branches merged into mythical beasts. Consoles carved as wild creatures support balconies displaying delicate wrought-iron balustrades.

And now out from this city came the edicts. Overnight, thousands of stark posters were pasted onto the tufa walls of boundaries and buildings in the villages and countryside. It seemed that any stone with a flat surface wide enough to take the breadth of a paste brush supported a dire warning.

> NO MILK OR FRESH CHEESE SHOULD BE CONSUMED.
> NOR GREEN VEGITABLES EATEN NEITHER RAW NOR COOKED.
> PREGNANT WOMEN AND CHILDREN SHOULD STAY INDOORS.
> DO NOT WALK IN THE LONG GRASS.

At home we could only pick at our food in the candlelight.

*

Rad. The word abounded in the newspapers. Previously unused, today's vocabulary espoused the word and 'Rad' was liberally sprinkled all over the pages of the newspapers. We began to see the term so often it became as familiar as a word from a school lexicon. And with this recognition we thought we had an understanding. In reality, few of us had the foggiest notion what it was. Those who did were unable to clarify our minds.

'Rad is a unit of absorbed dose of ionizing radiation; e.g. X-rays equal to an energy of 100 ergs per gram of irradiated material.'

'An erg is equivalent to 10/7 joules, which is the SI unit of work or energy equal to the work done when a force of one Newton moves to its point of application through a distance of one metre.'

While 'Rad' maybe has the jaunty air of a nickname, what it stands for – Radiation – does not. The circles continued to spread out, like the ripples of a pebble thrown into a boundless lake. There was neither sight nor sound as they passed through us, their waves had travelled through the air, leaving no visible trace, no smell or mark other than that of fear.

Each of us had to try and understand this fear of the unknown.

*

Back in the village, I stopped at the hotel where the television flickered in the foyer, near the public telephone. I was anxious to learn how the already familiar concentric circles, now televised in movement and full colour, were affecting Britain.

A map of Europe showed the strange phenomenon of radioactive intensity taking on the exact shapes of countries. Whereas Scandinavia had been very hard hit, as had Italy, France and Britain appeared to have

little to worry about. In my ignorance I was selfishly relieved.

But weather is not known for abiding by the man-made borders between different countries. Soon, it became clear that politicians had the whip hand in the art departments of the continent.

While Britain and France have many nuclear power stations (some of which are not in their first flush of youth), Italy has not yet seriously entered the race. (Not that they can afford to be holier-than-thou, as they buy much of their electricity from ageing French power-stations.)

'Good Evening Comrades. All of you know that there has been an incredible misfortune: the accident at the Chernobyl nuclear plant. It has painfully affected the Soviet people, and shocked the international community. For the first time, we confront the real force of nuclear energy out of control.' The president of Russia had spoken, but we were hardly any the wiser.

Gathering up more newspapers, we returned home and spread the pages out on the marble tabletop. England was still sticking to its original party line and didn't appear to be too badly hit by radiation. Well, not if you were able to believe the numbers, that appeared to be on a fluctuating scale nobody understood. A day or two ago the number had been 1.6 compared to Puglia's 10 diminishing to 2. This had been overprinted with 1.8. But by the next day, the reassuring 1.8 had shot up to 400.

Nobody we spoke to had the least idea what these numbers meant.

The farmer from next door rushed round and sat with us under the fig tree. He smiled as he explained that now the wind was from the south, it would be fine to eat the lettuces. 'So soon?' we asked nervously. And the ricotta, if it had been freshly made.

Although longing to be more informed, we were hardly reassured by our neighbour's following explanation.

How similar the words *il ragnio* and *uranio* sound. These words for spider and uranium, rolled off the Pugliese tongue, were hardly distinguishable from each other. Any differences were blown away by the wind of the sirocco that afternoon.

'In the centre of the earth is this giant spider. So large and furious is this creature that he has broken through the first layer of the earth's crust.'

We too imagined the terrifying sight of a vast hairy leg of the outsized arachnid, trying to break into the world at Chernobyl.

'And the Russians are entombing it in a magnificent sarcophagus.'

Far-fetched, we may have thought, but Salvatore's explanation gave us a powerful image to attach to our wishful thinking. Now we could look at the sky and see the swallows wheeling overhead, and the birds of prey hovering, instead of searching the heavens for the invisible concentric waves of mysterious Rads.

But I still imagined the tall grass radiating beams of Strontium-90, rocks I felt were releasing heat rather that absorbing it from the sun. I listened to every misunderstood suggestion, and it put not exactly the fear of God into me, but something very similar.

Sitting outside had lost its appeal.

Market day came round. The streets were filled with people frowning with worry. The streets were rumoured to be radioactive; you could feel the heat radiating from the ancient walls of Presicce.

'It's always like this.'

'But now it's different. Feel the difference…'

And we were invited to feel the warmth of the walls, and we too felt the difference.

A new generation of posters now adhered to the fabric of this little town, threatening the market traders with extreme penalties for selling radioactive produce.

We looked for the lettuces and courgettes that would still be crisp with freshness. We searched for fresh cheeses with the patterns of their wicker moulds imprinted on their flanks. But we were too late. The posse of officials armed with municipal Geiger counters had already passed by.

The radioactive food, the contaminated vegetables, the Strontium-90 ridden ricotta, were already being shovelled into the back of an open truck to be dumped, but where, we asked ourselves?

Those that had milked the goats, made the cheese, picked their vegetables before dawn and brought this produce to market, now stood around in small subdued groups, bewildered and frightened. These people had unwittingly just become members of the criminal class.

As we turned to go home, I noticed another poster pasted onto a wall in the square. It fluttered in the breeze giving the impression that it wanted to escape before anybody had a chance to read its message:

DO NOT DRINK OR USE THE WATER
DRAWN FROM ANY CISTERN

The ancient method of ensuring a supply of cool sweet water during the hot dry summer had overnight become a thing of the past. Even though we knew it wasn't, it had become to feel like war.

It took some time to realise the severity of the nuclear accident in Chernobyl. To this day, the cisterns are filled by a water tanker.

GLOSSARY

Mexico

aguamiel	the sweet sap of the maguey plant
alfeniques	little sugar paste animals
amate	a paper made since before the time of the Conquest from the bark of the ficus tree
atoli	a maize drink
butaque	a Spanish style of chair
calaveras	decorated skulls often made from sugar
caldera	a lake or land formed in the crater of an extinct volcano
campesinos	local or small-scale farmers
dia de la Candelaria	Candelmas
caritas	prehispanic miniature clay portraits of the dead
cempasûchil	Mexican marigolds with a pungent smell
champurrado	a maize and chocolate drink
chapulines	edible chillied grasshoppers
chiquihuites	sturdy woven baskets
colonche	wine made from prickly pears
comal	a large clay disk used for cooking flatbreads
la comida	the meal, lunch
copitas	small glasses of mezcal or other spirits
el correo	the post office
el desayuno	the first meal of the day
día de los Santos Reyes	Epiphany, Twelfth Night, the Day of the Three Kings
los duendes	elves or goblins, also a local nickname for the little children of Las Brujas
ejido	communal land used for agriculture
huaraches	can refer to rustic sandals or maize pasties
huipil	a loose blouse often with intricate woven or embroidery designs specific to an area, village, or even a family

ikat	a dyed, patterned woven fabric
jícaras	drinking bowls made from the shells of calabash, often brightly painted with a scene and a swan
jumiles	a dish of grey-looking insects
locos	means 'mad' or 'crazy', also the local name for *gigantes*, the giant papier mâché costumes worn by dancers at fiestas
masa	maize dough
metate	a tiny three-legged sloping grinding table carved from volcanic rock
metlapil	a stone rolling pin accompanying the above
las milpas	small fields where maize, beans and squash are grown symbiotically
la misa	the Catholic Mass
molcajete	a three-legged stone mortar, often carved in the shape of an animal
molinillo	an intricately handcarved wooden whisk for frothing a chocolate drink
mozo, mesero, joven	a waiter
el dia de muertos	Day of the Dead
los niños limbos	the souls of infants in limbo
la ofrenda	a home shrine on display during the Day of the Dead
pan de muertos	sweet bread baked and decorated with symbols for the Day of the Dead
pancita rellena	stuffed belly
papel picado	strings of brilliantly coloured paper or plastic flags, cut out to illustrate every fiesta
paseo	a throng of people out for an evening stroll
petate	a bedroll made from woven palm, then traditionally used as a shroud
piloncillo	unrefined brown sugar cones
piñata	a clay pot, often decorated as a seven-pointed star to symbolize the seven deadly sins, filled with sweets. It is suspended on ropes and broken open by blindfolded children wielding long sticks
posada	one of the ritual re-enactments held in the nine days before Christmas, to commemorate Mary and Joseph's search for a place to stay
presebre	meaning 'manger' is a nativity scene, also known as *naciemiento*
pulque	lightly fermented drink made from the sap of the maguey
pulquerias	drinking establishments usually only for men

noche de los rábanos	night of the radishes, 23 December, a festival in Oaxaca
rebozo	a finely-woven *ikat* shawl used by women to carry all sorts of things, from babies to potatoes
rosca de los reyes	Three Kings bread, a circular loaf with a crown, bejewelled with glace fruit. Inside are tiny baby dolls 'hiding' from Herod. The recipient of one of these dolls is expected to host or finance the feast of *Candelaria*.
los Santos Inocentes	the day of the Holy Innocents, 28 December, to commemorate the male infants massacred by King Herod
soplador	a fan woven from palm used to control the flames of an oven or grill
tamales	maize dough filled with meat, beans or cheese, wrapped in a corn husk or banana leaves before poaching
tejolote	a pear-shaped stone pestle
il templo	a church
tenates	circular woven baskets with lids, used to keep tortillas hot
tinacal	a *pulque* processing plant
voladores	a ritual with flying acrobats
zócalo	town square

ITALY

Ape	the three-wheeled, scooter-based pickup truck made by Piaggio that is almost ubiquitous in southern Italy
la cena	dinner or supper
cernia	a grouper fish
contorni de verdura	vegetable side dishes
contadini	local or small-scale farmers
finnochio	sweet fennel, also slang for a gay man
fiore del fiscoli	first oil that exudes from the paste of crushed olives
fiscoli	woven coir mats about 60 cm in diameter between which ground olives are pressed
orecchiette	typical ear-shaped pasta from Puglia
passeggiata	an evening stroll, the social event of the day when young and old promenade up and down their main street
prosciutto crudo	dry-cured ham (usually served uncooked)
sarracchiu	a pruning saws
runcedda	small billhook or pruning knife
taralli	a doughnut-shaped biscuit
trappitu	an underground olive oil mill

LIST OF ILLUSTRATIONS

Frontispiece: Contemporary clay figure made in Ocotlan, Oaxaca
Dedication: Marzipan cake

THE VILLAGE IN THE VALLEY

Introduction: 9, Map of Mexico; 10, Prehispanic dance; 11, Aztec grass symbol; 12, Floral façade for the San Miguel fiesta; 13, Wheat grown on clay animals, a symbol of bread at the Easter Eucharist

Chapter One: 14, Fountain in the courtyard of El Museo de la Ciudad de Mexico; 15, Flint knife; 16, Street performer; 20, Harvesting cocoa beans; 21, Chocolate jug and whisk; 22, Quetzalcoatl as an Axolotl; 28, Painted clay crucifix by Josefina Aguilar; 29, Wedding cake; 30, Child street juggler; 31, Aztec diorite serpent

Chapter Two: 32, A colonial kitchen; 33, Aztec rain symbol; 36, A colonial ladle rack; 41, Prehispanic terracotta receptacle

Chapter Three: 42, Casita Azul kitchen; 43, Aztec flower symbol; 47, Coconut shell masks; 51, Turkey from the Codex Florentino; 52, Tezcatlipoca Smoking Mirror; 53, Mexican counterattack, Codex Duran; 54, *Metate* and *metlapilli*, grinding stone and roller; 55, *Molcajete* and *tejolote*, mortar and pestle; 56, Woman making tortillas, a prehispanic plate; 59, Moctezuma divining news of the Spanish invasion

Chapter Four: 60, Franciscan monks expunging demons, from an Indian drawing; 61, Aztec symbol for water monster; 64, Franciscan Monks burning idols; 68, Terracotta figure; 71, *Molcajete*, a volcanic stone mortar

Chapter Five: 72, Clay figure by Señora Blanca Azompa; 73, Aztec wind symbol; 75, Humming birds; 78, Prehispanic goblet with humming bird; 81, Quetzalcoatl, the plumed serpent; 83, Prototype bed made in Las Brujas; 87, Prehispanic clay pot

Chapter Six: 88, Sousaphone players; 89, Aztec symbol for house; 94, Stone altar to the dismembered body of the moon goddess Coyolxauhqui; 96, Eclipse of the sun, Codex Laudianus; 101, Prehispanic clay pot with serpents;

Chapter Seven: 102, Three fancy dress 'Spaniards' at a fiesta; 103, Aztec vulture symbol; 109, 'The Scream'; 110, Chicomecoatl ('seven serpents'), revered deity of the *campesinos*; 111, Prehispanic clay vessel

Chapter Eight: 112, Man with cured vanilla pods; 113, Melipona bee, a pollinator of vanilla; 114, Stages in the life cycle of vanilla; 115, Pollinating vanilla by hand; 117, Vanilla pods drying in the streets of Papantla; 118, Flying *Voladores*

Chapter Nine: 124, San Miguel Archangel; 125, Aztec symbol for death; 127, Long distance travel before the Spanish Conquest; 131, Quetzalcoatl costume made from *amate* and feathers; 132, *Torelito* – a little bull – dressed with fireworks; 133, Tortoise hobby horse at a fiesta; 135, Papier mâché *locos* dancing

INDEX

ACKNOWLEDGEMENTS

There are many who have helped me with this book and I would like
to thank them.

I am truly indebted for the practical help and support of my
daughter Rosy who cheerfully undertook the task of scanning all the
illustrations without realizing that it wasn't to be a swift job.

Alexandra Robinson who with great diplomacy, corrected several of
my blunders.

Dorrie Peat for her translation of the mayor's epic poem 'Ode to El Oro'.

Nick Gray for casting his knowing eye over 'The Preamble' to the tales
of Italy.

Roderick Barker Benfield, the computer wizard from next door,
who patiently helped me out of numerous holes where my technical
incompetence had landed me.

Edward Behr for kindly allowing the inclusion of adaptations of articles
about Chapulines and Vanilla that had been previously published in his
magazine, *The Art of Eating*.

It has been a pleasure to work with Catheryn Kilgarriff of Prospect
Books and I would also like to thank Brendan King for his invisible stitching
as he edited the various parts together.

I am really indebted to the kindness of the many people I have met in
passing who have unwittingly contributed to my patchwork understanding
and endless sense of wonder during my travels.

To the friendly care of our neighbours in Mexico, who not only kept
us under their wings, but with consummate discretion eased us into the
mysteries of ritual and protocol that prevented us from being totally
bewildered.

It is with special fondness I remember the warm didactic friendship of
Dolores and Felice in Las Brujas.